SAGAS OF GIANTS AND HEROES

SAGAS OF GIANTS AND HEROES

translated by Ben Waggoner

Troth Publications
2010

Published by The Troth
24 Dixwell Avenue, Suite 124
New Haven, Connecticut 06511
http://www.thetroth.org/

ISBN-13: 978-0-578-05933-4

Cover emblem: Giantess riding a wolf. Design from the 11th-century Hunnestad Monument, Marsvinsholm, Sweden

Troth logo designed by Kveldulf Gundarsson, drawn by 13 Labs, Chicago, Illinois

Cover design: Ben Waggoner

Typeset in Garamond 18/14/12/10

Dedicated to Diana Paxson:
author, wise woman, colleague, friend

CONTENTS

INTRODUCTION

Huge and strong, sometimes grossly stupid or hideous or lewd, but possessing awesome powers and priceless treasures—such are the giants of the sagas. Giants are frequently hostile to mankind, and they are fearsome opponents in battle. In the myths, giants challenge even the gods, and though the gods fend off their challenges by fair means and foul, the giants are fated to rise up and overthrow the cosmic order. Yet in a sizable number of sagas, a hero with sufficient strength and luck manages to befriend a giant. Some of these alliances are so close that the human becomes adoptive kin of the giant partner, in a relationship known as *fóstra*, "fosterage". The hero may have to fight the *fóstra*, but once beaten, the *fóstra* may show great good will towards the hero, giving him treasures and wise counsel. The *fóstra* may side with the hero against the *fóstra*'s own kinfolk, helping to kill his or her parents and siblings. If the giant *fóstra* is female, the human hero may sire children on her. Yet even after the human hero abandons his giant *fóstra* and seeks a human wife, the *fóstra* may continue to help the hero achieve greatness.

The four sagas and six shorter tales in this book span several genres of Icelandic literature and range from the 13th to the 18th century, but they all place human-giant relations at the center of their plots, and almost all contain some variation on the theme of the giant *fóstra.* Nor are these the only ones that portray giant fosterage. The first chapter of Saxo Grammaticus's *History of the Danes* depicts the *fóstra* relationship between the human hero Hading, the giant Vagnhofdi, and his daughter Harthgrepa.[1] Many *fornaldarsögur* or "legendary sagas" depict giant fosterage or something close to it. So do five of the traditional corpus of "knightly sagas" or *riddarasögur.*[2] Several sagas and tales of Icelanders not included here either depict giant fosterage, or depict human foster-mothers who resemble giantesses in significant ways.[3] Finally, the major source texts for Norse mythology, the poems of the *Poetic Edda* and Snorri Sturluson's *Prose Edda*, also mention giant fosterage.[4]

All these texts collectively attest to the great popularity and durability of the theme of the giantess *fóstra* throughout medieval Iceland. It's not a trivial question to ask what this theme must have meant to the many authors and copyists who created and preserved these sagas and tales. The sagas that contain such fantastic episodes were long scorned as second-rate compared to more realistic, novel-like sagas, often labeled "dreary," "decadent," "degenerate," and even "pernicious".[5] Some contemporary authors still express bafflement that such sagas were so popular: Kathryn Hume asks, "Why is such supernatural material—with a few exceptions—so trivial and artistically uninteresting in most of Icelandic literature? . . . We may lament that an original and sophisticated literary form should give way to a formulaic and naïve one and wish that focus on varied and complex people had not yielded to a taste for faceless superheroes and monsters."[6] And Sandra Straubhaar wonders, "Twenty-first-century readers may well ask themselves: how could the dismemberment of unwashed, foreign-favored women possibly have been considered by any audience at any time as entertainment?"[7] Why did Icelanders write, read, and enjoy stories of giants for so long, and what did such stories mean to them?

Sagas and their Genres

It's usual to divide the Norse sagas into several classes, four of which concern us here. *Íslendingasögur* relate the lives of the first generations of settlers in Iceland; *konungasögur* tell the lives and deeds of Norse kings; *fornaldarsögur* or "sagas of old times" are set in Scandinavia, usually in the legendary past, and relate the deeds of heroes; and *riddarasögur* or "knightly sagas" are either translations of continental European chivalric romances, or original compositions set in the same milieu. There has been much debate over whether this is an adequate classification, or indeed whether it's possible to devise a firm typology of sagas at all.[8] A great many sagas blend elements from different classes; certainly all of the sagas and tales selected for this volume do so.

The first tale in this book, *Hálfdanar þáttr svarta*, is taken from the great manuscript *Flateyjarbók*, copied and illustrated by two Icelandic monks between 1387 and 1390.[9] Much of *Hálfdanar þáttr* is textually very close to *Hálfdanar saga svarta*, the biography of the Norwegian king Halfdan the Black, as it appears in the compilation *Heimskringla*.[10] Both the saga and the tale contain an episode in which:

1. The food and drink vanish from Halfdan's Yule feast.
2. Halfdan tortures a Finn whom he suspects of having stolen the food.
3. Halfdan's son Harald frees and runs away with the Finn.
4. Harald lives in the wilderness with the Finnish chieftain.
5. The chieftain sends Harald back, and promises him the kingship of all Norway.

In the *Heimskringla* saga, Harald returns home to find that his father is dead and that he is now king. In *Hálfdanar þáttr svarta*, however, the episode is doubled; Harald returns to his father, but much the same story happens again:

1. Wealth vanishes from Halfdan's treasury.
2. Halfdan captures the giant Dofri, whom he suspects of having stolen his wealth.
3. Halfdan's son Harald frees and runs away with the giant.
4. Harald lives in the wilderness with the giant.
5. The giant sends Harald back, and promises him the kingship of all Norway.

It's likely that the compiler of *Hálfdanar þáttr svarta* included two different versions of a story involving Harald's fosterage in the wilderness. As we will see, "Finns" and giants are conceptualized in very similar terms in these sagas.

Hauks þáttr hábrokar, also taken from *Flateyjarbók*, hints at a tradition that Harald Fairhair had also been fostered by a female giant—not in the Dovrefjell, but on the coast of the White Sea, a favored haunt of monsters in the legendary sagas. Harald's own fosterage is not described, but he sends his right-hand man Hauk High-Breeches to visit his *fóstra*, the crone Heid. This part of the tale has no parallel in *Heimskringla*, but the tale ends with the story of Harald's bewitched love for the Saami girl Snjofrid, which is also told in *Heimskringla.*[11]

Harald's fosterage by Dofri is mentioned in a nominal *Íslendingasaga*, *Bárðar saga snæfellsáss* (not included in this volume). Here, the half-giant, half-human Bard Dumbsson is fostered by Dofri, but has a prophetic dream that King Harald will later be fostered there.[12] Other *Íslendingasögur* also refer to Harald as *Dofrasfóstri.*[13] But the tradition of Harald's fosterage is presented most clearly in *Kjalnesinga saga*, which relates the lives of the early generations of Norse and Irish settlers in the area around Kjalarnes on the west side of Iceland[14]. Like many *Íslendingasögur*, it begins with the settlement of a region as the settlers establish and name their farms and the features of their landscape. The saga describes the Kjalarnes area accurately and in detail; its author must have known the region well.[15] As in so many sagas of Icelanders, conflict arises over legal matters, and then over a desirable woman, and the protagonist must leave Iceland for a while. His beloved must stay faithful to him for three years when he has to leave Iceland, but she is taken by another man when false news comes that her lover is dead or lost.[16] All this is typical *Íslendingasaga* fare, but the saga veers off into *fornaldarsaga* territory when the hero is sent into the wilderness to find the giant Dofri; he befriends his daughter Frid and begets a child on her.[17] Unlike many of the female giants in these sagas, Frid is quite beautiful and well-dressed, although evidently much larger than Bui (she refers to Bui as a "bearded baby"). When Bui leaves Frid behind, pregnant with his child, Frid is not happy but does not object, as is usual with giantesses who foster male heroes. However, the tale ends tragically; Bui returns to Iceland and lives there in peace and honor for years, but when he refuses to recognize his son by Frid, he is killed in a wrestling bout. The deadly conflict between Bui and his son has a close parallel in Irish legends of Cú Chulainn and his son Connla, although in the Norse text it is the father, not the son, who is killed. Kjalarnes was allegedly colonized by Irish settlers (including Bui's father), and it's tempting to assume that their traditions were incorporated into the saga, although other explanations are possible.[18]

The oldest text of *Kjalnesinga saga* claims that no one knows what happened to the son of Bui and Frid. But a later author saw fit to compose a "sequel" to *Kjalnesinga saga* telling what became of him.

Jökuls þáttr Búasonar is traditionally placed with the *Íslendingasögur*; but in subject matter, setting, and style, *Jökuls þáttr* is very far from the sagas of Icelanders, and really belongs with the *fornaldarsögur*. Its author certainly knew *Hálfdanar saga Brönufóstra*; not only do both include a female named Marsibil, but the plots are much the same in outline.[19] The final scene in Serkland (technically the Middle East, but in the tale simply a distant and exotic land) also shows influence from the *riddarasögur*.

Like *Jökuls þáttr Búasonar*, *Brandkrossa þáttr* is dependent on a larger saga; it was written as a "prequel" to *Droplaugarsona saga* (not included in this book).[20] The fantastic element is rather muted in this tale; the author is skeptical of the giant-episode, and the giant figure, Geitir, is not explicitly said to be a giant. Nonetheless, the basic outline of Grim and Thorkel's adventure is much like the giant encounters in *Kjalnesinga saga* and *Hálfdanar þáttr*. An alternate version of the giant-tale in *Brandkrossa þáttr* forms an episode in *Fljótsdæla saga*, one of the latest of the "classical" sagas of Icelanders, dated no earlier than the end of the 15th century. The giant in *Fljótsdæla saga* does not foster the hero, and unusually for giants, he bears some resemblance to the walking dead (*draugar*), which are usually treated as a separate category of beings. However, the rescue of the jarl's daughter does resemble episodes in several other sagas of giants, notably *Hálfdanar saga Brönufóstra* and *Jökuls þáttr Búasonar*.

The next three sagas in this book are part of the traditional corpus of *fornaldarsögur*. *Hálfdanar saga Brönufóstra* and *Sörla saga sterka* are paired; not only does the hero of *Sörla saga* defeat the hero of *Hálfdanar saga*, but the two sagas contain similar objects (a cave with a window, a ring made of several parts screwed together), and the heroes' encounters with their fostering giantesses are broadly similar. The heroes also meet in *Sörla þáttr* (not included in this book), which summarizes their conflict and its aftermath and continues the tale into the next generation.[21] It's worth mentioning that *Hálfdanar saga*'s tale of the fight against two giants in a cave has been called closer to *Beowulf* than any other Norse saga.[22] *Sörla saga*, even more so than *Hálfdanar saga*, contains a large store of themes and images from the courtly *riddarasögur*.

Illuga saga Gríðarfóstra is not connected with any other saga in the corpus, although two very minor characters appear in other sagas. The oldest manuscript of *Illuga saga* dates only to about 1600, and it may in fact be post-medieval. It is atypically short for a saga, consisting mostly of one episode.[23] The plot revolves around a noble lady turned into a hideous giant, whom the hero frees from her enchantment. The theme is related to a well-known folktale motif known as the Loathly Lady, although in typical Loathly Lady tales, the hero must embrace the hideous woman himself in order to free her, which does not happen in *Illuga saga*.[24] The Loathly Lady motif may be the result of Celtic influence; it is well known in Irish mythology, where the Loathly Lady turns out to be the embodiment of Sovereignty, and the hero's embrace of her grants him rulership.[25] In *Illuga saga*, there is no question of sovereignty, as Illugi is not a king; nonetheless he may be said to come into full manhood from the encounter, winning the right to marry a princess and eventually becoming the sworn brother of a famous king.

The final story in this book, *Inntak úr söguþætti af Ásmundi flagðagæfu* ("Summary of a Saga-Tale of Asmund Ogre-Lucky"—henceforth referred to as *Söguþáttr* for short), is all that remains of a lost *fornaldarsaga*-like narrative. At one time, there was apparently a saga about Asmund Ogre-Lucky, and a set of *rímur* (long ballad-like poems) derived from the saga, but these have been lost. The *Söguþáttr*, which includes a few verses from the *rímur*, was written down around 1700 by Reverend Eyjólfur Jónsson, based on stories that he had heard from his mother and maternal grandmother. His grandmother had learned the saga from an old vellum manuscript. It is an open question how much of the story we have came from this manuscript, how much is derived from the *rímur*, and how much was added by Eyjólfur. That said, many of the themes in the *Söguþáttr* have close parallels in other sagas: the unpromising "coal-biter," the idea that promising men could make a name for themselves by serving the king of Norway, and so on. Even the wording of many expressions in the *Söguþáttr* is close to phrases found in other sagas.[26] While the *Söguþáttr* draws on several saga genres, there's no reason not to include it in the corpus of *fornaldarsögur*.[27]

Although Asmund Ogre-Lucky is not said to be fostered by a giant, the *Söguþáttr* nonetheless shows a number of parallels with the tales of giant fosterage. The tale is divided into four episodes: Asmund's early life as a *kolbítr* ("coal-biter," an unpromising lad who does nothing but lie by the fire); his defeat of the giant Nadd; his contest with Thorgerd Holdatroll; and his encounter with the family who worships Völski. Nadd and Thorgerd are more or less stock giants, but the Völski episode is bizarre: the hero encounters a family that worships a severed horse penis that they have magicked into a being that walks by itself, serves them at the table, and steals wealth and brings it to them. When the inevitable showdown comes, it takes four men and a dog to kill this monster. This seems to be a blending of at least three different sources:

1. *Völsa þáttr*, in *Flateyjarbók*, purports to be an account of pagan worship in a remote part of Norway. The mother of a family takes a severed horse penis and preserves it until it is able to stand up on its own. She names it Völsi, and in a religious ritual, requires her family to pass it around, reciting verses that contain the repeated line "May the Mörnir [probably giantesses] take this blessing."[28]
2. Two tales from *Flateyjarbók*, *Ögmundar þáttr dytts*[29] and *Rögnvalds þáttr ok Rauðs*,[30] feature wooden statues of gods coming to life, moving independently, and doing their worshippers' will. A third *Flateyjarbók* tale, *Þorleifs þáttr jarlsskálds*, depicts evil magic used to animate a wooden man and send it to assassinate an enemy. The Christian writers of *Flateyjarbók* interpreted these stories to mean that devils were living inside the idols.
3. Icelandic folklore mentions the *tilberi* ("carrier"), a magically animated being that a witch can send out to steal milk and wool from neighboring farms. The *tilberi* is made from a human rib wrapped in wool, brought to life by the witch spitting Communion wine on it three times, and nourished by the witch's own blood. Elsewhere in Scandinavia, magically animated "troll-cats" and "milk-hares" were sent out by a witches to steal from their neighbors.[31]

What, If Anything, Is A Giant?

Tröll kalla mik
tungl sjöt-Rungnis,
auðsúg jötuns,
élsólar böl,
vilsinn völu,
vörð náfjarðar,
hvélsvelg himins.
Hvat er tröll, nema þat?[32]

Trolls call me [or: They call me a troll,]
moon of the dwelling-Rungnir,
giant's wealth-sucker,
storm-sun's grief,
seeress's companion,
fjord-corpse's guardian,
heaven-wheel's swallower.° *heaven-wheel*: sun
What is a troll, but that?

This verse, allegedly spoken by a troll-woman to the poet Bragi and quoted in Snorri Sturluson's *Edda*, is difficult to understand, and several of its figures of speech remain obscure. Nonetheless, it alludes to many of the characteristics of giants in the sagas. Many giants live along fjords, and many draw vast wealth to themselves. Some can call up winds and storms; some have powers of prophecy or foresight. The last name, "heaven-wheel's swallower," and possibly also the fourth line, "storm-sun's grief," refers to the myth that giants in the shape of wolves follow the sun and moon and will eventually swallow them.

Old Norse had a surprising large vocabulary to denote the beings that are usually called "giants" in English. *Jötunn, risi* and *þurs* are the most common words to denote a humanoid of unusual size. *Bergbúi*, "mountain-dweller," and occasionally *hraunbúi*, "lava-field dweller," are also found, although not in the sagas presented here. Female giants have their own special tems: *flagð*, translated here as "ogre," is grammatically neuter, but a being called a *flagð* is a always female, and nearly always hostile. The same is true for the *syrpa* and the *skersa* or *skessa*, which are used for female giants but also for coarse, unladylike women, making it difficult in some cases to decide exactly what sort of being is meant. *Kerling* usually means "old woman," but it can be applied to giantesses as well (in which cases I have usually translated it as "crone" or "hag"). *Gýgr* and *íviðja* are also used for female giants, although these words do not appear in the texts presented here. A very common word for both male and female giants is *tröll*, with the female form *tröllkona*.

A few texts draw distinctions between different types of beings. *Bárðar saga snæfellsáss* makes a point of mentioning that *risir* are more handsome and easier to deal with than their adversaries, *tröll* and *þursar*.[33]

In *Þorsteins þáttr bæjarmagns,* Goðmundr, a legendary ruler in the far north, is said to rule *Risaland*, distinct from *Jötunheimar.*[34] Several other sagas mention the unusual beauty of the *risir*; *Þorsteins saga Víkingssonar* calls them more beautiful than the elves[35], while *Örvar-Odds saga* calls them "more handsome than most other people. . . but they aren't any more intelligent."[36] However, most sources use these words more or less as synonyms. The Eddic poem *Þrymskvíða* calls the giant Thrym the *þursa drottinn* ("lord of *þursar*"), but calls his realm *Jötunheim* and has him address his subjects as *jötnar.*[37] Another Eddic poem, *Helgakviða Hjörvarðssonar*, mentions a being named Loðinn ("hairy"), who is called *jötunn*, *þurs*, *hraunbúi*, and *maðr* ("man"), all in the same verse.[38]

The texts in this book show a great deal of this semantic overlap, but some distinctions are usually made. In *Hálfdanar þáttr svarta*, Dofri is referred to as a *jötunn*, *tröll*, *dólgr* ("monster"), and *karl* ("old man"). The names seem chosen to fit the tone of the saga at that point: Dofri's antagonist King Halfdan calls him a *tröll*, but Dofri is called a *karl* when he bawls over the stunned Harald. The same is true of *Hauks þáttr hábrokar*; the antagonists call Heid a *tröll*, but Harald Fairhair simply calls her *mín fóstra. Kjalnesinga saga* never uses any of the words for "giant" for Dofri; his daughter is only said to be *mikil á allan vöxt*, "large in all dimensions," and the men in his hall are *heldr stórleitir*, "quite large-faced." *Jökuls þáttr Búasonar* uses *syrpa* for the female beings that the hero first encounters, and *flagð*, *jötunn*, and *tröll* for beings encountered later. In *Brandkrossa þáttr*, as in *Kjalnesinga saga*, the giant figure Geitir is never directly called a giant; the only clue that he is not wholly human is his name—Geitir appears as a giant's name in poetry[39]—and his statement that *var móðir mín vel mönnuð, en föður átta ek heldr stórfengan*, "my mother was well-born, but I had a rather huge father." The narrator of *Fljótsdæla saga* calls Geitir a *jötunn* and a *dólgr*, but characters within the story, notably the princess whom he has kidnapped, refer to him as *tröll.*

Turning to the wholly legendary sagas, *Hálfdanar saga Brönufóstra* uses *tröll*, *karl*, *kerling*, and *flagð* (and *jötunn* exactly once) for hostile beings, but none of these names are used for Brana once she has befriended the hero Halfdan and become his *fóstra. Sörla saga* uses both *jötunn* and *risi* for the hostile giant Skrimnir (where we might expect *þurs*). It usually uses *kerling* for his wife Mana, but also uses *tröllkona*, *flagð*, *flagðkona*, and *skessa. Illuga saga* uses *tröllkona* and *skrípi*, "monster," for Grid (who appears ogre-ish but is "really" a human), and *flagð* for the servant Sunnlod and the queen Grimhild (who appear human but are "really" trollish). *Sögupáttr* uses both *maðr*, "man," and *risi* for the first giant encountered, while Thorgerd is named *Höldatröll* but is not directly called a giant; her daughter only says *Lítt mun móðir mín eðli eiga við aðra menn, og mun hún hníga til ættar sinnar*—"My mother's nature is little suited for other people, and she will turn to her own kin." The strange magic monster Volski in the last section is called a *kvikindi*, "beast," but he "turns into a troll" (*tryllist*) on being attacked, whereas Olaf calls the old woman that created Volski a *flagð* after he has killed her.

To complicate matters further, any firm definitions of these types of being tended to blur and shift over time. In the primary mythological texts, the *jötnar* are on the level of gods, along with the Æsir and Vanir. Far from being brainless lummoxes, giants like Mímir and Vafþrúðnir have deep learning and wisdom. Odin in particular desires this wisdom: he exchanges his eye for a drink of wisdom and reason (*spekð ok mannvit*) from Mimir's Well in the keeping of the frost-giants,[40] learns nine powerful songs from his giant uncle,[41] and sleeps with Gunnlöð and is given the mead of poetry in exchange.[42] The giants are also fecund, and gods repeatedly take wives or lovers from among the *jötnar*. Freyr falls in love with the giant-maid Gerðr;[43] Njörðr is chosen by Skaði (who becomes Odin's concubine after her marriage fails);[44] and even Thor, who is renowned for bashing giants, has a giant-concubine, Járnsaxa (Iron-Knife), and has friendly dealings with several other giants. The exchange is one-way only: giants who try to gain brides from the Æsir end up defeated and killed. Nonetheless, there is no "species difference" between gods and giants; they mingle, they can interbreed, and they share many functions, although the gods are more closely aligned with human beings.[45]

In the later legendary sagas and in folklore, giants and trolls are scaled down to the human world. Although they are still powerful and dangerous, it is possible for strong or crafty humans to beat them. Yet it's not clear where the "greater giants" of myth leave off and the "lesser giants" of the sagas begin. Both have deep wisdom, great treasures, and fertile wombs, which they may kindly bestow, or be tricked out of, or be fought for. Arinnefja in *Egils saga einhenda* has been the lover of both Odin and Thor, like many other female giants in the mythology, but she also has friendly dealings with humans. Skrimnir is a giant who gets the better of the god Thor; a giant with the same name is summarily killed by the hero of *Sörla saga.* Surtr appears in mythology as the giant who will one day kill the god Freyr and set the cosmos aflame. However, a giant sharing his name is killed by the hero of *Jökuls þáttr Búasonar*; another giant of that name appears in *Bárðar saga* and the post-classical *Hellismanna saga* as an inhabitant of Iceland; yet another Surtr is killed by the hero of *Ketils saga hængs.* When an Icelander goes up to a cave and recites a praise-poem to Surtr,[46] it's not clear whether the mythic Surtr or a "lesser" Surtr is meant.

The names and concepts of giant beings evolved differently in different parts of the Norse world. In Iceland, for example, all the large, powerful land-beings apparently ended up classified as trolls,[47] while in parts of mainland Scandinavia names like *jätte*, *jætte*, *jutul*, or *jøtul* persisted.[48] Perhaps the most extreme shift occurred in Sætersdal, Norway, where the Norse word *þurs* evolved into *tusse* and came to mean a helpful farm-spirit, like the *nisse* elsewhere in Norway or the brownie in English folklore. Despite this very complex taxonomy, a few trends may be distinguished. Lotte Motz has noted that in modern Scandinavian languages, words derived from *þurs* usually imply stupidity (e.g. Danish *tosse*, "to act foolish"; Danish *tosse*, Norwegian *tosk*, Swedish *toss*, all meaning "simpleton").[49] Words derived from *jötunn* pertain to great size and strength (e.g. Danish *jætteagtig*, "gigantic"), and also to ancient features in the landscape (e.g. Danish *jættestue*, "giants' chamber," for a prehistoric burial mound; Danish *jættegryde*, "giants' cauldron," for a large rock hollow; Swedish *jättekast*, "giant's throw," for an isolated boulder).[50] *Risi* has left relatively few cognates, which overlap with *jötunn* in pertaining to great size and landscape features (e.g. Swedish *resehög*, "giants' mound," for a prehistoric burial mound).[51] Cleasby and Vigfusson's *Dictionary* quotes an Icelandic saying, *hár sem risi, sterkr sem jötunn, heimskr sem þurs*—"tall as a *risi*, strong as a *jötunn*, stupid as a *þurs*"—which seems to agree with Motz's conceptions of the defining feature of each type of giant.[52]

Motz also notes that words derived from *tröll* pertain to magic (e.g. Danish *trolddom*, "sorcery"; *trylle*, "to enchant"; *tryllekreds*, "magic circle").[53] *Tröll* in Old Norse is itself derived from *trylla*, "to madden; to enrage; to fill with furious power."[54] This is borne out by the sagas, in which not all trolls are giants, and not all giants are trolls. *Hrólfs saga kraka* uses *tröll* for a flying man-eating beast, of which it is said that "it is not an animal, rather it is the greatest of trolls"—evidently, being a troll goes beyond being merely a monster.[55] In *Eyrbyggja saga*, a man-killing bull of uncanny birth is called a troll.[56] Several people in various sagas, while fully human according to their genetic descent, are called trolls because they are large, ugly, ill-tempered, skilled in magic, or, usually, all of the above: to give just one example, in *Kjalnesinga saga* both Bui and Esja are called *tröll* by their adversary Kolfid. Legendary sagas sometimes use *tröll* for someone who is seemingly human by birth, but who comes from a distant land, is supernaturally strong, and is otherwise uncanny; examples include Gardar and Tofi in *Sörla saga sterka*, whereas Sóti and Snækollr in *Hálfdanar saga Brönufóstra* should probably be classified as *tröll* even though the word is not specifically used for them. Ögmundr in *Örvar-Odds saga* is half-human, half-ogre (*gýgr*), but it's not until he is enchanted with spells and sacrifices that he is turned into a *tröll*.[57] Finally, in *Flateyjarbók*, King Óláfr Geirstaðaálfr warns his people not to sacrifice to him after his death, because dead men who are worshipped are *trylldir*, "turned into trolls".[58] Thus, the semantic field of *tröll* overlaps humans, giants, animals, monsters, mythical hybrids, and the dead. What's common to all of them is that a *tröll*, regardless of species, is hostile to ordinary humans, and uses uncanny strength and magic against them.

One "species" of *tröll* that deserves comment here is encountered in *Kjalnesinga saga* and *Sörla saga sterka* in this book, as well as in many other legendary sagas: the *blámaðr* or "black man." A few sagas, such as *Orkneyinga saga*, record crusades or raids in the Mediterranean region, and in these sagas, *blámaðr* is used for the black Africans that the Norse heroes occasionally encounter. Although they may fight against the Norsemen, these African *blámenn* are not depicted as especially uncanny[59]. In legendary sagas, however, *blámenn* have virtually nothing to do with actual Africans; they are more or less stock monsters, usually in the service of a powerful king, overlapping somewhat with the concept of berserks. They are hideous and immensely strong, and they howl and gibber but never say anything intelligible. Though difficult to kill, they are always defeated by the hero after an exciting battle scene.

Finally, the concept of "giants" in Iceland also overlaps that of *landvættir* or "landwights," spirits associated with the land itself and its natural features. A well-known passage in *Óláfs saga Tryggvasonar* in *Heimskringla* relates how King Harald Gormsson sent a sorcerer to spy out Iceland invisibly; the sorcerer encountered *landvættir*, including a hostile dragon, bird, bull, and *bergrís*, "mountain giant". Each had similar *vættir* in tow; the *bergrís* was supported by a host of *jötnar*.[60] A similar word to *bergrís* is *bergbúi*, "mountain-dweller," which certainly seems to refer to a giant in some texts, notably the short story *Bergbúa þáttr*. At the same time, *Landnámabók* tells how a *bergbúi* went into partnership with the early settler of Iceland Bjorn Gnupsson and caused his goats to breed so rapidly that Bjorn amassed a huge flock and became known as Hafr-Bjorn, "Buck-Goat Bjorn". When Bjorn attended the Althing, all the *landvættir* followed him, both great and small.[61] These examples suggest that at least some *jötnar* could be seen as land-dwelling beings—perhaps of unusually large size or strength, and living in wild places, but not qualitatively different from other *landvættir*.

Innangarðr and Útgarðr

In a well-known analysis of medieval Icelanders' conceptual models of space and time, Kirsten Hastrup has shown that the Icelanders' world could be divided into two concentric zones: *innangarðs* and *útangarðs*, "inside the yard" and "outside the yard". On Icelandic farmsteads, the farm buildings and home fields were *innangarðs*; the unclaimed land outside the fence was *útangarðs*. This arrangement was repeated within the farm, where the living quarters belonged to the category *innihús*, "inner house," while the barns and storehouses were the *útihús*, "outer house". The arrangement was repeated on a larger scale in the Icelander's view of the known world: the countries of northern Europe where familiar human societies and languages were found were *innangarðs*, while the wild Scandinavian mountains, northern Russia, Siberia, Greenland, Labrador, or Africa were *útangarðs*.[62] Finally, the same model appears in mythology; the giants come from the *Útgarðr* that surrounds *Ásgarðr*, the gods' enclosure.[63]

Hastrup emphasizes that the definition of *innangarðs* does not necessarily depend on its arrangement in space. What defines *innangarðs* is law.[64] Icelanders used the same expression to refer to their land and to their society: *vár lög*, "our law".[65] As Njál's wise saying goes, *með lögum skal land várt byggja, en eigi með ólögum eyða*—"with law shall our land be built, but with lawlessness be laid waste."[66] What is *útangarðs* is also *útlaga*, "out of law" (literally, "lying outside"); for better or for worse, law simply does not apply there. This concentric "horizontal model" repeats itself at different geographic scales, like a fractal pattern. Outlaws, vagrants, people of very different cultures, and the giants of legend and mythology were all fundamentally similar, as they were all *útangarðs*. *Sörla saga sterka* makes this point well when it describes a hostile force of *blámenn ok bannsettar hetjur*, "black men and banished warriors".[67] The concept was too fundamental to be eradicated by Christianity.[68]

The *Útgarðr* was seen as dangerous and hostile. Yet *Útgarðr* is also fundamentally necessary to *Innangarðr*. They relate to each other through exchange: each has things that the other needs. The division between *Innangarðr* and *Útgarðr* is not the same as the Christian concepts of Heaven and Hell: the boundary between *Innangarðr* and *Útgarðr* must remain flexible and porous, and interchange across that boundary must be possible for both realms to survive. The stories that we have tend to be told from the perspective of the *Innangarðr*, and they generally privilege *Innangarðr* over *Útgarðr*: free farmers over outlaws, Norsefolk over foreigners, and gods over giants. Beings of the *Innangarðr* are often shown trying to imbalance the exchange by taking more than they give: traders in Bjarmaland plunder their former trading partners once their truce is finished,[69] crusaders in the Mediterranean plunder towns and trading ships,[70] voyagers to the ends of the world slaughter giants, and the Æsir gods break their agreements with giants by trickery, seduction, or force.[71] Yet this masks the fundamental dynamic of reciprocity between *Innangarðr* and *Útgarðr*: powerful Norsemen make mutually beneficial alliances with distant peoples,[72] voyaging heroes help giantesses in need, gods accept giants into their own society and do favors for them,[73] and gods— sometimes—pay the full price for what they take from giant keepers.[74] Even hostilities may start as friendly encounters.[75] As the giantess Brana tells the human Halfdan, *mun ek gott af þér hljóta ok svá þú af mér* —"I will gain good from you, and you from me as well."[76]

In Norse mythic thought, there is a tendency for distinct and separated elements on one level to be fused into one, by a mediating element at a higher hierarchical level.[77] Those who could mediate between the inner world and the outer world, who could cross the boundary and return, could potentially bring back great benefits for those who stayed behind. Outlaws have their uses: Grettir the Strong lived as an outlaw in the Icelandic wilderness, but was known to re-enter human society, not always to rob and kill, but to do heroic deeds, killing monsters and even entertaining feast-goers with feats of wrestling. Even great kings like Sigmund the Völsung might have to "do time" as outlaws.[78] Trading expeditions to the far north of Scandinavia and Russia might have to risk both natural and supernatural hazards, but return with valuable cargoes. The gods who travel the most into the *Útgarðr*—Odin, Thor, and Loki—run risks from the beings that they encounter, but they gain great benefits as well: a giantess gives Thor magical gloves and a staff,[79] and the gods all feast well with the giant Ægir.[80] When the giants do not give their benefits freely, they may be tricked or forced into giving them up, as in the myths of the building of the walls of Asgard, or the theft of the mead of poetry. The pattern is the same for the giants in the sagas in this book: However frightening they may be, they may also give help and treasures (freely or not) to the heroes who can navigate the dangerous boundary between *Innangarðr* and *Útgarðr*.

Giants as Social Others

The giants of these sagas, living in one or another level of *Útgarðr*, are consistently depicted as Other—as being markedly different from the culture that the saga authors knew. Giants are not always physically different from humans, except for their size. Even size is not always a distinguishing feature; some giants are not said to be especially large, and some human heroes are said to be of giant size. Sigurd the Völsung was said to be so tall that he could walk through a field of full-grown rye and the tip of the sword at his side would graze the tops of the rye stalks;[81] his horse's tail hairs were seven ells long (well over three meters).[82] Lotte Motz has pointed out that with a few exceptions, giants in the myths are not depicted as consistently larger than the gods,[83] while Harthgrepa in Saxo's *History of the Danes* assures her human lover Hading that her kind can assume whatever size is required.[84]

Sometimes giants are not only large but handsome and imposing, such as Frid in *Kjalnesinga saga*. However, it's more usual in the legendary sagas for giants to be physically different from humans to the point of being hideous. Grid in *Illuga saga Gríðarfóstra* is probably the most extreme, bearing a striking if coincidental resemblance to Lena the Hyena; Heid in *Hauks þáttr hábrokar* and Gnipa in *Jökuls þáttr Búasonar* are more or less tied for second place in the ugly contest. Giants occasionally have unusual numbers of body parts; Brana's fellow giants in *Hálfdanar saga Brönufóstra* have two heads, and her father Jarnhaus has three. Thor is said to have bashed the nine heads of the giant Þrívaldi[85] and torn off the extra arms of the six-armed or eight-armed giant Starkaðr,[86] whereas a "three-headed *þurs*" is mentioned in *Skirnismál*,[87] and a giantess with nine hundred heads appears in *Hymiskviða*.[88]

Whether hideous or beautiful, giants do not follow human ethics. Some giants eat human flesh, such as Sleggja and Jarnnef in *Hálfdanar saga Brönufóstra*. This trait certainly marks them as Other—although not all giants eat humans, and giants that do are not depicted as imminent threats to the social order, in the way that Grendel is in *Beowulf*.[89] More generally, beings of *Útgarðr* do not show the moderation of egotistical impulses that is expected of residents of *Innangarðr*. Giants tend to act impulsively, taking things and people simply because they want them. And while power struggles among humans are supposed to be settled by law and precedent, struggles among giants are settled violently, with the strongest winning all.[90] As discussed below, giantish sexuality is also unrestrained and immoderate, especially among female giants. But perhaps most shocking for Norse audiences, giants are willing to ignore their own ties of kinship. Once a hero shows up and proves his mastery, giants seem to have few qualms about letting the hero get away with killing their relatives, or even enlisting the hero's help to kill their own kin. In this book alone, Mana forgives Sorli for killing her husband Skrimnir in *Sörla saga*; Brana helps Halfdan kill her father and family in *Hálfdanar saga Brönufóstra*; and Gnipa helps Jokul wipe out not only her own family, but most of the giants of Greenland, in *Jökuls þáttr Búasonar*. Given the importance of kin ties in Norse society and law, with the relatives of a slain man obliged to take revenge or accept compensation, there could be no clearer way to demonstrate to a Norse audience that giants are ethically and socially "out of law."

Another marker of otherness is weaponry. Giants usually fight unarmed, by grappling. When they fight with a bladed weapon, it is generally a *sax*, a single-edged long knife/short sword (translated "knife" here for simplicity) or else a *skálm*, another word for a short blade. Mana in *Sörla saga sterka* and the seven ogresses in *Illuga saga Gríðarfóstra* wield *skálmir*, while Grid in *Illuga saga*, Eitil in *Jökuls þáttr Búasonar* and Brana in *Hálfdanar saga Brönufóstra* each wield a *sax*. Giants may also wield clubs—Brana gives iron clubs to the sworn brothers in *Hálfdanar saga*, and the *blámenn* in *Sörla saga* wield steel-studded cudgels. In the Eddas, the sagas, and later folklore, giants and trolls fling huge stones.[91] In several sagas not included in this book, giants fight with polearms: the troll in *Grettis saga* wields a *fleinn* (usually translated as "pike"), also called a *heptisax*, "hafted knife"[92]; the trollish Harek Ironskull wields a double-pointed pike in *Þorsteins saga Víkingssonar*[93]; a huge *risi* carries a staff with a double-edged point in *Hjálmþés saga ok Ölvis*[94]; and the giant Grimnir in *Hrólfs saga Gautrekssonar* says that he has neither axe nor sword, but kills men with a forked iron poker.[95] Such giantish weapons are rarely wielded by humans, who bear swords, axes and spears while wearing shields and armor. Giants may have such things in their caves, and may give them to favored humans (or lose them to human looters), but rarely use them in battle.

Yet another marker of otherness is the games that giants play. The giant couple in *Hálfdanar saga Brönufóstra* play a peculiar game of turning somersaults while the iron hook in one giant's nose is hooked into the iron ring in the other's nose.[96] Other sagas depict giants playing violent throwing games, dangerous to humans who try to take part.[97] Even the relatively cultured Dofri in *Kjalnesinga saga* suggests that Harald should retire from the feasting-hall in the evening because his retainers will be getting boisterous.[98] Giants' wrestling, whether in play or in deadly combat, includes tricks that humans refuse to use: Högni in *Sörla saga sterka* wrestles with Sorli but refuses to bite out his throat "as a troll does."[99] Giantish wrestling also includes tearing flesh; just as Harthgrepa in Saxo's *Gesta Danorum* dies when "lacerated by companions of her own race. . . the savage nails of her assailants,"[100] Mana in *Sörla saga* has "the flesh pulled from her bones."[101]

Even more so than male giants, female giants are set apart from humans. Simply by living in the wilderness, female giants are radically Other. Women were conceived of as associated with the hearth, the center of *Útgarðr*; those women who left it, or were driven from it, risked becoming trolls. This happens in *Bárðar saga snæfellsáss* to Bard's daughter

Helga and to the farmer's daughter Jóra, both of whom go off alone into the wilderness after suffering deep disappointments, eventually turning into trolls.[102] Women living alone can be dangerous even if they still live within human society, such as Esja in *Kjalnesinga saga*, who is called a troll by her adversaries. Icelandic women who traveled from one farm to another brought news, and sometimes spoke prophecies or worked magic, but they might be feared as much as welcomed, as they too partake of the trollish nature of *Útgarðr*.[103]

Female giants are further set apart from humans by their unrestrained sexuality.[104] Even in cases where the giantess is much larger than the human, size disparity is no obstacle to sexual relations, as seen in *Kjalnesinga saga* among others. The sexually charged encounters between Illugi and Heid in *Illuga saga Gríðarfostra*, Hauk and Heid in *Hauks þáttr hábrokar*, and Jokul and Gnipa in *Jökuls þáttr Búasonar*, also hint at the wanton nature of female giants. In sagas not included in this book, a scantily clad giantess in *Hjálmþés saga ok Ölvis* makes an indecent proposal to the hero,[105] one in *Sturlaugs saga starfsama* expresses infatuation for a human,[106] and yet another in *Egils saga einhenda* is driven by such strong urges that she "can't seem to live without a man."[107] The hero of *Örvar-Odds saga* is smaller than a newborn giant and yet "played all the games he felt like" with a female giant, managing to impregnate her despite only coming up to her mid-thigh.[108] Excessive eagerness for sex was considered disgraceful in women; it was called *ergi*, the same insult that implied cowardice and passive homosexuality when applied to men.[109]

Another marker of otherness that especially applies to female giants is clothing. While some giants dress well by human standards, others dress in ways that violate Norse cultural standards. Sagas repeatedly describe female giants wearing skin tunics that hang down in front but nearly bare the buttocks; Geit and Gnipa in *Jökuls þáttr Búasonar* and Grid in *Illuga saga Gríðarfóstra* are examples in this book. Some giants in other sagas wear less than that: the members of a troll family in *Gríms saga loðinkinna* wear such scanty skin tunics that the hero sees *hversu þau váru í sköpun bæði í millum fótanna*, "what the genitals of both of them were like, between their legs"[110], and a giantess in *Egils saga einhenda* wears such scanty clothing that *mátti þar sjá viðrlita mikil sköp, því at hún var stuttklædd*, "there one could see her huge genitals, because she was wearing short clothes."[111] That this was not purely a late literary convention may be seen in the carved stone from the 11th-century Hunnestad Monument in southern Sweden, depicting a giantess riding a wolf and wearing only a tunic that comes to above her knees.[112] On the other hand, human women in Viking-era art are virtually always depicted wearing multiple layers of clothing extending down to the ankles. In fact, some women's outer garments were relatively short in front but trailed in back—the diametric opposite of the giantesses' skin tunics.[113] Furthermore, spinning, weaving cloth, and making clothes were never-ending tasks of every Norse woman;[114] the fact that giantesses wear skins and do not spin, weave, or sew, further emphasizes their Otherness. The giantesses who do wear fine cloth dresses are either half-human (Brana in *Hálfdanar saga Brönufóstra*) or relatively civilized *risar* (Frid in *Kjalnesinga saga*). Finally, in contrast with the near-nudity of the giantesses, living human females are almost never depicted nude in the sagas. There are several cases of dead human women appearing nude as undead beings or in dreams, and the effect is terrifying instead of sexy.[115] Female nudity emphasizes otherness, whether the naked woman is a giantess or a dead apparition.

Giants as Ethnic Others

Given that both non-Norse peoples and giants were seen as *útangarðs* at different levels, it's not surprising that giants show a number of the features of exotic cultures.

Probably the strongest parallels can be drawn between the giants and the Saami. The Norse and the Saami lived in adjoining regions, and where the two came into contact, there was considerable cultural symbiosis between them. The *Historia Norvegiae* explicitly states that the Norsemen of Halogaland "often live together with the Lapps and have frequent commerce with them."[116] Ohthere, a Norseman from Halogaland, described his life and his trading among the Saami and other Finnic peoples to King Alfred; he engaged in reindeer herding, implying that he had adopted some Saami ways.[117] *Óláfs saga Tryggvassonar* mentions Raud the Strong, a wealthy Halogalander with a great number of Saami retainers who "followed him whenever he needed them."[118] Several other sagas mention trading and alliances, as well as raiding, between Norse and Saami or other Finnic peoples.[119] Modern genetics confirms that there has been interbreeding between the western Saami

Left: Giantess riding wolf using snakes for reins; stone DR 284, Hunnestad Monument, Marsvinholm, Skåne, Sweden. Right: Silver figurine of a woman wearing multiple layers of flowing clothing; from Grödinge, Södermanland, Sweden. In addition to the contrasting dress styles, compare the poise of the human woman with the giantess's wild energy.

and their Norse neighbors.[120] Perhaps most interesting of all, a male skeleton from a ship-burial in Halogaland had physical features typical for the Saami; yet he had been buried in typical heathen Norse fashion, implying an interchange of religious concepts.[121]

Nonetheless, there seems to have been lingering unease among the Norse. Saami women are depicted as using magic to bring about their enemies' or even husbands' downfall, such as Vanlandi's wife Drífa and Agni's wife Skjalf in *Ynglinga saga*,[122] Harald's wife Snæfrid in *Haralds saga hárfagra*,[123] and Eirik Bloodaxe's wife Gunnhild in several sources.[124] Magic aside, Saami society was more flexible in some gender roles than Norse society was—women could fish, hunt, and ski, for example—and it's possible that the "unladylike" nature of giants in the sagas is ultimately based on Norse reactions to Saami society.[125] Else Mundal has also suggested that the Saami in the Middle Ages may have had a custom of offering transient sexual relationships to male visitors.[126] If true, this might be reflected in the stories of male giants offering their daughters to humans, or at least not objecting to such transient relationships, as in *Kjalnesinga saga* among others.

Evidence for this view comes from texts that conflate the Saami with uncanny beings. In the first version of the doubled story of Harald's fosterage in *Hálfdanar þáttr svarta*, the abductor is a "Finn," but he is replaced by a giant in the second version. In *Hauks þáttr hábrokar*, Svasi, the man who bewitches King Harald, is called a "dwarf," while in the parallel account in *Heimskringla*, he is a "Finn."

The likeliest case of a giant-fosterage tale reflecting real-world ethnography would be *Ketils saga hængs* (not translated here). The protagonist Ketil, from Hrafnista in northern Norway, travels north and encounters a man named Bruni. Bruni offers him his daughter Hrafnhild, who is large, strong, and "has a face an ell wide." She functions as a fostering giantess, becoming his lover, becoming pregnant with his son, and then being left behind when Ketil's father makes a more suitable match for him with a Norse girl. But she is never explicitly stated to be a giant (although Ketil's exasperated father calls her a "troll" at one point) and Bruni later becomes king of the "Finns". *Ketils saga hængs* also describes certain "Finns" as *eigi mjóleitir*, "not narrow-faced," paralleling a passage in *Kjalnesinga saga* in which the giant Dofri's people are called *stórleitir*, "big-faced". This saga is not set in impossibly ancient times—Ketil is said in several sagas to be the cousin or the grandfather of early settlers of Iceland, which would put him in the early- to mid-9th century to the extent that he can be dated at all. It's quite possible that this saga, stripped of its supernatural events, is based on family traditions about Norse-Saami relations in Halogaland. To this day the Saami are stereotyped (not especially accurately) as having broad faces and flat noses.[127] Since Ketil himself is said to be the son of Hallbjorn Half-Troll, he may himself be of mixed Norse and Saami descent. Thus, some degree of Saami influence on the image of giants cannot be ruled out. Lotte Motz has suggested cultural and ethnic parallels between the giants and several Eurasian cultures, not just the Saami.[128]

Influence from other ethnic groups can also be detected. For example, giants and humans with giantish ancestry are often said to be dark or swarthy.[129] The troll-like beings called *blámenn*, "black men" appear in several sagas, as has been noted. The *blámenn* of the legendary sagas have little to do with actual Africans. In fact, they are not always found in Africa; Snorri Sturluson placed them in Siberia.[130] Nonetheless, whether the portrayal of giants in the sagas contains any real ethnography or not, it tends to project supernatural traits onto people of non-Norse ethnicities.[131] The same thinking may be seen in the treatment of other ethnicities: for example, saga characters of Celtic descent are often portrayed as being swarthy, ugly, unpleasant, and/or workers of hostile magic,[132] and the North American natives of the Vinland sagas are also described as swarthy, ugly, and hostile.[133]

Giants as Religious Others

What role did giants play in the religion of the Norse peoples? It was long assumed that giants never received offerings or worship of any sort. Anne Holtsmark even made the lack of worship part of the definition of "giant," writing that "The giants differ from the *vettir* [spirits of the land] in that they never receive offerings."[134] Countering Holtsmark's assertion, Steinsland has argued that giants did receive worship in the Viking era. He discusses Skaði, who is said to be the daughter of the frost giant Thjazi—yet she has *vé ok vangr*, "temples and fields,"[135] and place-name evidence suggests that she was worshipped in south and central Sweden and southeastern Norway.[136]

A problem with the premise of the entire argument is that, like the word *tröll*, the words *goð* and *áss*, "god," do not refer to a "biological species" or lineage of spiritual being. Most of the Norse gods were said to have giant ancestry. Rather, *goð* and *áss* often refer to a being's orientation towards humanity. A being who is helpful and beneficial to humans when called on, regardless of "descent," is inside *Innangarðr* and may be called an *áss* or *goð*. Skaði may be a giantess "by descent," but when she enters Asgard and wins a place there, she enters *Innangarðr*, even though she is still said to live in her father's home Þrymheimr.[137] Snorri Sturluson lists her as one of the gods without comment.[138] *Bárðar saga Snæfellsáss* describes Bard Dumbsson, of mixed giant and human descent, who lives as a human for a while, but eventually goes off into the glacial wastelands and lives among giants and trolls. Yet he is helpful to people who call on him; he is called *Snæfellsáss*, "god of Snæfell," and the saga calls him the *heitguð* or "oath-god" of the people who live nearby. Defined by their function rather than their "descent," gods are what people worship in hope of benefits. A giant who was worshipped and who benefitted his or her worshippers would no longer be a giant, but a god.

At the end of *Kormaks saga*, the hero, raiding in Scotland, encounters a *blótrisi*, literally "sacrifice-giant." The word appears nowhere else in Old Norse, but it can be compared with *blótnaut*, which can mean "cow that is to be sacrificed," but in some legendary sagas means "cow that is worshipped and receives sacrifices." A *blótnaut* that receives sacrifices is always described as uncommonly strong, hostile, and hard to kill—in a word, trollish.[139] In the same way, Kormak's enemy *blótrisi* is said to be *tröllaukinn*, "made greater by a troll," which seems to mean possession; he certainly has the hostility and strength associated with trolls in the sagas. We see the same attitude in *Ólafs þáttr Geirstaðaálfs* in *Flateyjarbók*, which states that dead men who are worshipped are *trylldir*, "turned into trolls."[140] The common theme is that worshipping something makes it more powerful, and this is not always a good thing. The *blótrisi* is presumably a giant who has been worshipped and received sacrifices. But to Kormak, the *blótrisi* is not a *goð*, because he is in Scotland and is presumably worshipped by the natives. As such, he is wholly a creature of *Útgarðr*, and is hostile and dangerous to Kormak.

The most commonly cited instance of a giantess who was worshipped is *Þorgerðr* or Thorgerd, variously known as Hölgabrúðr, Hörgabrúðr, Höldabrúðr, Hölgatröll, Hörgatröll, and Höldatröll. In part because of the variation in her name, and in part because she does not appear in the *Poetic Edda* and *Prose Edda*, there has been some controversy over what sort of being she was. Lotte Motz has argued that Thorgerd was in fact a giantess who received worship; originally associated with wild nature, she became the tutelary goddess of the petty kingdom of Hálogaland[141] However, Gunnhild Røthe has exhaustively reviewed the evidence and concluded that Thorgerd was in all likelihood the *fylgja* (protective spirit and ancestress) of the ruling family of Hálogaland, the Jarls of Hlaðir.[142] Thorgerd's worshippers probably did not see her as a giantess; she was part of their own *Innangarðr*, the "patron goddess" of their land and family. Olaf Tryggvasson's defeat of the Jarls of Hlaðir banished

Thorgerd to *Útgarðr*, and Christian writers who were partisans of Olaf Tryggvason would have used the old conceptual categories to deal with her. In *Ketils saga hængs* she is called Þorgerðr Hörgatröll ("altar-troll") and listed with a group of trolls who engage in nocturnal *gandreiðir*, "magic riding" or "witch-riding".[143] By the time that *Söguþáttr* was written, she has become Þorgerðr Höldatröll, "man-troll," defeated and banished for her refusal to pay tribute to King Olaf.

Thus there seems to be no conclusive evidence for a cult of the giants. However, Lotte Motz has pointed out a parallel between giants in the sagas and Inuit belief. Among the Inuit, it was believed that spiritual power was conferred by close contact with the forces of nature. The highest deity spoke to men through storms and winds, and his name appeared in words for "thought" or "intelligence." To gain shamanic powers, it was necessary to travel far from human dwellings and endure loneliness and hardship in solitude; only then would one of the holy powers speak to the would-be shaman.[144] Motz has compared this belief with the kennings "wind of giantesses," "storm of troll-women," and their variants, all meaning "mind," "thought," "emotion," "courage," or related concepts. She adds that both in myths and in legendary sagas, giants often have the power to summon storms,[145] and that they possess much knowledge which they can teach to favored humans.[146] Icelandic laws used the phrase *útiseta at vekja tröll upp*, "to sit outside to wake up trolls," to mean a form of magically seeking knowledge that Motz compares with shamanic practices. She concludes that Germanic religion once encompassed beliefs similar to Inuit beliefs: Contact with the forces of wild nature, personified by the giants, was necessary to gain certain kinds of power and wisdom. A young man might have to suffer great ordeals to encounter the wilderness powers (shipwreck, cold, hunger, battle), but if he survived, he gained supernatural aid and power, and might bear a new name (such as *Brönufóstra*, *Gríðarfóstra*, and so on) as a token of his transformative experience.[147]

Elsewhere, Motz has argued that the saga giants share traits with various beings worshipped by north Eurasian peoples, from Finland to eastern Siberia, often those known as "Masters of the Forest" or "Lords of the Wilderness".[148] She has argued that giants show features typical of Eurasian shamanism, such as the ability to shape-shift, an association with iron, and the teaching of wisdom to young protégés.[149] She concludes that the giants were originally honored by an earlier, non-agricultural people of Scandinavia related to the northern circumpolar cultures, who had been pushed back by the ancestors of the Norsemen.[150]

Motz's ideas are not always supported: some of the sagas that she cites were written very late, after the Protestant Reformation, and/or have been influenced by European romances or other external sources. Motz herself admits that it is not clear how much the situation in the legendary sagas, written well after Christianization, might mirror the actual living faith of pre-Christian times.[151] And not all giants and giantesses in the sagas seem to have much to do with shamanistic initiation; as Sandra Straubhaar points out, some seem to function primarily as grotesque figures for the hero to brutalize and kill entertainingly.[152] Nonetheless, several other scholars have suggested that combats between humans and trolls, berserks, or other monsters in the sagas may go back to a tradition of initiation rituals.[153] The sagas of giant fosterage may ultimately go back to a related tradition of "vision questing"—perhaps learned from the Saami, or from other peoples of the Arctic cultural complex.

Giants as Psychological Others

John McKinnell has analyzed the relationship between beings of *Innangarðr* and *Útgarðr* using the psychoanalytic theory of Jacques Lacan.[154] Lacanian psychology analyzes the unconscious as the desire of the Self, or the Subject, for the possession of the Other, an entity that is radically different and fundamentally separate from the Self. The Subject must reject the Other to maintain its selfhood, and yet the Subject continues to desire the Other. Furthermore, the Subject desires control over the Other's responses—yet paradoxically, the Other must act freely, or its responses are valueless.

Whatever the value of Lacan's concept of the Other for psychology, McKinnell applies it fruitfully to the study of Norse mythology. Giants, trolls, dwarves, workers of magic, and the dead belong to the Other. Men and gods must be opposed to them if the order of the universe is to persist, and yet they need what only the beings of the Other can provide. Thor is noted for slaying giants, but has giant concubines and accepts gifts from friendly giants; Odin also kills giants, and yet has giant concubines and seeks out wisdom from giants and from the dead. The human heroes of these sagas and tales do the same; while they may slay giants, berserks, and trolls, they also ally with them, accepting wisdom and treasures from them.

McKinnell points out that in the myths in which the gods encounter the giants, Odin usually seduces female giants, gaining from them something that the gods and/or men need; Thor usually kills both male and female giants, although he may also seduce or befriend female giantesses to gain something of value; and the tribe of gods known as the Vanir—in the Norse sources, the god Njörðr and his children Freyr and Freyja—are the only ones who marry giant spouses. These patterns extend to legends and tales of human heroes, who may follow an Odinnic, Thorian, or Vanic pattern, or a mixture.

The general Thor pattern, best exemplified by the myth of Thor's encounter with Geirrod, is as follows:

1. The hero makes a journey to fight a giant.
2. He has one or more companions, but they contribute little.
3. They are all badly received at their destination.
4. The hero is attacked by at least one giantess and one giant.
5. He destroys both, in fights that involve wrestling.

McKinnell subdivides the "Thor pattern" into two variants, the basic Thor pattern and the "Bear's Son" pattern. The basic Thor subtype is as follows:

1. The hero is tricked into making the journey.
2. He is helped by a friendly giantess.
3. He or his associate has a sexual partner.
4. He must cross a dangerous river, a boundary between worlds.
5. Both fights take place in a cave.
6. The hero fights with either his bare hands or with crude weapons.

The "Bear's Son" pattern is exemplified by the first half of *Beowulf* and two episodes in *Grettis Saga*. This pattern is close to what Michael Stitt calls the "Two-Troll Tradition," and has been studied intensively because of its close parallels with *Beowulf*.[155] It goes as follows:

1. The hero comes to fight a male and female monster.
2. He may have associates, but there is no friendly giantess.
3. The first combat occurs when one of the giants attacks the hall.
4. The second combat occurs when the hero enters a dangerous lake or waterfall.
5. The hero's associates may assume that the hero has died during the second combat and abandon him.
6. The second combat takes place in a cave and may involve a special sword.
7. There may be a bright light after the hero kills the second giant.
8. The hero may decapitate the second giant.
9. The hero returns by his own efforts.

None of the sagas in this book fits either pattern perfectly, but *Hálfdanar saga Brönufóstra* and *Sörla saga sterka* are both blends of motifs from the "basic Thor" and "Bear's Son" patterns. In *Hálfdanar saga*, a friendly giantess helps the hero (basic Thor pattern) by giving him a magic sword (Bear's Son pattern); all the fighting takes place in caves (basic Thor pattern), and in the end both giants are decapitated (Bear's Son pattern). *Sörla saga* is probably based on *Hálfdanar saga* and shows much the same mixture of subtypes, although here there is no explicitly stated sexual relationship between the hero and a giantess.[156] *Söguþáttr* departs far from the pattern, but Asmund does have some Thor-like traits; he defeats Thorgerd in a contest involving red-hot iron, as Thor does in his contest with Geirrod.[157] The *Fljótsdæla saga* extract might be considered a "basic Thor" tale, although there is neither a friendly nor a hostile giantess; it may be closer to myths in which Thor does not play a prominent role, such as the kidnapping and rescue of the goddess Idunna.

McKinnell's "Odinnic pattern" derives from the myth of Odin winning the mead of poetry and from related myths. It may be summarized as follows:

1. The hero is associated with Odin, whether as a protégé of the god, as an opponent of his or an opponent of paganism in general, or less directly.
2. The hero is rescued by a hospitable giant.

3. The giant is basically friendly, although there may be tension.
4. The hero spends the winter in the giant's household.
5. There is a sexual relationship between the hero and the giant's daughter; she becomes pregnant, but the hero leaves.
6. The giant gives the hero a valuable gift.
7. The child is a son, and is later sent to his father.
8. The hero makes a conventional marriage with a human later.

Kjalnesinga saga is the best example of this type in this book; others include *Ketils saga hængs* and parts of *Örvar-Odds saga.*[158] *Hálfdanar þáttr svarta* is of this type, except that the fostering giant has no daughter. However, in *Hauks þáttr hábrokar*, Harald is said to have married Snjofrid the daughter of Svasi, who magically subjugates him; this may be a displacement of this element of the Odinnic pattern. The Odinnic pattern appears to some degree in *Hálfdanar saga Brönufóstra*, although in this case the hero's offspring is a girl who never appears in the saga. *Brandkrossa þáttr* is also of this type, except that the hero takes the giant's daughter (who is mostly of human descent in any case) with him, he does not marry again, and there is no son who turns up later. *Illuga saga Gríðarfóstra* contains elements of the basic Thor pattern and the Odinnic pattern, but both patterns are altered; notably, the hero's sex partner is the giantess's daughter, not the giantess herself.

An additional narrative pattern, the "helpful giantess," is often grafted on to these basic patterns. An example from the mythology would be the god Thor receiving gloves and a staff from the giantess Grid before he goes to battle Geirrod. McKinnell notes that a helpful giantess may function as a mother-figure, giving a hero gifts, wisdom, and self-confidence. This is fundamentally different from Odin's relationship to giantesses, because mothering giantesses may continue to aid their human partners even after the humans leave.[159] Even when the hero's mother or foster-mother is human, she is often somewhat uncanny. In *Kjalnesinga saga*, Bui's human foster-mother Esja knows sorcery; she teaches Bui, protects him using magic, and also stage-manages his conflicts. Grima in *Hálfdanar saga Brönufóstra* also uses her magic to protect young Halfdan. *Söguþáttr* hints that Asmund's own ancestry is somewhat uncanny, since his mother has a *lífsteinn* ("life-stone") and dies when the stone is split.

Alternatively, the helpful giantess may be the mother of the hero's associate or sexual partner, as in *Illuga saga.* The helper may be what McKinnell calls "the incongruous partner," functioning both as mother and as lover; this is clear in *Hálfdanar saga Brönufóstra* and implied in *Kjalnesinga saga* when Frid calls Bui a "bearded baby". Similar "incongruous partners" include Harthgrepa in Saxo's *History of the Danes* and Hildigunn in *Örvar-Odds Saga.* In *Hauks þáttr hábrokar* the *fóstra* relationship between Heid and Harald is not seen; however, Heid not only gives motherly aid to Hauk and Vighard, but feels their naked bodies in a sexually charged scene, and she may be classified with the "incongruous partners." Finally, the helpful giantess may be in need of liberation from her giant status. This is clear in *Illuga saga*, in which the giantess is a human lady under a spell. Similar enchanted princesses appear in *Þorsteins saga Víkingssonar*[160] and *Gríms saga loðinkinna.*[161] In texts with heavy Christian influence, the giantess figure may need baptism in order to enter the human, Christian community; this is Hladvor's fate in *Sögubáttr.*[162]

Conclusion: What are Giants?

Ek var austr
ok jötna barðak
brúðir bölvísar,
er til bjargs gengu;
mikil myndi ætt jötna,
ef allir lifði,
vætr myndi manna
undir Miðgarði.

I was in the east
and beat evil-minded
brides of giants,
who went to the cliff-face;
great would be giants' kindred
if all lived,
naught would be man's [kindred]
in Midgard.

Giants are Other, beings of *Útgarðr*. Often they are adversaries of gods and heroes, and there is no sign that they were ever recipients of organized worship in Norse religion. Yet giants must never be eliminated completely. The above extract from *Hárbarðsljóð* makes this clear. So does the much later Icelandic folktale in which a huge hairy hand stops the saintly Bishop Gudmund from sprinkling holy water on a certain sea-cliff, because "the wicked need a place of their own, too."[163] The same theme can be found, transposed into different keys, from primary mythic texts to legendary sagas to folktales. And the creators of all of these used *Útgarðr* and its dwellers to reflect on the world that they knew. Legendary sagas in general reflected the values that Icelandic chieftains and their retainers were expected to have in the Sturlung age.[164] Myths of gods taking giant concubines, but resisting marrying giant wives or giving their women to giant husbands, parallels medieval Icelandic society in which high-ranking freeborn landowners tried to maximize their power and position through control of their women's' marriages.[165] Other myths of gods and giants in conflict may well have reflected the feuds and power-politics of 13th century Iceland. Far from being escapist literature, the legendary sagas of giants reflect very real fears and hopes at a time when the political center of Iceland was under constant stress.

Giants are absolutely necessary in the Norse worldview. *Útgarðr* must not overwhelm *Innangarðr*, for that would bring down Ragnarök. But without *Útgarðr*, there would be no *Innangarðr*; without the periphery, there would be no fixed center. *Innangarðr* may oppose and encroach on *Útgarðr*, but at the same time *Útgarðr* and *Innangarðr* reflect each other, and each one slips into the other's territory.[166] Many of the great figures of legend, whether male gods and warriors or female goddesses and wise women, are liminal beings, who can cross the boundary in either direction, face the dangers that they encounter, and return with the boons that they have won.

Notes on the Texts

The first two tales in this book are taken from *Óláfs saga Tryggvasonar in Mesta* (*The Longest Saga of Olaf Tryggvason*), a saga related to Snorri Sturluson's *Óláfs saga Tryggvasonar* as found in *Heimskringla*, but greatly expanded by the interpolation of many additional tales and even whole sagas.[167] Specifically, the tales in the book are taken from the version of *Óláfs saga in Mesta* found in the manuscript *Flateyjarbók* (GkS 1005 fol.). Most of *Flateyjarbók* was written or copied by two Icelandic monks and priests, Jón Þórðarson and Magnús Þórhallsson, between 1387 and 1390.[168] *Hálfdanar þáttr svarta* appears as chapters 450 through 456 of the *Flateyjarbók* version of *Óláfs saga Tryggvasonar in Mesta. Hauks þáttr hábrokar* follows *Hálfdanar þáttr svarta*, comprising chapters 465 through 469 of the *Flateyjarbók* version of the saga. The texts were translated from Sigurður Nordal's normalized edition of *Flateyjarbók*[169], and checked against Vígfusson and Unger's diplomatic edition.[170]

Kjalnesinga saga and *Jökuls þáttr Búasonar* were translated from the Íslenzk Fornrit edition. Internal references in *Kjalnesinga saga*, such as the mention of Bishop Arni Thorlaksson who is known to have died in 1298, suggests that the saga was written late, probably in the 14th century. There are four groups of manuscripts, called A, B, C and D; the oldest surviving manuscript, the primary basis for the Íslenzk Fornrit text, is the parchment AM 471 4to, dated to the latter half of the 15th century, and the only manuscript in Group A.[171] Group C manuscripts of *Kjalnesinga saga* not only include several insertions, they add *Jökuls þáttr Búasonar* as a continuation. *Jökuls þáttr Búasonar* was probably written in the 15th century, presumably by someone who knew *Hálfdanar saga Brönufostra*; the plots are similar in outline, and both feature princesses named Marsibil. The end of *Jökuls þáttr* is indebted to the "sagas of chivalry" or *riddarasögur*. The Íslenzk Fornrit text is primarily based on AM 504 4to.[172]

Brandkrossa þáttr and the extract from *Fljótsdæla saga* were also translated from the Íslenzk Fornrit edition. Both texts are closely associated with the better-known *Droplaugarsona saga*: *Brandkrossa þáttr* was written as a "prequel" to *Droplaugarsona saga*, and *Fljótsdæla saga* narrates many of the same events as *Droplaugarsona saga*.[173] Neither *Brandkrossa þáttr* nor *Fljótsdæla saga* are completely consistent with each other or with *Droplaugarsona saga. Brandkrossa þáttr* has been dated as no younger than the second half of the 13th century; it exists only in 17th-century paper manuscripts, all of which seem to have been copied from the same original source, now lost. The Íslenzk Fornrit edition is based on five manuscripts, three of which (JS 435 4to, Thott 1768 4to, and AM

164k fol.) were copied by Árni Magnusson's assistant Ásgeir Jónsson.[174] *Fljótsdæla saga* was not originally written as an independent narrative, but as a continuation of *Hrafnkels saga Freysgoða*; the main manuscript source is the damaged AM 551c 4to, with emendations from a copy made when the manuscript was less damaged (AM 451 4to).[175]

The texts of the three *fornaldarsögur* are taken from Jónsson and Vilhjálmsson's three-volume edition, *Fornaldarsögur Norðurlanda.* Jónsson and Vilhjálmsson's edition closely follows Rafn's 1829-30 edition, also called *Fornaldarsögur Norðurlanda.* Rafn's base text for *Sörla saga sterka* was an 18th-century Icelandic paper manuscript known as Rask 32, in the University of Copenhagen Library. A longer recension of this saga, with more narrative details and a less positive attitude towards its female characters, was published by Biörner in 1737, in his *Nordiska Kämpa Dater.* Other recensions exist; as yet there is no critical edition.[176] The other *fornaldarsögur* are based on manuscripts in the Arnamagnæan collection; Rafn's base text for *Hálfdanar saga Brönufostra* was AM 152 fol., and his base text for *Illuga saga Gríðarfóstra* was AM 123 8vo.

Finally, *Inntak úr söguþætti af Ásmundi flagðagæfu* was translated from the version published in the 1862 first edition of Jón Árnason's compendium *Íslenzkar Þjóðsögur og Æfintýri.*

Notes on the Translations

Many features of Old Norse saga style do not make for readable English if translated literally. Verb tenses flip from present tense to past; passive constructions abound, such as "and so it was done, that. . ."; and repeated independent clauses are typical: "And. . . and then. . . but then. . . and so. . ." Any translator must make a judgment call on how much to "smooth out" the prose. While there has been a trend away from the archaisms and calques of Victorian translators towards more plain and colloquial English, the pendulum may be beginning to swing the other way.[177] A translation that completely smoothes out all foreign-sounding stylistic quirks may be as undesirable as a slavishly literal trot.[178]

But sagas were often read aloud as entertainment in Iceland, not just in medieval times, but as late as the early 20th century. In that spirit, I've tried to stay true to the original meaning while also creating something that will work well as spoken prose—to capture something of the flavor of a tale that might have told around a fire in the depths of winter (with periodic questions, comments, and even heckling from the audience, which the reader may freely supply).

Sörla saga sterka shows a great deal of influence from the *riddarasögur*: its exotic settings in Africa, its magic items and treasures owned by legendary personages, its scenes of combat on horseback, and its exotic lions and elephants. *Sörla saga*, and to a somewhat lesser extent *Hálfdanar saga Brönufóstra*, use relatively many foreign words to convey a certain noble atmosphere: *prakt* from Middle High German *praht*, "magnificence"; *riddari* from MHG *ritter*, "knight"; *burt-reið* from MHG *buhurt* or Old French *behourd*, "joust"; *kurt* and *kurteis* from Old French *cortesie*, "courtesy, courtliness"; and so on. To bring out this chivalric flavor, I have translated some expressions in these sagas with English expressions that wouldn't fit a more historical saga, such as "Prince" for the repeated title *könungsson*, "king's son". In general, I've tried to keep a "statelier" tone in these two sagas than in, say, the more matter-of-fact *Kjalnesinga saga*, while also trying to avoid pseudoarchaic "yea-and-verily" language.

In all of the texts, I have anglicized the spelling of Norse names by dropping diacritics, replacing *þ* with *th* and *ð* with *d*, and dropping the masculine nominative case ending, whether *-r* or a geminate consonant. Place names have been translated by their modern equivalents when possible, and anglicized when the modern equivalent is unknown. The name ending *-fiðr* often alternates with *-finnr*; thus *Kjalnesinga saga* names the same person *Kolfinnr* and *Kolfiðr*, and *Hálfdanar saga* alternates between *Þorfinnr* and *Þorfiðr*. I have standardized such forms to the majority usage in the text I was working from.

I thank Dan Campbell, Thomas de Mayo, Paul Montgomery, and Sue Nilsson for their ever-helpful comments and critiques of my drafts. Any mistakes that remain are entirely mine. I thank Zoe Borovsky, Sean Crist, P. S. Langeslag, Stefan Langeslag, Andy Lemons, Carsten Lyngdrup Madsen, and Jon Julius Sandal, who have created free electronic resources that were absolutely crucial for my work. Last but not least, I thank Patricia Lafayllve for her encouragement, and Amanda Waggoner for her unfailing love and support.

Hafi hverr þökk, er hlýðir ok sér gerir skemmtan af,
en hinir ógleði, er angrast við ok ekki verðr at gamni.

THE TALE OF HALFDAN THE BLACK

Hálfdanar þáttr svarta

CHAPTER I

Halfdan the Black took the kingship of Agder eighteen years after the death of his father Gudrod the Strong, the Hunter-King.[1] He was tall and strong from an early age. He invaded neighboring kingdoms and conquered them. He invaded Romerike and fought a battle with King Sigtrygg the Strong. In the end, King Sigtrygg fell, and Halfdan took Romerike.

Soon afterwards, he fought a battle against King Eystein at Hedmark, and he won a victory. King Eystein fled to Hadeland to join the hersir[2] Gudbrand, and there he built up his forces. They went down to Hedmark in the winter and encountered Halfdan the Black on a large island. There they fought a great battle, and many men fell on both sides. There Guthorm fell, the son of Gudbrand the hersir, who was considered the most promising future chieftain in Oppland. King Eystein fled, and in the spring he sent tribute to Halfdan; then Halfdan granted Eystein half of Hedmark, on account of their kinship. Halfdan then laid Toten and Hadeland under his rule, but he gave Vestfold to Olaf Geirstad-Alf, his brother.[3]

Then Halfdan the Black took a wife. He married Ragnhild, the daughter of Harald Gold-Beard the king of Sogn, and he had a son by her, who was named Harald. He was raised in Sogn with his mother's father Harald until he was ten years old, and then Harald Gold-Beard granted him the kingdom and the royal title. A little later, Harald Gold-Beard died. That same winter, death took Queen Ragnhild. The following spring, King Harald of Sogn died of an illness. As soon as Halfdan the Black heard that, he readied large forces for an expedition northward to Sogn. There he was well received. He said that he had to claim the kingdom on behalf of his own son. There was no resistance to him, and Halfdan laid that kingdom under his rule.

Halfdan's good friend Atli of Gaular came to him. King Halfdan set Atli to be the jarl over the shire of Sogn, to sit in judgment and collect the king's tribute. King Halfdan went to Oppland, to his own kingdom.

CHAPTER II: King Halfdan won Vingulmork

The next autumn, King Halfdan was residing on his estates in Vingulmork. One night, around midnight, a man who had been standing guard on horseback came and told him that a host was approaching. Halfdan stood up at once and ordered his retainers to arm themselves, and they went out into the courtyard. At that moment, Hysing and Haki[4] came with large forces. There was a great battle. Before King Halfdan could be overwhelmed, he fled to the woods, and he lost many men.

Olvir the Wise, his foster-father, heard the news, and he summoned large forces and went to meet King Halfdan.[5] He went right away against the sons of Gandalf. They met at Eide, near an island, and fought there. Hysing and Helsing fell there, but Haki escaped and fled. After that, King Halfdan laid all of Vingulmork under his rule and took tribute.[6]

One year later he went up to Heidmork. The same winter, Halfdan married Ragnhild the daughter of Sigurd Hart, and then he took possession of Romerike and Hadeland. As soon as Halfdan the Black had left Vingulmork, Gandalf and his son Haki went to Vingulmork and subjugated many people and raided far and wide. There was great enmity between King Halfdan and King Gandalf for a long time afterwards.

King Halfdan and Ragnhild had a son who was named Harald.[7] There was one extraordinary thing about Halfdan: he never dreamed. He brought the matter before a man named Thorleif the Wise, and asked for advice on what he might do about it. Thorleif told him what he did: when he wanted to enquire into some matter, he went to sleep in a pigsty[8], and he never failed to dream.

CHAPTER III. The Dream of King Halfdan

King Halfdan now did this. He went into a pigsty and soon fell asleep. A remarkable vision appeared to him: it seemed as if he had the thickest hair of any man, and his hair was in locks so long that some reached the earth. His locks were of every color, but one lock excelled all the others in its beauty and brightness. His locks seemed to be of very unequal lengths: some hung down to the ground, some fell to the middle of his leg or to his knee or his torso, some hung down no farther than his neck, and some just stuck up from his head like short horns. He told Thorleif the Wise this dream, and Thorleif interpreted it in this way: a great progeny would come from him, and his descendants would rule the lands with great glory, yet not all with equal glory. But one would come from among his descendants who would be greater than all of them, mightier and more renowned. And men have believed it to be true that that lock signified Olaf Haraldsson, who is greater than all the kings of Norway in holiness, and brighter in heaven and on earth, so that all men may know.

Halfdan was a most wise and fair man. He established laws, and minded them himself, and compelled others to keep them. So that tyranny might not overturn the laws, he himself set the penalties under the law, and arranged the rules of conduct for each person according to his nobility and worth.

CHAPTER IV: About King Halfdan

It happened one Yule evening that when King Halfdan and all his household had come to the table where the Yule feast was prepared for him, all the provisions disappeared from the table—food and ale and all the fare that had been meant for the feast. King Halfdan was very grieved at this. Everyone else set out for his own home. And so that he might find out what had caused this happening, he investigated in many ways.

There was a certain Finnish sorceror with King Halfdan. The king had him seized and tortured to make him confess, but he couldn't learn anything. The Finn sought help, mostly from Harald the son of King Halfdan. Harald went before his father and begged him for mercy, but it wasn't granted.

Then Harald set the Finn free, and he fled with the Finn himself. Once they traveled to where a chieftain was holding a feast. They were both warmly welcomed, and when they had been there for a while, the chieftain spoke with Harald: "Your father did himself a great disservice, for it was I who took from him the provisions which he had intended for his own Yule feast. But I shall repay you for that.[9] If you would take my advice, you must first go home for now, because he will be in dire straits. But you alone are meant to be saved, and you will get the most benefit, because you are destined to be the high king over all Norway." Then Harald prepared to go home.

Now it must be told for what reasons the heathens held their Yule, because that is very different from what Christians do. They hold their own Yule for the Nativity of our Lord, Jesus Christ, but heathen men hold their feast for the honor and majesty of the evil Odin. Odin is called by many names: he is called Vidrir and Har and Thridi and Jolnir.[10] He is called Vidrir because they said that he rules the weather; Har, because they said that every man would become higher because of him; Jolnir, because they derived that name from Yule; and Thridi, because they had become aware that He who is greatest is both one and three, and they had some knowledge of the Trinity, but turned it into heresy.[11]

CHAPTER V: Harald Releases Dofri

Now there is this to tell about King Halfdan: he stayed quietly at home in Oppland. A strange thing happened: much wealth and many fine treasures disappeared from the king's treasury, and they didn't know what could have caused it. The king gave this close attention, because he realized that the thief would visit him again. He had preparations made, with such crafty spells and powerful incantations that whoever should enter the hall and try to take the money would be forced to stay there and wait for men to come. The king realized that the one who was playing these wicked tricks must be both large and strong, so he had a fetter forged from the strongest steel, and had it wrapped with the heaviest lead bands.

This is what happened: Early one morning, when men came to the treasury, they saw an enormous giant there, a monster both broad and tall. Many men flung themselves on him and put the fetter on him, but he was very strong in his hands. It took sixty men before he was fettered. Now they bound his hands tightly behind his back with lead bands, and he was brought low.

King Halfdan asked him his name. He said that he was called Dofri and had his home in the mountains that were named for him.[12] The king asked whether he had stolen his gold. He said that it was true, and begged for a pardon, and offered to bring back three times as much gold. But the king said that he should never be pardoned, and that he should wait, bound there, for the assembly to be summoned, and it would sentence him to the most shameful death. He also said that no one should offer him help, nor give him food, and whoever did so should be punished with nothing less than the loss of his life. Then the king went home, and Dofri stayed behind, bound.

A little later, Harald came home. He heard what had happened and what his father had decreed. He realized that it would not do for him to beg for Dofri. Harald was five years old at the time. Right away, he went to where Dofri was sitting. Dofri wore a very sullen and downcast expression.

Harald said, "You're in a bad way. Will you accept life from me?"

"I'm not so certain whether I want to bring you into such great danger," said Dofri, "because of your father's proclamation."

"What will you need to deal with that?" said Harald. He drew the knife he kept with him, made of the finest iron, which the Finn had given him. He cut the fetter and the leaden bands from Dofri. And when Dofri had gotten loose, he thanked Harald for saving his life and left the place at once. He didn't take the time to tie his shoes, but turned tail and fled, so that no one saw hide nor hair[13] of him.

CHAPTER VI. Dofri Sought Harald and Kept Him With Him

Not long after, men went searching for Dofri. The king asked what the truth was about this deed, and Harald said that he had released Dofri. The king became so furious that he drove his own son Harald away, but said that he could not bear to have him killed. But he gave a strict order that Harald should not receive help. He told him that he could get help from wherever that troll Dofri was.

Harald now went off into the forest. He stayed outside day and night. When five nights had passed, Harald was staying in a grove, and he had become very weak from both hunger and thirst. Then he saw a huge fellow walking, and he thought he recognized the troll Dofri.

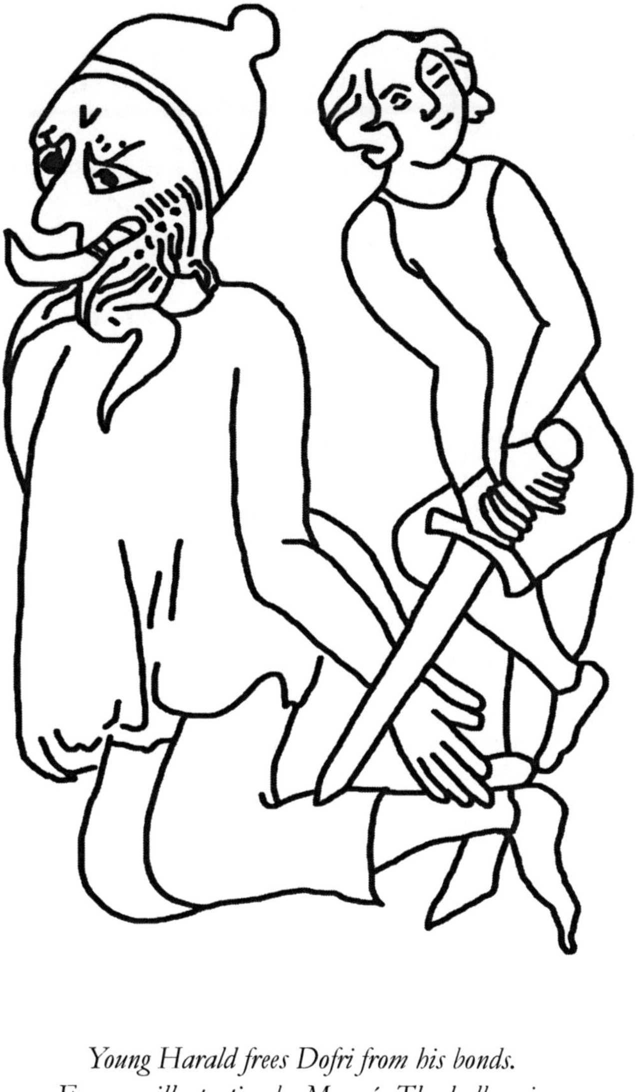

Young Harald frees Dofri from his bonds.
From an illustration by Magnús Thorhallson in
Flateyjarbók *(GkS 1005), written 1387-1390.*

Dofri said, "As it stands, you're not in a good way now, king's son. I dare say that you'll be better off with me. Don't you want to come with me now to my household?"

Harald said yes. Dofri picked up Harald in his arms and went striding along with him all the way, until he came to a huge cave. He carried the boy on his arm, but when he went into the cave, he stooped less than he meant to and struck the boy so hard against the rock that he was knocked unconscious. It seemed to Dofri that it would be a terrible misfortuned if he had killed the boy, and it grieved him so much that he bawled over him. But as he was grimacing and shaking his head, Harald came to, and he looked up at old man Dofri, who looked quite hideous as he twisted his mouth and bulged out his cheeks and rolled his eyes back in his head.

Harald said, "It's true what they say, my foster-father, that 'few who cry are pretty', because you look quite dreadful and monstrous to me. Cheer up, because I'm not hurt."

Then Dofri cheered up and let Harald down into his cave. Harald was there for five years, and lacked nothing that he needed. Dofri loved him so much that he could not let anything happen to him. Dofri taught him much knowledge, and also took pains to teach him skills. Harald grew in both size and strength.

It is said that Dofri came to speak with Harald one day, and he said, "Now I think that I have rewarded you for the gift of life, because I have brought you to the kingship—for your father is dead, and I was not far away. Now you must go home and claim your kingdom. I lay this on you, that you must not let either your hair or nails be cut before you become the sole king over all Norway.[14] And I shall be in your ranks and go into battle with you. That will benefit you, because I will be a dangerous fighter, since I will be invisible. Fare hale and well now, and may you go on to glory and prosperity, fame and fortune, not least because you have been with me." Dofri was greatly affected when they parted.

And when Harald came home, he was raised to the kingship over all the shires that his father had ruled before. He told his men where he had been those five years, and then he was named Harald Dofri's Fosterling.

CHAPTER VII. The Death of Halfdan

King Halfdan met his death in this manner: he was being driven from a feast in Hadeland over the lake called Rond. When he came to Rinkil Bay, the ice broke beneath him and he perished there, along with many of his men, because the ice had recently been broken through to water cattle. King Halfdan was forty years old. He had been king for twenty-two years.

Of all kings, Halfdan was the most blessed with bountiful harvests. Men found that so admirable, that when it was heard that he was dead, and his body was brought from Ringerike for burial, leading men from Vestfold and Vingulmork and Romerike came up at once, and they all asked to take the body with them and bury it in their own shires. They felt that that would make their lands fruitful. They came to this agreement: the body was divided into four pieces. The head was laid in a mound at Stein in Ringerike, but every chieftain took his portion with him and had a mound raised in each shire. These were called Halfdan's Mounds. Many men kept up sacrifices and worship there, before that was banned by his kinsmen.[15]

THE TALE OF HAUK HIGH-BREECHES

Hauks þáttr hábrokar

CHAPTER I

Bjorn on the Mound[1] was king over Sweden when Harald assumed kingship over Norway. After that, Onund was king in Sweden for forty winters or longer, and then Eirek his son. He married Ingigerd, daughter of Harald Fairhair. The Swedes sacrificed to her and carried her off to a certain island, but Halfdan the Black, her brother, brought her away with him. After that, relations were strained between King Harald and Eirek the King of Sweden for a long time.

One summer, King Harald summoned the dearest of his men, Hauk High-Breeches, and said, "Now I am free of all war and violence in my lands. We will now relax and amuse ourselves. We want to send you into the Eastern realms this summer, to buy me some precious treasures, rarely seen in our lands."

Hauk asked the king to arrange this matter, as he did others. The king gave his men leave to travel to other lands. Hauk had had them with him before. Hauk took one ship and a good company of men, and went east to Novgorod[2] in the autumn, and stayed there for the winter. He came to where a market had been set up. A great crowd of people from many lands had gathered there. The champions of King Eirek at Uppsala had come: Bjorn Blue-Sides and Salgard Tunic.[3] They were overbearing men, and they lorded it over everyone else.

One day, Hauk went around the town with his company of men, and he wanted to buy some costly treasure for his own lord, King Harald. He came to where a Russian man was sitting, and there Hauk saw a costly cloak[4], sewn all over with gold. Hauk bought this cloak and paid a pledge, and left to get the money. Earlier that day, Bjorn had asked to purchase this cloak for the King of Sweden, but he was outbid.

When Hauk had gone, Bjorn's servant boy came and told the merchant that it wouldn't do if Bjorn could not have the cloak. But the merchant said that the deal had to stand. The boy went away and told Bjorn, and at that moment Hauk came with the money for the cloak and paid for it. He took the cloak and went out. Then Bjorn and Salgard came to meet him. They asked why he had the cloak that they had bought. Hauk said that he had bought it, and he would keep it. Bjorn said that King Eirek had the first claim on treasures, as was fitting for the greatest king in the Northlands.

Hauk replied, "King Harald is not accustomed to giving up what is his for the King of Sweden."

He sent a boy home with the cloak, but an argument broke out among them. Salgard said that he wanted them to fight over who should have the cloak, and thus over whose king should be called the greatest.

Hauk said that they might well fight over the purchase of the cloak. "But I am not willing to stake my king's honor on my own weapons," he said.

Then a man came up to Hauk, short and stout. Hauk asked him his name. He said that he was called Bui, "and here's a sword that I will give you, if you intend to fight with Bjorn and Salgard. It's not unlikely that it will bite."

Hauk accepted it, and tested it, and said, "You have my thanks, but I will not accept it. I have enough weapons that will bite, if my heart and courage aid me. But I will call you Bui Sharp-Sword."

Bui answered, "King Harald would not refuse it, if I offered it to him. What will be, will be—but you'll be glad to have it later." Then he turned away.

Now a battle broke out between them. Hauk had more friends and got more help. Several men fell there, and many were wounded. Hauk won a victory, but the locals got between them and separated them. The Swedes weren't pleased with this, and they went home, leaving matters as they stood. The news of how Salgard had proposed conditions for the battle was heard in Norway, and King Harald was very angry.

Hauk now came home and met the king. Harald was very hostile, and he asked, "Is it true, Hauk, that you staked my honor on your weapon?"

"That's not so, lord," said Hauk, and then he told everything that had happened.

King Harald was very pleased, and he said, "You must have really been flaunting your high breeches[5], Hauk, when you beat King Eirek's champions."

"That was true," said Hauk, "but no less so than in England, when I set your son Hakon on the knee of Athelstan, king of England."[6]

Then the king smiled. Ever since then, Hauk was called High-Breeches.[7] Men say that no better treasure than the cloak had ever come to Norway.

Bjorn and Salgard came to meet King Eirek, and they told him what a terrible insult Hauk had done to him, and how King Harald did not seem to be the lesser king in any way. King Eirek was displeased, and thus a quarrel came about between him and King Harald.

CHAPTER II: Vighard comes to King Harald and Hauk Habrok

It so happened one winter that King Eirek held a Yule feast. He had taken the high seat, with his householders arranged around him. The men who were standing guard outside saw a man skiing. He came towards them swiftly, and stepped out of his skis. He was a tall man in a short wolf-skin cloak. They greeted him well. He took off his cloak and was wearing a scarlet tunic underneath; he had a helm on his head and was girded with a sword. He was the most handsome man; he had long fair hair and was the tallest and strongest of all men. He went before the king and greeted him. The king welcomed him and said that he was a man of noble appearance. He asked his name, family and kin.

The man gave his name as Vighard, and said that his family was from Halogaland. "I have come to find out if you will accept me, in the same way that Bjorn and Salgard were accepted before."

The king replied, "Certainly you are a handsome man. But I can hardly value you, who are untested, as much as those who have often risked their lives for me and are the boldest champions."

Vighard said, "Farewell, lord!" He went out at once and took his gear and stepped into his skis.

King Harald held a Yule feast in Gudbrandsdal to the north. On the second day of Yule, it happened that the king's men were standing outside and holding their games, and the king sat next to the playing field. The king's estate lay near a mountain.

Then the king said, "What is that now that looks like a whirlwind on the mountain? Can it be a man skiing?"

The powdery snow was loose and formed a cloud, but the wind neither increased nor decreased, and so they saw that it had to be a man—yet few men would make the run down that slope.[8] The man approached them quickly. He came up to the games and went before King Harald and greeted him. The king accepted his greeting, and saw that he must be a mighty man.

The man said that his reason for coming was to offer his services to him, if he would take him into fellowship with his champions.

The king answered, "If your accomplishments match your appearance, it would be a great honor to have you."

The king called Hauk over, and asked if he would accept this man into his companionship and fellowship. He agreed to the king's will. They were equally great men. Now he was accepted into fellowship with the king's champions.

CHAPTER III: Harald Sends Hauk and Vighard

One summer, King Harald said that he wanted to send Hauk north to Bjarmaland[9] to bring back pelts. When Vighard heard that, he said that he wanted to go. The king replied that he wouldn't begrudge him that honor. He had one of his ships prepared for each of them. When they were ready, the king gave them dinner, and said that he was sending men whom he felt he would miss more than many others. "But it seems likely to me that King Eirek has heard about your voyage, and will remember you, Hauk, since you took the cloak from Russia. I know about the sacrifice that King Eirek will hold beforehand to get help. But I'm sending you to my foster-mother, whose name is Heid. She lives to the north, on the shore of the White Sea.[10] Follow her advice. I'm sending her a gold ring that weighs twelve ounces, two sides of aged wild boar bacon, and two barrels of butter."[11] Now they sailed away, with good men and weapons.

King Eirek found out about their journey, and he told Bjorn and Salgard that he wanted them to travel north to Surtsdal[12] and Bjarmaland. At the beginning of summer, King Eirek had a feast prepared at Uppsala. Then he had two wagons driven to the place where he sacrificed to the god named Lytir.[13] It was the custom that the wagon should stand there through the night, and Lytir would come to it in the morning. But this time, Lytir didn't come as he usually did, and the king was told that Lytir was unwilling. The wagon stood there for two nights, and he didn't come. Then the king performed many more sacrifices than before, and on the third morning, his men became aware that Lytir had come. The wagon was so heavy that the harnesses burst before they came into the hall with it.

Right away the wagon was set in the middle of the hall floor. The king came with a horn of drink and welcomed Lytir, and said that he would drink a toast to him. He said that he thought it was very important for Lytir to undertake the journey, and he promised to give him great gifts, as before.

Lytir answered, saying that he was unwilling to undertake this voyage. He said that he had once gone north from there, "and there I encountered such a great troll that I have never met the like before. It was old then, and I would not go there again if I knew that it was alive, but I expect it must be dead now."

The king agreed that it must be dead. Lytir said that the king was a worthy man, and he said that he would go.

Two ships were now made ready for Bjorn and Salgard. When they sailed out of Lake Mälaren, a dragon-ship covered with a black tent sailed ahead of them. They didn't see anyone holding the ropes. It sailed no matter what wind was blowing. They sailed north along the coast.[14]

CHAPTER IV: Hauk's Battle against Bjorn and Salgard

Now there is this to be told about Hauk and Vighard: they traveled north to the White Sea and went to the home of Heid, King Harald's foster-mother. Six men from each ship went. She was sitting by the fire, yawning hugely.[15] She was wearing a tunic of skins with sleeves down to the elbows. Hauk brought her greetings from King Harald.

She said, "King Harald's greeting seems good to me," and she said that she wanted to go to the ship with them. She begged them to turn back, and said that their journey would turn out badly.

Hauk didn't take her advice; he was the greatest of men. First he gave her the ring. She said, "Health to King Harald!" and put it on her hand.

"And here are two sides of bacon that he sent you," said Hauk.

"It's good of him to send these," she said.

Then he gave her the barrels of butter. She said, "King Harald is unlike other men. These are excellent treasures, and I've never received the like. I must reward him."

She took a barrel under each arm and threw the bacon on her back, and said that this gift seemed better than the other two. "My fosterling remembers what I like best. Have my advice, and come with me!"

And so they did. She made a fire and sat on the opposite side. They noticed that she had a most hideous mouth, for one lip hung down to her chest and one spread up to her nose.

She removed Hauk's clothes and felt him all over,[16] and said, "You're a stout-hearted man, with a lucky look about you."

She asked him to kiss her, and he did. Then she asked Vighard to take off his clothes. He was hesitant. Hauk ordered him to, and he did.

She said, "A tall man, well-bred and uncommonly strong." She asked him to kiss her.

He said that all trolls could kiss her.

She replied, "You could stand to be more handsome yourself!" and told him that worse things would happen to him than kissing her. She gave Hauk two spheres, "and if Bjorn and Salgard attack your ships, fling them over the side of your ship."

Now they sailed north to Bjarmaland. One evening they saw a sailing ship rounding an island, and they intended to meet the men and exchange news. Hauk recognized that they were Bjorn and Salgard. Few greetings were spoken before they anchored their ships next to each other and fought. Now they saw that a dragon-ship was anchored by the island, and arrows flew from it, and each one was aimed at a man. Hauk forgot that he had the spheres that the old crone had given him. Men fell all along the gunwales of both ships.

Both Hauk and Vighard went onto Hauk's own ship, because Vighard's ship was cleared of men. Vighard got into the prow and leaped onto Bjorn and Salgard's ship, and so did Hauk, and they pressed forward to the mast. Bjorn and Salgard came against them there, and they began fighting. It wasn't long until all who were left standing were wounded. Bjorn charged down from the afterdeck at Hauk, and now the four of them fought, and in the end Bjorn fell. Vighard attacked Salgard, but when he was least aware of it, an arrow flew from the dragon-ship into Vighard's breast, and he fell down dead.

Just then Hauk remembered the spheres, and he angrily threw them overboard. They came down next to the dragon-ship, and a fire blazed up between the prows of the ships. Hauk killed Salgard because he was blinded and it wasn't possible for his men to help him.

Hauk put his weapons and clothes into a small boat, and didn't stop until he had come back to Heid the crone and told her the news. She was glad that he had come back. She healed him, and she went with him to where there were merchants. She put him on a ship with men who were intending to travel south along the coast. She turned back, but he didn't stop his journey until he met King Harald and told him the whole story. The king was pleased that he had returned.

But it is said about Lytir that he came back and met King Eirek, and told him that he could never be helpful to him from then on, because of the injuries that he said they had received from the great troll in Norway.

CHAPTER V: About King Harald's Appearance and Height

Eirek was king of Sweden for forty-seven years.

King Harald was the most handsome and noble of all men in appearance. He had hair as fair as silk or beaten gold, and it hung down in long locks, and it was so long that he could tuck it under his belt. He was also the strongest and tallest of all men, as may still be seen from his hill in Haugasund. To the west of the church lies a slab that lay over his grave, and it is thirty-five feet long. And two stones stand in the churchyard there; one stood at his head and the other at his feet, and the slab was lying there between the stones, over the king's grave, when his mound was torn down. The stone that had lain over his grave is so thick that it would come up to the middle of a man's thigh.

When the sad tidings came out that King Harald was near death, he was eighty-three years old. He died of an illness in Rogaland, and is buried at Haugar along Karmtsund. King Harald was much mourned by everyone, and all the people said the same: there would never be anyone like him in wisdom and all accomplishments, in generosity and the honors that he bestowed on his men.[17]

He was on his guard against all sorcery and magic, ever since he managed to break free from the delusion of Svasi the dwarf,[18] who came to him one Yule evening and turned the king's thoughts to a Finnish woman named Snjofrid. Such ardent passion struck him that he went to marry her and loved her more than anything, for she seemed to him to be lovelier than every woman on account of Svasi's spell. He had sons with her, as was said before.[19] At the end of their fated life together,[20] Snjofrid died, and the burial shroud Svasi's Gift was spread over her. Such great magic was concealed in it, that King Harald found her body bright and beautiful, so that he wouldn't let her be buried. He himself sat by her for three years and went out of his mind with grief, on account of his excessive love for her in death. King Harald then recited a poem for her, which was called *Snjofrid's Praise-Poem*, and this is how it begins:

I'll ever hold in my heart
fear and hurt, for—*Men, hear*—
I cannot wake the woman.—
waves of the lord of graves.° *lord of graves*: Odin; his *waves*: poetry
From song-ground° my praise surges, *song-ground*: mouth
slipping through Dvalin's° grip; *Dvalin*: a dwarf
I'll draw for doughty heroes
true draughts of Regin's brew.° [21] *Regin*: a dwarf; his *brew*: poetry

A wise man with King Harald, named Egil Wool-Shirt, suggested that the shroud should be taken off the body, and it was done. The body was obviously rotted and foul-smelling, and it was buried at once, according to the old custom. After that, King Harald became so angry with incantations and spells and all magic that he let none of those men prosper in his kingdom; they were either killed or exiled. Then this was said:

A long time ago things weren't so bad,
but the Finnish girl drove Harald mad.
He thought she shone like the sun's rays.
Such things happen to many, these days.[22]

So ends the story of King Harald.

THE SAGA OF THE PEOPLE OF KJALARNES

Kjalnesinga saga

CHAPTER I

Helgi Bjola,[1] the son of Ketil Flat-Nose, laid claim to Kjalarnes, between Leiruvag and Botnsar, and lived at Hof on Kjalarnes.[2] He was a most worthy man. He followed the old religion, though he wasn't much for sacrificing, and he was wise and kindly to everyone. Helgi married Thorny, the daughter of Ingolf of Viken, the first man to settle in Iceland. Their sons were Thorgrim and Arngrim. They were both tall and strong, and the most valiant of men.

Helgi divided among his ship's crewmen the lands he had claimed. He settled Thrand at Thrandarstadir, Eilif in Eilifsdal, Hæking in Hækingsdal, Tind at Tindsstadir, and everyone there as he saw fit.

There was a man named Orlyg, entirely of Irish descent. At that time Ireland was Christian, and King Conchobar was Ireland's ruler. This man who has been named was a target of the king's anger. He went to find Bishop Patrick, his kinsman, who told him to sail to Iceland, "because many powerful men are now sailing to that place," he said. "But I want to lay this duty upon you: that you bring three things with you. They are consecrated earth, which you are to lay under the corner pillars of the church, and a plenarium[3], and a consecrated iron bell. You will approach Iceland from the south. Then you must sail westwards to where there is a great fjord that cuts into the land from the west. In the fjord you will see three high mountains and valleys in all of them. You shall steer towards the southernmost mountain. There you will find a good harbor, and a wise chieftain named Helgi Bjola. He will receive you, for he is not much given to making heathen sacrifices, and he will give you a place to live, south of the mountain that I just told you about. There you shall have a church built, and dedicate it to Saint Columba.

Now farewell," said the bishop, "and keep your faith well, though you come among heathens."

After that, Orlyg prepared for his journey. And the main thing to tell about his journey is that everything went as the bishop had said. He reached harbor in Therneyjarsund. He went to meet Helgi Bjola, who welcomed him warmly. There Orlyg built a farm and a church, and he lived there afterwards, until he was old.[4]

CHAPTER II

Towards the end of Conchobar's days, a ship came into Leiruvag. There were Irish men on board. One man was named Andrid; he was young and unmarried, tall and strong. There was also a woman on the ship named Esja, a widow and very wealthy. A man named Kolli was on the ship with them.[5] Helgi welcomed them all. He settled Kolli at Kollafjord. Because Orlyg was old and childless, he gave up his land and farm, and Esja took him in. She settled at Esjuberg. All of these people were said to be baptized, although many said that Esja knew the old magic. Andrid went to Hof and lodged there over the winter, and he swore brotherhood with Helgi's sons.

Andrid asked Helgi to get him a farm and a wife. He had plenty of money. At the time, all of Kjalarnes was overgrown with forest, so that the only clearings were where men cleared to build farms or roads. A great road had been cleared from Hof through the woods. Helgi and Andrid rode that way in the spring. And when they came out onto a hill, Helgi said, "Here I will give you land for you to build a farm, Andrid. I believe that my sons would want you to live nearby."

After that, Andrid built a farm along the road and called it Brautarholt, because the forest was so thick that he felt that building his farm anywhere else would be harder.[6] Andrid built a stately farm there.

There was a man named Thormod, who lived in Thormodsdal. With him was his sister, named Thurid. She was beautiful and wealthy. Helgi asked for this woman to marry Andrid, and she was promised to him. And that summer, Helgi's son Thorgrim was engaged to Arndis, the daughter of Thord Skeggjason from Skeggjastad.[7] Both weddings were held together at Hof, and celebrated with the greatest enthusiasm. Many people attended.

After the wedding, Thurid went to Brautarholt and took over managing the household. It was soon evident that she was a strong-willed woman. They had many livestock, and they all grazed with almost no supervision, out in the woods on the cape. That autumn, they were missing a dark-colored cow, three years old. She was called Mus. This cow was found three years later on the cape that extends westward from Brautarholt. She had two calves with her by then, one a yearling and the other one born that summer. For that reason, they called that cape Musarnes.

Helgi Bjola died during the first winter that Andrid settled at Brautarholt. People felt that that was the greatest loss, for he was the most well-liked of men.

In the spring, the brothers divided their inheritance from their father. Thorgrim had their father's estate and the chieftainship, because he was older, but Arngrim got the outlying lands. He raised a farm along the fjord, which he called Saurbaer. He married a woman named Olof from Borgarfjord. They had two sons, named Helgi and Vakr. They became valiant men, but were not very large.

Thorgrim raised a farm in the spring at Hof. It was grandly built in a short time, for many people supported him, friends and kinfolk. He became a powerful man in his district. He held the chieftainship all the way to Nyjahraun, which was called the Brundal chieftainship. He was called Thorgrim the Godi.[8] He was a great man for sacrifices. He had a great temple raised in his fields. That temple was a hundred feet long and sixty feet wide. All the people had to pay a temple-tax. Thor was the most highly honored god there. The inside was built in a semicircle, like the apse of a church, and was all hung with tapestries and set with windows. Thor stood there in the middle, with other gods on both sides. In front of Thor there stood an altar, made with much craftsmanship and plated over with iron. On it there had to be a fire which should never be extinguished; they called that the hallowed fire. On the altar there had to lie a great ring made of silver. The temple priest had to wear that on his arm at all meetings. All men had to swear oaths on it in all legal cases in which the evidence was circumstantial.[9] On that altar there also had to stand a great bowl made of copper. All the blood had to flow into it from those cattle, or men, which were given to Thor. They called that "the portion" and the bowl was the "portion-bowl."[10] They had to sprinkle the sacrificial blood over men or animals. Those animals that were offered there had to be eaten in feasts when the sacrifices were celebrated. But the humans that they sacrificed had to be plunged into the bog that lay outside, next to the doors, and they called that Blotkelda.[11] The cross-beams in the hall at Hof had been in the temple when Olaf Jonsson[12] had it torn down. He had them all split, but they were still quite thick.

Thorgrim established a Spring Assembly on the south side of Kjalarnes, along the coast. One can still see where the shelters were. Minor cases had to be prosecuted there, and only those cases which couldn't be prosecuted there, or which were too important, had to be presented at the Althing.[13]

Thorgrim and Arndis had a son together. He was named Thorstein. He was a very quarrelsome man from an early age, and he felt that everything was beneath him.

Kolli lived at Kollafjord, as was said before. He married a woman named Thorgerd, the daughter of Eilif from Eilifsdal. Together they had a daughter named Olof. Her beauty was renowned, and for that reason she was called Olof the Fair.

CHAPTER III

When Andrid and his wife had lived for several years at Brautarholt, they had a son. He was sprinkled with water and named Bui.[14] He soon far surpassed the other young men; he was bigger and stronger that other men, and more handsome to look at.

Esja lived at Esjuberg, as was said before. She asked to foster Bui Andridsson, and he was raised at Esjuberg. Bui was said to be self-willed as he grew up. He never wanted to sacrifice and said that it seemed unmanly to creep before idols. He also never wanted to go around carrying weapons. Instead, he went around with a sling, and always knotted it around himself.

There was a woman named Thorgerd. She lived at the farm called Vatn, which since then has been named Ellidavatn. Her son, who was named Kolfid, grew up with her. He was large and ugly at an early age, with dark hair. He lay in the fire-pit and bit the bark of charred branches and tended his mother's kettles. Thorgerd thought this was a great shame, yet Kolfid preferred it.[15]

Thorgrim the Godi kept a close watch on men who didn't want to sacrifice. They had to put up with harsh terms from him. He and his son Thorstein spread much gossip about how Bui didn't want to sacrifice, and they called him Bui the Dog.[16]

In the spring when Bui was twelve years old, but Thorgrim's son Thorstein was eighteen, Thorstein summoned Bui to the Kjalarnes Assembly on the charge of incorrect belief, and said that it was punishable by permanent outlawry.[17] Thorstein prosecuted the case, and Bui was sentenced to become a permanent outlaw.[18] Bui gave no sign that he acknowledged the sentence, and he arranged all his journeys as before. He always went to Brautarholt to see his father and mother, and he continued to do so. Because of all this, there was great animosity between the families.

It's said that when spring was ending, Bui went to Brautarholt. He always went by himself. He carried no more weapons than before; he had knotted his sling around himself. Thorstein saw Bui traveling and recognized who he was. He went to his father and said, "How long will this go on, father—that this dog whom I drove into the woods last summer should walk past our farmyard as freely as if he had nothing to answer for? It seems to me that if you put up with such an insult from your neighbors, others wouldn't think it a great matter to disobey your orders or ignore our rulings."

Thorgrim said that he made a strong argument—"but what do you want to do now?"

Thorstein said, "It's clear what I need to do. I want you to give me men. I will take Bui's life when he goes home. I don't think we need to consider that his father would ask for any compensation for him."

The father and son agreed to do this. They waited to hear that Bui was passing by on his way home.

Bui stayed for several nights at Brautarholt, and as he was preparing to leave, his mother Thurid came to him and said, "My son, I don't want you to leave so heedlessly. I've been told that Thorstein has spoken harsh words to you. I want you to let at least two strong men go with you, and for you to be armed and not go weaponless like women."

Bui said, "I'm obliged to do as you wish, but it's hard for my foster-mother to take care of any more people like me. But even if I should happen to meet Thorstein, it's not clear which of us will live to tell about it, even if I have to fight several of his men. I will go alone, as I have planned."

After that, Bui went on his way eastwards along the shore, and at once Thorstein heard about it. Thorstein and his men, twelve all together, took their weapons. By then Bui had come to a hill called Kleberg, when he saw his pursuers. He made a stand and gathered some stones. Thorstein and his men came fast, and when they crossed the brook that was there, they heard the whirring of Bui's sling, and a stone went flying. The stone struck one of Thorstein's men in the chest and killed him at once. Bui flung several stones, and each one hit a man. By then, Thorstein and his men had come very close to Bui. He turned and left the high ground by another route, and only the hill stood between them. At that moment, such a darkness descended that no one could see in front of his toes.

Thorstein said, "We've got an uphill battle[19] if we're dealing with both a dog and a troll. We'll go back for now, but I still want to have a meeting with Bui—the sort that we will not both be able to tell about afterwards."

After that, they turned back, and carried their followers back with them. They were not at all pleased with their journey. People said that the expedition had gone all wrong for them.

CHAPTER IV

Bui went home, and his foster-mother Esja was outside. She greeted Bui warmly, and he responded in kind.

Esja said, "Didn't you think for a while that you were short of men?"

Bui said, "I didn't need any more."

Esja said, "You weren't completely alone, fighting against them all."

Bui said, "I think it's good to benefit from good things."[20]

Esja said, "Aren't you tired of Thorstein pursuing you?"

"I'd be more certain of that," said Bui, "if I could expect any help."

Esja said, "There are always risks to be run."

After that, their conversation ended.

Now the year passed until winter. Then Bui went alone, late in the evening, out to Brautarholt, and stayed there through the night. Just before dawn, he went out walking. He turned and headed eastwards to a hill from where he could clearly see the farm at Hof. The weather was clear and bright. He saw that a man from Hof was coming out early, in his linen underclothes. The man went out of the gate and turned down the path that led to the temple. Bui thought that he recognized Thorstein. Bui headed for the temple, and when he came there, he saw that the fence was unlocked, and so was the temple. Then Bui went into the temple. He saw that Thorstein lay groveling before Thor. Bui walked silently until he came to Thorstein. Then he gripped Thorstein in such a way that he got one hand under the backs of his knees and the other under his shoulders. In this way, he heaved Thorstein off the ground and drove his head so hard against a stone that his brains were splattered on the floor. He died instantly. Bui carried him out of the temple and threw him against the fence. Then he went back into the temple. He took the sacred flame and stoked it, and then he carried the fire around the temple and touched it to the hangings. One after another quickly caught fire, and in a short while the temple was burning from the inside. Bui went out and locked both the temple and the fence, and tossed the keys into the fire. After that, he went on his way.

Thorgrim the Godi awoke in the morning and looked outside. He could see the fire on the temple. He called to his people, both women and men, to come running with jugs of water and save the temple. He also called to his son Thorstein, but he couldn't be found anywhere. When they came to the fence gate, their way was blocked because the gate was locked, and they couldn't find the keys anywhere. They had to break down the gate because the fence was so high that they couldn't get over it. They broke down the gate. When they came in through the gate and into the courtyard, they saw where Thorstein was lying dead. The temple was locked, so they couldn't save what was inside. Grappling hooks were readied and the temple was pulled down, and some of the timbers were saved.

Now there is this to be said about Bui: he came to the farm called Holar. There he announced the killing of Thorstein at his hands.[21] After that he went home. Esja was on the west side of the yard and greeted Bui. He responded warmly to her greeting.

She said, "Have you been chased by Thorstein at all this morning, or has the provocation had an effect?

Bui said that he wouldn't deny that something of a dust-up seemed to have happened to the people at Hof.

Esja said, "Have you announced the killing at all?"

He said that he had.

Esja said, "I have no confidence that I can protect you from Thorgrim without a place to hide, because I know that he'll come here today."

Bui said, "Won't you arrange things as you think best?"

They turned and left the farmyard and went along the mountain and over the river. Then they took a path so narrow that they had to walk single file,[22] up the mountain onto the peak called Laugargnipa.[23] In front of them there was a fine cave that gave good shelter. Down below, there was an excellent hot spring for bathing. In the cave were food and drink and clothing.

Esja said, "First you must stay here."

Bui said that it should be so.

Then Esja turned and went home. As soon as she came home, she had fires kindled in the farm buildings with wet peats, which smoldered and made the greatest smoke and stench.

CHAPTER V

When Bui had left, the farmer who lived at Holar rode to find Thorgrim the Godi, and he told him the message Bui had brought. As soon as Thorgrim found out, he sent for men: for Helgi and Vakr the sons of his brother Arngrim, and for many others, making thirty men all together. Thorgrim rode to Esjuberg with this troop. When Esja saw them coming, she had the floor sweepings brought to the fire and burned, but she stood outside the doors when Thorgrim and his men arrived.[24] Esja greeted them and invited them to stay.

Thorgrim said that they had other business there than dining. "We want you to give up Bui the Dog, your foster-son," he said, "and we will give him a wretched death, as he deserves."

Esja said, "What has my foster-son done, that he should be put to death?"

Thorgrim said, "That can't be completely unknown to you; you know how to do many things. He has done deeds so monstrous that it would be better if nothing like them happened again. He has killed my son Thorstein, and done something even more monstrous than that: he has burned up the temple and our gods."

Esja said, "Even if my foster-son Bui were here and had done something that deserved death, I would never give him up for you to kill him. But Bui hasn't come here since yesterday, when he left."

Thorgrim said, "We don't believe that he isn't here, and we want to search for him."

Esja said, "Now I'm sure that your father Helgi Bjola is dead. My house would never be searched if he had anything to say about it. There's such a difference in power between us that you'll do as you wish. But I want no more than five of you to go through my house."

Thorgrim said that it would be so. He went inside with four other men. Esja stood in the doorway and told the housemaid to carry a light in front of them. But when Thorgrim and his men came in, the buildings were full of smoke and such a great stench that they could hardly take a breath unless they pulled their clothes over their heads. The housemaid took a long time to kindle the light, but eventually a feeble light was carried before them. Yet they were inside for a much shorter time, and went into fewer places, and made less of a search than they would have if they could have put up with conditions inside. After that they came out and said that the place wasn't passable for any man.

Thorgrim said, "We believe it's true that you've hidden Bui, Esja. We would now be at odds if you hadn't been on good terms with my father, and if it weren't pointless for me to capture you. "

Esja said, "You won't find Bui here, because he hasn't come today."

After that, Thorgrim rode away to his home. Then he said to his men, "All of that together bothers me so much that I have to do something to soothe my anger. I'll go to Brautarholt and kill Andrid."

Helgi and Vakr said that killing an old man was an evil deed. Thorgrim said that it had to be done. They rode to Brautarholt, and there was no resistance, for Andrid was captured in his high-seat and led out. Thurid, the lady of the house, offered money for the life of her husband, but it wasn't accepted. Thorgrim got a man to kill him, and he faced his death bravely. After that they rode away. Thurid had Andrid's body prepared, and he was carried to an island that lay off the coast and buried in a mound there. That island has been called Andridsey ever since.

CHAPTER VI

That same autumn, a ship came in. The steersman was named Orn, a native of Viken in Norway. Orn the steersman went to lodge at Kollafjord. But the Norwegian[25] hadn't been there long before the beauty of Kolli' s daughter Olof attracted his attention. He got in the habit of sitting and talking with her every day. Kolli had a grand household, and he wanted to keep up good cheer for the sake of the steersman, so he held games there. When the young men of the district heard that, they crowded there, and a great many people competed in the games.

Esja soon came to meet her foster-son Bui and told him about the killing of his father. Bui didn't show emotion at that, and said that an old tree could be expected to fall.[26]

It's said that Esja came to meet Bui one day. He asked what news she had to tell him. She said that games were being held at Kollafjord. "What's more," she said, "Orn the steersman sits and talks with Olof the Beautiful every day, and people suppose that he'll seduce her."

Bui said that she would make a good marriage.

Esja said, "Sometimes you say the most completely idiotic things, seeing as how I have intended this woman for you. Now I want you to go straight to the games and risk your life. There's no way to protect you if you're fated to die."

Bui said that it was her decision.

The next morning, Bui went to the games at Kollafjord. He arrived rather late, and the games had begun. He wore his usual clothes, with his sling wrapped around him. Olof sat on a dais, and Orn the steersman was at her side, and they were conversing with each other. Bui went to the dais and pulled the two men on Olof's other side out of their seats. Then he sat down and stayed there that day. In the evening he went home to his cave. He behaved the same way the next day, and then the next. Orn the Norwegian kept on doing as he had been, but neither one spoke to Olof so that the other one couldn't hear.

CHAPTER VII

Now the story relates that Thorgerd the housewife was at Vatn. She went into the hearth-house[27] one day. Kolfid her son was lying there, stretching his long legs out all the way.

"There is a great difference," she said, "between what men are born into the world for, and what they become known for. Two men are sitting at Kollafjord and competing for Olof the Fair, and it's said that they've done many manly deeds. Now all the young men are going to the games, but you are so worthless that you lie in the fire-pit, breaking your mother's heart. It would be better if you were dead, rather than for me to witness such a shame and disgrace to our family."

Kolfid said, "You're upset now, mother, but things will soon get better."

Thorgerd turned and left. A little later, Kolfid stood up and went outside and looked around and saw that it wasn't late. Kolfid was dressed like this: he was wearing a hooded cloak,[28] and he'd tied the flaps between his legs. He wore long breeches and had hairy calfskin shoes[29] on his feet. A woodpile stood in the yard; he went there and took a long log in his hand, and then he turned and left the farmyard. He threw the log in front of him and ran after it, and he traveled very fast.[30] He didn't stop until he came to Kollafjord.

By that time the games had begun. Olof sat on the dais, and Orn the Norwegian and Bui were sitting on either side of her. When Kolfid came into the room, dressed as described, most people thought he looked quite ridiculous.[31] He stood still on the floor and looked around, and saw a chair standing on the floor. He went up and took the chair and set it down in front of where Olof was sitting. Kolfid sat down and stayed there all day.

In the evening he went home. He went into the main room. His mother greeted him and asked where he had been, and he told her. She said, "How did you like it?"

"Fine," he said.

"Will you go there more often?" she said.

Kolfid said, "I don't think I'm fickle in my conduct. I suppose I'm expected to grant you this much: to go there for a while."

She said, "But I want you to have suitable clothes, my son, and good weapons, and a man to go with you."

"I don't want that," he said. "I want to keep my clothing as it is, and I won't take anyone with me."

"It's up to you," she said.

The next morning, Kolfid went to Kollafjord, and he acted just as he had on the previous day. And so these three men made these trips until the beginning of winter. None of them said either good things or bad things to another, and no one said anything to Olof that no one else could hear. She answered them all courteously.

Thorgrim the Godi found out about what Bui was doing. But because he had done him injury by killing his father, he did nothing to him, and so matters stood for a while.

CHAPTER VIII

It is said that on one occasion, Orn the Norwegian came to speak with the farmer Kolli. "Here's how matters stand, Kolli," he said. "This would be a good household, and it's all your doing that it's good. But it seems quite unendurable that these two men have gotten in the habit of coming here. I could tolerate Bui behaving himself in that way, as bad as that is—but as for that that filth who sits there and listens in on people's conversations, I am done putting up with that any longer."

Kolli answered, "I want you to arrange matters as you please."

That same afternoon, Orn ordered his servant to take their weapons and go south of the hayfield and wait for him there. Since there was a great bustle as many men were getting ready to leave, no one paid attention to where the Norwegian was going. The Norwegian turned south across a hill, and there the two of them sat and waited for Kolfid.

After the games, Kolfid left as usual and went on his way. But when he came south of the hill, Orn the Norwegian and his servant rushed out and attacked him. Kolfid defended himself with a cudgel and parried their weapons; he was harder for them to overcome than they had thought. And when they had fought for a while, Kolfid struck the servant and knocked him out, and both shield and sword flew out of his hands. Kolfid snatched up both of them, and then attacked Orn the Norwegian, and in the end Orn fell, but Kolfid was wounded. At that moment, the servant came to his senses, but Kolfid didn't want to hurt him further. He went on his way. The servant saw that the Norwegian had been killed. He tossed a shield over him and then went home to Kollafjord. Kolli had his body brought home and prepared according to custom.

Now it's time to tell about Kolfid's journey. He was badly wounded, as was said. There were large rivers in his way, and when he came out of the Leiruvag River, it made him very cold and stiff. There was some frost on him.

There was a man named Korpulf who lived at Korpulfsstad. He was an old man and was said to know quite a lot of the old ways. He had a son named Grim; he was young and quite a promising young man. Korpulf was Kolfid's mother's brother. Kolfid turned and headed that way, and was well received. Korpulf bandaged his wound. Kolfid stayed there for a while, but sent word to his mother of where he was staying.

The morning after Orn was killed, Esja came early to her foster son. He welcomed her warmly and asked for news. Esja told him about the killing of Orn the Norwegian and all the circumstances. "Now I want you to change your outfit. Here I have a shaggy cape that I want you to wear, and also a shirt. I think it probably won't be cut soon, either by weapons or magic.[32] The third possession I have for you is a knife. I expect that it will never be stopped in its stroke, because you will soon have to find out how the weapon cuts for you."

Bui said that it was up to her. He went on his way to Kollufjord, and now there was no crowd next to Olof on the dais. She treated Bui in the same way as before.

When Kolfid's wound was healed, he said to his kinsman Korpulf that he wanted to meet with his mother. Korpulf said that was up to him—"but I've decided that you shouldn't have these rags any longer. I want you to have good clothes and weapons, which I will give you. You'll need them soon. Along with that I want to give you my son Grim to go with you and be your follower."

Kolfid said that it should be so.

After that, the kinsmen went to Vatn to meet Thorgerd. She was glad to see them, and asked what Kolfid wanted to do.

Kolfid said, "I intend to meet Bui now. We two shall no longer sit together to talk with Olof."

Thorgerd said, "This plan of coming to blows with Bui isn't promising, given Esja's magic and Bui's toughness."

Kolfid said, "Every danger has two possible outcomes. Either I'll live or die."

"It's your decision, my son," she said.

CHAPTER IX

In the morning, the kinsmen set out early and came to Kollafjord. Men were getting ready for the games. Bui was sitting on the dais next to Olof.

Kolfid entered the room and went up to the dais where Bui was sitting, and said, "There are two choices before you. One is for you to give up coming here altogether. The other is for you to fight a duel with me in the morning, on the island that lies to the south in the Leiruvag River."

Bui said, "The less equal the choices, the easier to choose. I've made my own decisions so far about where I go, and I intend to do so still. But I'll offer you a duel as soon as you want."

After that they joined hands and swore a binding agreement between them. Kolfid and Grim turned and left; they went to Korpulfsstad in the evening, and told Korpulf what had happened. He said, "Now you're not setting a promising course, kinsman. More distinguished men than ourselves have had a hard time dealing with Esja. But now it must go on as it's fated to go."

They stayed there for the night. As they were getting ready, Korpulf said, "I can't offer you much help, Kolfid, but there's a sword here which I will give you. I carried it in my younger days, but it won't be much help for you this time." After that, the kinsmen went on their way.

Bui stayed behind at the games once he and Kolfid parted. He didn't go home before his usual time. Eaja was there ahead of him and greeted her foster son, and asked whether he'd been challenged to a duel. He said that it was true.

Esja said, "Kolfid is a tough and vigorous man. I will sleep next to you tonight."

She fixed a bath for him, and she stroked every one of his limbs.[33] Then in the morning she dressed him as she liked, and wished him well. Bui now traveled until he came to the island. Kolfid was there ahead of him, along with many men, because people had a great curiosity to see the fight of these young men, both of whom were strong.

It was the custom at that time to spread a cloak under the fighters' feet. It was their law that the one who stepped off the cloak had to redeem himself with three marks of silver, and the first one whose blood fell on the ground was out of the fight.[34] After that was done, the laws of single combat were recited between them. Bui had to strike first, since he was the one who had been challenged. Both of them had good shields and other weapons.

Bui struck at Kolfid. Kolfid warded off the blow with his shield, but his shield was sheared off on one side of the handgrip. After that, Kolfid struck a similar blow at Bui. Then Bui struck at Kolfid and destroyed the shield he held and gave him a great wound on the arm, and Kolfid was out of the fight. Men rushed between them and separated them. Afterwards, each went his own way. Kolfid went to Korpulfsstad, and Korpulf bandaged his wound and said that this was only to be expected when dealing with Bui. Kolfid stayed there for a while.

Bui went from the duel back to Kollafjord. Olof was washing clothes, and she greeted Bui. He returned her greeting, and said, "Our meetings have come to this, Olof: I won't go to my cave alone, and I find it tiresome to come here every day to talk with you. You must come along with me now."

Olof said, "That won't please my father."

Bui said, "He's not going to be asked."

Then he took Olof on his arm and went on his way. They traveled until they came to Bui's cave. Esja was there ahead of them and greeted them. "You seem to me to have done well in your courtship, Bui, to have protected Olaf from those worthless people and brought her away from their harassment. My dear Olof, you shall be welcome here."

Olof said that Bui would decide where to live for the present.

Kolfid soon heard that Olof had been taken. He said to his uncle Korpulf, "I was far away. Olof should not have left that way. I shall search for Bui as soon as my wound is healed."

"You're wrong to set your heart on Olof," said Korpulf. "And I don't advise you to search for Bui, unless you have many men."

CHAPTER X

Now the winter went on, and Kolfid's wound healed. Then he said, "Now I will go to meet my mother and get men from there. Your son Grim must be waiting for me at the Leiruvag River in the morning, along with the men that you send to help me."

Korpulf said that it would be so.

In the morning the kinsmen that Kolfid had summoned met up; there were fifteen men all together. Then they all went on their way until they came to the foot of the mountain where Bui's cave was. There was a steep, narrow path leading up. There were two well-armed men keeping watch above them, with plenty of stones. Kolfid saw that there was no way they could get up the narrow path. Then Kolfid called out, and he said, "If Bui can hear my words, let him come down this path if he has a man's heart instead of a mare's."[35]

Bui heard Kolfid's words clearly. He jumped up and seized his weapons, and said that he would never tolerate Kolfid's shameful insults. Olof said that it was ill-advised to go up against that the forces that would be there. Bui said that he didn't care about that. But when Bui was armed, such a pain struck both his eyes that he had to grab at them with both hands. Olof asked what had happened to him.

Bui said that his departure was delayed. "I suspect that my foster-mother is meddling," he said.

Olof said that was a good thing.

When Kolfid realized that Bui wasn't coming out, he and his men turned away. He didn't stop until he came home, and wasn't satisfied with his journey. As soon as Kolfid turned away from the narrow path, the pain in Bui's eyes subsided. Now the winter passed.

CHAPTER XI

When summer began, Bui and Esja made plans together.

"Now I don't want you to stay here longer," she said. "Instead, you must go north to Hrutafjord. A ship has been laid up on shore over the winter, at Bordeyri. You must travel to foreign lands and find out what lies in store for you there. I've grown old, and I have few years left to live."

Next she prepared him for the journey, and she gave him a man to go with him and three horses. Olof had to go home to Kollafjord and wait for him for three years. As soon as Bui was ready, he went along the path down the mountain. Esja his foster-mother went with him, and she was greatly affected on parting with him. Then Bui went on his way, and when he had come to the Blikdal River, he met a shepherd from

Saurbaer. The shepherd asked who these men were. Bui told him the whole truth.

As soon as they parted and a hill blocked the line of sight between them, the shepherd raced home and told the brothers Helgi and Vakr everything about Bui's journey. They thanked him for his efforts. At once they had horses brought and summoned the men of their household. They armed themselves quickly and rode hard, twelve men all together.

Bui didn't see the pursuit before he came over Skeidhlid. Then he rode until he saw a hill in front of him, which has been called Orrustuholl[36] ever since. He made a stand there, and ordered his companion to see to the horses and baggage. Bui climbed the hill and carried stones up with him. He had good weapons all, and the shirt that his foster-mother had given him. The brothers came upon him, and leaped from their horses and came after Bui with a fierce attack. Bui defended himself bravely, and at first he let stones fly. By the time Bui was out of stones, four of the brothers' men had fallen. Then he took his shield and sword. The brothers attacked with great bravery, because they were both stout-hearted. Two more of their followers fell. The brothers and all their men were wounded. Bui was still not wounded, but was terribly weary.

At that moment, Eilif the farmer from Eilifsdal arrived with six men and got between them. Because Helgi and Vakr were wounded, they gave up fighting. Eilif told Bui to be on his way, and he left. Eilif had the dead men buried, and he had the others' wounds bandaged.

Afterwards, the brothers went back to Saurbaer and weren't pleased with how the journey had gone. Bui didn't stop traveling until he came north to Hrutafjord. He took passage there, and when they were ready they sailed out to sea.

The brothers Helgi and Vakr took passage that summer in Kollafjord, and both sailed away. They came to Norway and went to the household of King Harald Fairhair. They were with the king through the winter, and they were well thought of by every man. They told the king about their encounters with Bui. The king said it was a bad thing that Bui had burned the temple, and he called that a cowardly deed.

CHAPTER XII

Now there is this to be told about Bui: the sailors had light winds and reached the Orkneys late in the autumn. Jarl Einar Rognvaldsson ruled the islands at the time.

Bui came to the jarl's household and went before him and greeted him. The jarl asked who he was. Bui told him quite clearly—"and I would like to take winter lodging with you, lord."

The jarl said, "You will be good company. You shall certainly stay with us this winter, if you wish."

Bui stayed with the jarl's household over the winter. Jarl Einar had much trouble over the winter, and Bui was the most fearless in all trials. But in the spring, when the ship that Bui had come on was preparing to head for Norway, Bui went before the jarl and asked for leave to go.

The jarl said, "It seems more advisable to me, Bui, for you to stay with us. We have tested you and found you to be a bold man. We will take you into the fellowship of my household, and grant you other honors, if you will stay here."

Bui thanked the jarl with fine words, but said that he preferred to go to Norway. The jarl said that it had to be so. After that, they sailed to Norway and arrived in the northern part of the country. They heard that King Harald was residing in Trondheim.

Bui went to Trondheim on a cargo ship, and when he came to Steinkjer, he went before the king who was sitting at the table, and greeted him well. The king asked who this large man might be. Bui told him the whole truth.

The king asked where he had been over the winter. Bui told him."And I have come here, lord," he said, "because I want to offer you my service."

The king said, "Do you have the right to come here freely?"[37]

Bui said that he didn't know.

The king had Helgi and Vakr summoned. And when they came before the king, he said, "Do you recognize this big man at all?"

"Yes," they said, "and he would be hard-pressed if you were not so near. We urge you to give us permission to avenge our grief on him."

The king said, "I will not behave shamefully to any man who comes into my power, and I see no good outcome for you, even if you contend with him on equal terms. But because you, Bui, did that unworthy deed and burned our gods, who are worthy of worship from all men, inside their temple, I would have to have you killed if you had not placed youself in our power. Now you must redeem your head with a quest. You must fetch the game board[38] from my foster-father Dofri and bring it to me."

Bui said, "Where should I go?"

The king said, "Figure it out yourself."

Bui said, "Many would say, lord, that you are sending me to my death, but nonetheless I will accept. And I want you to promise me a truce until I can return."

The king said that he would do so.

Bui then left the estate and stayed in Trondheim for the summer. He asked about old place names, and he was told where the Dovre Mountains were.

CHAPTER XIII

Early in winter, when snow lay on the mountains, Bui headed up into the settled regions. He stayed for a while in the remotest inhabited lands with a farmer named Raud. Bui asked Raud whether he knew any advice that he could give him so that he might succeed in his journey.

Raud said, "The king has sent many men on this errand, and none has come back. It's obvious to me that the king wants you dead. But I know that none of them had any chance of finding out where Dofri rules, except for King Harald. Still, since you've sought me out, I can tell you something. I will show you the path to the Dovre Mountains, to the peak where most men suppose that Dofri's caves must be. Arrange it so that you come to the base of the peak on the evening of Yule. Then you'll have to look around. I can do no more for you."

Bui asked him to accept his thanks for that, and gave Raud a fine large gold ring. Raud thanked him for the gift—"and come back here, Bui," he said, "if you return, as unlikely as it is."

Bui said that he would do so. He arranged everything as Raud had said. On the eve of Yule he came to the bottom of this peak, and stayed there for a while, and saw nothing that was likely to be a door. Bui struck the crags with the pommel of his sword and said, "You, Dofri, open up your hill and let in a man who's come a long way and is weary from traveling. That befits your honor."

And when Bui spoke these words for the third time, there was a noise in the cliff like a clap of thunder. At that moment the cliff sprang apart and became a door. Just then, a woman came to the door. She was very large in every way; she was beautiful to see and well dressed, wearing a red tunic[39] worked all over with lace and a broad silver belt around her waist. She had loose hair, as is the custom for maidens, and it was long and fair. She had fair hands and many gold rings on them, and strong arms. She was quite magnificent in appearance.

She greeted the newcomer and he warmly accepted her greeting. She asked him his name. He told her, and asked, "What is your name and kinfolk?"

She said, "I am called Frid, the daughter of King Dofri. But why are you knocking on our door, man?"

"I want to meet your father, and ask him for lodging over Yule. He is the most famous king of all."

Frid said, "You're not an unpromising man to look at. I say it's best for you to come inside with me."

Bui did so. Frid commanded the cave to close up, and it did. Then they walked for a while by firelight. She turned towards the cave wall at one point; there was a door before her, and another, and then they came into a small chamber, all hung with tapestries and splendidly furnished.

Frid said, "Here you must sit down and wait, Bui, and take off your weapons and wet clothes."

He did so. Then she placed a fine table before them and set it. She brought him a basin of silver and a costly towel, and then she invited him to sit and eat.[40] She brought fine food and excellent drink. All the tableware was made of silver and ornamented with gold, all the dishes and goblets and spoons. Frid sat down next to Bui, and they ate and drank together. She asked him to tell her all about his journey. Bui did so, and told her everything about how he had come there.

"Now you've done well," she said, "by not concealing the truth from me, and it may be that you won't suffer harm by coming here. But I think I knew the truth already. King Harald has sent many men after this game board, and my father has destroyed them all. Now I must go and find him and tell him what has happened."

Frid went away, and was gone for a while. Bui greeted her when she returned, and asked what her father had said about them.

She said that she had told him that a little bearded baby had arrived.

He had said that he wanted to see it. "I said that it had to be put to bed for the night. Now you shall sleep in my chamber tonight."

He said that that would please him well. They amused themselves there[41] throughout the evening.

CHAPTER XIV

Bui awoke in the morning, and it was daylight. Frid asked how he had slept. He said that he had slept well. She brought him fine clothing and said, "Now you must bear yourself well when you go before my father. Ask him for lodging over Yule, and be bold."

They went forward into the cave. She went ahead until there were doors before her, and then they came into a great chamber all hung with tapestries, with straw on the floor. A man sat in the high seat on the far bench, tall and handsome; he had a great beard, hoary white. This man was dressed in finery and looked entirely like a chieftain to Bui. Both of the benches were filled with people, and many had huge faces. The women sat on the other side of the chamber, and the fairest of them all sat in the middle. Tables were laid throughout the chamber, and foods were set out that were suitable for men to enjoy at that season. Young men were going around and serving drink.

Frid went before the man in the high seat and greeted her father. This bearded man answered his daughter warmly; Bui realized that this must be Dofri. He went before him and spoke these words: "Be well, King Dofri, with your merry household!"

Dofri responded well to his words and said to his daughter, "Is that the bearded baby that you told me about yesterday?"

"So it is, father," said Frid.

Dofri said, "Few such come from the lands of men, except for King Harald my foster-son. He is far above them all. But why have you come to us?"

Bui said, "I have come here to ask for Yule lodgings from you. I am a foreigner, but I have heard much spoken about your fame. It would seem foolish not to behold such a noble chieftain."

Dofri said, "You speak well. I want you to stay with us. You shall drink with us in the hall through the day; we wish to converse with you. You shall be seated in the opposite high seat.[42] But in the evening you and my daughter Frid shall amuse yourselves in her room, because the men of my household will seem rather boisterous to you."

Bui thanked him with fine words for this noble invitation and excellent arrangement. Then he went to the other side of the floor, and Frid went with him. She asked the three who had been sitting there to stand up, and they did. Then she had a fine pillow placed beneath them, and they sat down on it, and stayed there throughout the day. Dofri asked Bui many questions, and Bui had a ready answer to them all. When the evening began, they went before Dofri and wished him well. He bade them go in peace. Then they went to Frid's chamber and stayed there through the night. In this manner, Yule went by.

On the last day of Yule, Bui went before Dofri and said, "You have treated me nobly, as I expected. Now although I find it good here, I shall not tarry here with you."

Dofri said, "Bui, you shall be welcome here throughout the winter, if you prefer."

Bui thanked him for this new favor. He and Frid carried on as they had been doing, as said before.

Now the winter passed, and when few days were left until summer, Bui said to Frid, "How do you suppose my errand will turn out? I want to ask you to have a few words with your father."

Frid said, "Didn't it enter your mind that you'll have been here all winter, so that you would have no hope of going back to the world of men? I must inform you that I am pregnant with your child."

Bui said that he didn't want to deny it—"but still, I would hope that you could do me a favor."

Frid said, "It seems bad to me that you should be killed now, even if you were deserving of it. Instead, I will go to my father today and find out where your case stands."

That day, when people had taken their seats, Frid went to her father and sat on his knee and laid her arms around his neck and said, "How do you intend, father, to part company with Bui, your guest over the winter? It would be a noble thing to treat him well. Outstanding men will visit your household more willingly."

Dofri said, "How well do you want me to send him off?"

Frid said, "Give him splendid gifts, father. Then it will be obvious that he has visited the home of a great and noble chieftain."

Dofri said, "What should I choose?"

Frid said, "Give him that game board that King Harald has often sent for, and a gold ring along with that. Then he can redeem himself from the king with the gaming board, and keep the ring as a memento."

Dofri said, "It's up to you, daughter, because I can't deny you."

"You do well, father, as always."

She went to her seat.

The days passed until summer, and on the first day of summer, Frid said to Bui, "Now we two will eat in my room. Then take your clothes and weapons and keep them ready to hand. You won't have long to wait once you and my father part company."

After that, they went to meet Dofri. He had just sat at the table. Dofri greeted them and asked them to sit and drink, and they did. Then Dofri said, "Bui, you have stayed well here over the winter, to the best of my knowledge. And we want it to be evident from trustworthy tokens that you have visited us. Here is a game board that I will give you. I know this to be a treasure that my foster son King Harald has his heart set on. And you shall accept this gold ring from me."

Bui thanked him for this favor and for the great honor he had done him, with many fair words, and wished that he might reign as the most fortunate of all kings. After that, they received permission for Bui to go, and they turned and went away.

As they came to the cave doors, the cave opened up. Frid went outside and said to Bui, "Now it has happened, Bui, that I am pregnant with your child, as I told you. I must now tell you what the arrangement will be. If it is a girl-child, she shall stay here with me, but if it is a boy, I will send him to you when he is twelve years old. You must welcome him, and if you don't, you will meet your fate. I won't come with you. Farewell."

And then they parted.

CHAPTER XV

Bui went on his way and didn't stop until he came to Raud. Raud welcomed him and asked about his journey, and Bui told him the truth.

Raud said, "You've had great luck on this journey, but you'll have to brace yourself that King Harald won't be satisfied with only this from you, because now he will make you fight the troll that I know to be the largest in Norway. That's a black man[43] who has been the bane of many men. Now I will give you a wrestling jacket that you should have, and then I expect that you won't feel it very much wherever he puts his paws on you, because he breaks most men's bones if he doesn't kill them."

Bui thanked Raud for his good deed. He stayed there for several nights, and then went down to Trondheim. He heard that the king was at Steinkjer. When Bui arrived, he went to meet the king and greeted him. The king looked at him and said, "Is that you, Bui? How did Dofri receive you?"

"Yes, lord," said Bui, "and I had an advantage, thanks to you, because Dofri treated me well."

The king said, "Were you with Dofri over the winter? And did you get the game board?"

"Yes, lord," said Bui, "I got the game board."

The king said, "Come to me in the morning with it."

Bui said that he would.

The next day, Bui came before the king as he sat at the drinking table, and brought him the game board. When the king saw it, he said, "You are an excellent man, Bui. You have true tokens that you have met Dofri. He has never wanted to let me have this game board. But as worthy as you are, we must see something of your strength. You shall wrestle with our black man."

Bui said, "I thought that if I brought the game board, you would let me go in peace."

The king said, "It's no great matter to have one wrestling match."

Bui said, "The king's word is law. Now I want to stipulate with you, lord, that if I should beat him, which seems unlikely, you will release me from your anger and grant me leave to return to Iceland."

The king consented. Then the king stipulated a delay of two weeks before this bout was to happen, because he wanted as many people to witness it as possible. When the time had passed, the king had a trumpet blown to summon all the folk out to a wide field. Once the king and a great many people had arrived, Bui prepared for the bout. He went in the shirt that Esja had given him, which we mentioned earlier. He pulled on the wrestling jacket that Raud had given him. Then he went to the contest. The king had the black man led out, and four men were holding onto him. He howled fiercely and barked like a troll. The ground was arranged so that there was a flat field with high hills beyond it, and the people sat on the hills all around. On the field stood a great flat stone slab buried in the ground with its narrow edge pointing upwards; they called that the wrestling slab.

Bui went before the king and said, "Where is the man that you mean for me to wrestle, lord?"

The king said, "See where they are holding him back from the field."

Bui said, "That doesn't look like a man to me. It looks more like a troll."

The king said, "We shall test you for only a short time, if we see that you're not a match for him."

Bui said, "It's your decision."

After that, Bui went forward onto the field, and when the people saw him, many said that it was a bad thing for a troll to be made to fight such a gallant man. Then they turned the black man loose. He rushed at Bui, howling, and when they met, they began fighting most fiercely and briskly. Bui quickly realized that he was much less strong than this beast; he saved himself from falling, stayed on his feet, and dodged him all around the field. He realized that the black man was gripping him so hard that his bones would have broken if his clothes hadn't protected him. Bui realized that the black man wanted to bring him to the stone slab. But when they had been fighting for a while, the black man was terribly exhausted. Squeals were coming from him like the squeals of pigs when they fight each other, and he was foaming at the mouth. When Bui noticed that, he let himself be pushed back to the stone. The black man resumed pressing him hard, and his howls were horrible to hear, because he was nearly dead from the fight. But when Bui came close enough to the slab to touch it with his heels, the black man pushed as hard as he could. Bui made an unexpected move and leaped backwards over the slab, and the black man's hands came loose and slipped off Bui's wrestling jacket. Then Bui pulled the black man towards him as hard as he could, and the black man stumbled and fell onto the slab, so that his chest hit the stone where it was sharpest. Then Bui jumped on him with all his strength. The black man's chest was split apart, and he was dead. Many people said that this was a great deed of bravery.

Bui went before King Harald. The king said, "You are an excellent man. You may now depart from us and go to your native land in peace."

Bui thanked the king for that. Then Bui went to the coast and took passage to Iceland.

CHAPTER XVI

The summer when Bui left, Olof the Fair was pregnant with a child. In the autumn she gave birth to a girl which she knew to be Bui's, and the girl was named Thurid. Esja asked to foster the girl, and Kolli and Olof accepted.

But during the summer when Bui was in Thrandheim, Helgi and Vakr traveled to Iceland. They spread the news that Bui was lost, and that King Harald had sent him on a dangerous mission from which he hadn't returned. When that was made known, Kolfid want to Kollafjord and took Olof the Fair away by force, against her father's will. Kolfid took Olof out to Vatn, and she stayed there that summer and the following winter.

But the next summer, a ship came south to Eyrarbakki, into the harbor that's called Einarshofn. Word spread that Bui Andridsson was on the ship. And as soon as this news was heard on the other side of the mountains, Kolfid kept an eye on Bui's travels and found out that he had come to Olfus. Then Kolfid rode from his home up to the pass called Oxnaskard, with twelve men in all: his kinsman Grim and ten other men were with him. They lay in wait there for Bui.

At that moment, Bui rode down from the pass. He saw armed men and realized who they must be. Bui had all good weapons, and he was wearing his shirt, Esja's Gift. Bui rode towards a great boulder that stood below the pass, and got off his horse. They rushed towards him. Bui had a small thong-spear[44] in his hand, and he flung it at them. The spear hit the lower part of Grim's shield; it broke through the shield and plunged into Grim's leg above the knee and pierced it through. Grim was out of the fight. Bui turned his back to the boulder, because it was as large as a cliff, and then he could only be attacked from the front.

Then Kolfid said, "It's well that we've met here, Bui. Now the cave of that troll Esja won't shelter you as it did the last time."

Bui said, "I don't regret it. Our meetings have only ended with you accomplishing nothing. I expect that it'll still go the same way. But it's a manly deed for one to go against one."

Kolfid said, "We'll make use of the fact that we outnumber you."

Bui said, "I'll welcome that."

They attacked him, but he defended himself boldly. Kolfid encouraged his men, but he himself held back, because he meant to keep the odds in his favor. But Bui was hard for them to overcome, because although they landed cuts and thrusts on him, he wasn't wounded where his shirt reached. But wherever he landed blows, there was no need to bandage them. In the end, six of Kolfid's men had fallen and all the others were wounded. Bui was wounded on the leg.

Then Kolfid said, "You're a great troll, Bui, since you defend yourself for so long against so many."

Bui said, "You've held yourself aloof in this game, and it's cowardly not to dare to attack me."

Then Kolfid charged at Bui with a drawn sword, and each struck at the other. Bui protected himself with his shield. Kolfid struck hard and often, and attacked most boldly, and Bui's shield was mostly hacked to pieces. But when Kolfid slackened his strongest attacks and grew tired, Bui renewed his attack on him and moved away from the stone. He didn't strike many blows before he had destroyed Kolfid's shield. Then he gave Kolfid a blow that cut him in two at the waist. By then, Bui was also somewhat wounded on both his arms and legs, where the shirt hadn't protected him, and he was terribly weary from the fight.

Bui went over to Korpulf's son Grim and asked whether he would like a truce. Grim said that he would.

"Then you must swear to be true to me from now on," said Bui.

Grim said that he would. Kolfid's followers also accepted a truce from Bui. He told them to take Kolfid's body and see to it.

Then Bui took his horse and rode until he came down to Ellidavatn. Olof was outside, and she greeted Bui. He asked her to take her clothes and come with him. She did so, and she rode with Bui to Kollafjord. Kolli was outside and greeted Bui warmly and invited him to stay there. Bui said that they would rest for a while by the spring to bind his wounds, and this was done.

Then Bui said to Kolli, "Now it's true that my arrangement with Olof is known to you. I have paid Kolfid back for his impudence. But your daughter Olof must stay with you until someone offers to marry her, because I don't want to love her now that Kolfid has spoiled her." It had to be as Bui wished.

CHAPTER XVII

Then Bui rode to Esjuberg. Esja his foster mother was still alive, and she was glad to see him with all her heart. Bui soon went to Brautarholt to find his mother. She was still a strong woman then. Bui stayed there for a while.

Thorgrim was still living at Hof, and he was very old. He had one daughter, a girl named Helga; she was young and the strongest of women. His brother Arngrim was dead by that time, but Arngrim's sons had divided his inheritance between them. Helgi had the land in Saurbaer, but Vakr became a merchant and was thought to be the boldest of men.

In the end, wise men of good will came forward and brought about a settlement between Bui and Thorgrim. However long the discussions went on, it happened in the end that Bui and Thorgrim put their cases—all the events told of here—to the judgment of the best men. Their cases were brought up before the Spring Assembly. As the beginning of a settlement, they stipulated that Bui should marry Thorgrim's daughter Helga, and the money that was awarded to Bui shoud be Helga's dowry. They saw to it that Bui and his wife would have all of Thorgrim's money after he died. Arngrim's son Helgi was to marry Kolli's daughter Olof. After that, each pledged loyalty to the other. They held a great feast at Hof, because both weddings were to be celebrated there. Both of their marriages were brought about in the summer.

A little later, Esja died. She gave all her money to Bui and to his daughter Thurid. Bui took over the farm at Esjuberg and made it an excellent farm. After the wedding in summer, Helga went to Esjuberg with Bui, and it was soon obvious that she was the most strong-willed of women. Friendship now began to grow between Thorgrim the Godi and his in-laws. Thorgrim held Bui in the highest honor, and referred all his legal cases to him. Bui made good use of that; he became the most popular of men. Children were born to Bui and Helga; they had a son who was named Ingolf and another named Thorstein, and they had a daughter named Hallbera.

The next summer, Thorgrim fell ill and died. He was buried according to the custom of the time, and his inheritance-feast was held after him. At that time, Vakr left off travelling; he took over the land at Saurbaer, and Helgi took over the land at Hof from Bui. Bui took over the chieftainship all the way out to Nyjahraun and inland as far as Botnsar. Bui lived at Esjuberg for twelve years, and he had a great estate. At that time, Vakr married Thurid, the daughter of Bui and Olof.

CHAPTER XVIII

It so happened that a ship came north into Eyjafjord, and men from Trondheim were on it. On that ship was a man named Jokul, young and very well-dressed. As soon as Jokul landed, he hired a horse and followers. Then he rode south through the land, and nothing is told about his journey until he came to Esjuberg in the afternoon. He said little about himself. They stayed there through the night, because there was food prepared for everyone.

In the morning, Jokul went to speak with Bui, and he said, "The case is this: I have a reason for coming to see you, Bui."

Bui asked what that could be.

Jokul said, "I've been told that you are my father. My mother is Frid, the daughter of King Dofri."

Bui said, "That's an unlikely story that you are my son, because I would expect that a son of mine would be a brawny man, but you look quite feeble to me."

Jokul said, "I'm still not very old. But my mother told me to say to you, as a sign, that she told you that you would meet your fate if you didn't acknowledge our kinship."

Bui said, "I don't care about your stories; they mean nothing to me. I want us to wrestle, because you're no son of mine if there's no strength in you."

Jokul said, "It's unheard of that I, twelve years old, should need to wrestle with you, since you killed King Harald's black man with your wrestling tricks. Still, it's up to you."

Jokul and Bui went east, below the mountain, to a spring where there were fine fields. Then they dressed for the match, and began wrestling with all their might. It went on for a long time, and neither one fell. Bui was very weary.

Jokul said, "Let's not struggle any more. Accept kinship with me."

"No," said Bui. "One or the other of us must fall."

Jokul said, "That won't be better."

And then they attacked each other a second time. They had a hard struggle. Jokul was on the verge of falling, and at that moment it was as if both feet were yanked out from under Bui. He fell face downwards, and there was a loud and mighty crash.

Bui said, "That was quite a good fall. Your mother must not have held back from interfering."

Then other men rushed in and saw the deadly signs that Bui's ribcage had broken; there had been a stone underneath him. Bui said to Jokul, "Your mission here hasn't turned out as it should, because you would have been a promising young man, whereas now the story told about me will be shortened."

After that, Bui was carried home on a red shield. He lived for three days and then died.[45]

Jokul thought that his deed was so bad that he rode away at once to a ship which was ready at Eyjarbakki to the south. He left in the summer, and since then we have heard no tale of him.[46]

Helga Thorgrimsdottir lived at Esjuberg with the children that she and Bui had had. The church at Esjuberg, which Orlyg had had built, was still standing. No one paid attention to it, but since Bui was a baptized man and never made heathen sacrifices, the housewife Helga had him buried along the south wall of the church, and laid no wealth next to him except for his weapons.[47]

The very same iron bell was hanging in front of the church at Esjuberg when Bishop Arni Thorlaksson was in office[48] and Nikolas Petrsson lived at Hof. By then, it was rusted through.[49] Bishop Arni also sent the plenarium south to Skalholt. He had all the pages arranged and glued into the binding. There's Irish writing on them.

A great family is descended from Bui Andridsson.

And now we end the saga of the people of Kjalarnes.

THE TALE OF JOKUL BUASON

Jökuls þáttr Búasonar

CHAPTER I

Jokul felt that what he had done was wicked, so he rode away at once to the ship at Eyrarbakki, and sailed with Ulf the steersman. They had unfavorable winds, and darkness came up before them and they lost their way, so that they were at sea all summer. When autumn began, a storm blew up, with such great blizzards and frosts that every drop that fell into the ship froze solid. All the winds blew to the east, both night and day. In the end, everyone became quite exhausted and gave up, except for Jokul; he bailed out the ship all by himself for four days.

In the end, the ship was driven onto a great bank of rocks by the crashing waves. The storm was so powerful that the ship was smashed to splinters, and their cargo was lost. Jokul climbed up onto a rock with Ulf the steersman and some of the sailors, but the others drowned. All of them were overcome by exhaustion and cold, except for Jokul.

Jokul now asked Ulf what course of action they should take—"should we let the waves take us?"

"No," said Ulf, "that won't do any good. There's nothing for it but for you to search for shelter, seeing as how you still have your strength."

Jokul told them that it had to be so—"and now I'll head for land."

At once he plunged into the water and made for shore. There was such heavy surf and huge breakers that he had a difficult time getting there by swimming, and so he dove underwater to reach land. But when he came onto land, all his clothes froze solid around him. The storm was so powerful that he could hardly walk straight, and he never could tell where he was going. He staggered along the beach, and in the end came to a large old hut. It was locked, but the key was in a slot carved into a post. He opened the hut and went in. He felt his way ahead of him, and inside he found a large log that was still smoldering. At once he lay planks on the fire, and it quickly grew bright throughout the hut. He saw that there were two beds inside the hut. He realized that people had been inside, and he saw that he might live well there, if there were enough provisions. But then he thought that people would blame him if he abandoned his men that way. He turned back into the storm and retraced his steps, and swam out to the rocks and reached his men. Seven of them were dead, but eighteen were alive but worn out by the cold, except for Ulf.

Jokul said, "Do you intend to stay here any longer?"

Ulf answered, "Some other place would seem better to me than staying here longer."

"Will you trust my guidance?" he said.

They said that they would willingly. Jokul carried Ulf the steersman to land, and he didn't stop until he had brought all of them to land. Then Jokul led them to the hut, and they made a large fire. His companions quickly regained their hope of survival, but he felt that something was wrong: they didn't know where they had come to, and they had no supplies. So the evening passed.

Jokul asked, "Which of you lads is willing to stand watch tonight?"

Ulf answered, "I don't think I have the strength, but do you want me to stand watch?"

"No," said Jokul.

They lay down to sleep, and Jokul stood watch alone. He could see little by the light of the moon as it played to and fro. He strolled down to the sea and along the shore. He saw that much of their cargo had washed ashore. And then he thought he saw a pair of creatures gathering their cargo into a single pile. He stopped, paid attention, and listened, and he heard these two hags talking with each other.

Gnipa said, "Something was moving there along the sand."

"I don't know what it could be," said Geit.

"I think I know," said Gnipa. "Jokul has come here, the son of Bui and Dofri's daughter Frid. His fame has spread widely, and she who had such a man would be better off."

Geit said to Gnipa, "Let's go meet him and offer him two choices. One is that he marry one or the other of us. The other is that we kill him."

"Let's do it, dear sister," said Gnipa.

Then they strode towards Jokul with wide strides. They had scowling faces with long noses, and their lips hung down over their chests. They were dressed in skin tunics, so long in the front that they kept stepping on them, but hanging above their buttocks in the back. They smacked their thighs with their palms and behaved in a most unladylike manner.

Jokul saw that, and drew the sword that his mother Frid had given him. At once he struck at Geit's neck so her head flew off. Just then Gnipa came up and attacked Jokul, and the fiercest wrestling bout broke out. Nearly everything around them was knocked out of place. Gnipa attacked so fiercely that Jokul was powerless before her, and all his flesh became bruised and bloody. Jokul saw that this couldn't go on any longer, and he held Gnipa in a hip-lock. When she least expected it, he caught her with a hip-throw. First her head hit the ground, and then her body. That was a mighty fall.

Gnipa said, "Take advantage of the fall now, man."[1]

Jokul said, "You'll end up like your sister Geit instead."

Gnipa said, "You mustn't do that. You'll want to spare my life. Tell me what your men need."

"So be it," said Jokul, "but be true and helpful to me."

Gnipa agreed. She stood up and said, "You behaved unworthily just now, Jokul, when you killed my sister Geit, a child of twelve years old—and I'm thirteen. Now seven of us brothers and sisters are left, and I'm the youngest of them all."

"I don't bother about such things," said Jokul. "But where have my fellows and I come to?"

"You've come to the wildernesss of Greenland," said Gnipa, "into Ollumlengri Fjord.[2] It's not far from here to the home of my father, who is named Surt, and my mother is Syrpa. My father's quite old, and my brothers and sisters don't want me to have any of the inheritance. I'm not pleased about that, but I have to put up with it. We must part for now—to the sight, but not in our friendship."

Then Jokul went home to the hut.

CHAPTER II

Ulf awoke early in the morning, found Jokul and asked for news. He told him what had happened. "And it's time to search for provisions for ourselves," said Jokul.

When they went out, they saw that enough food and drink had been brought for them even if they were to stay there for the next twelve months. Then they went inside and sat down to eat.

When they were fed, Jokul said, "Now I must divide our men today. Ulf and I will go to the glacier together, but you lads should go along the beach and get our cargo together and carry it to the hut." They did so; each one went on his way.

Jokul and Ulf went onto the glacier, and it wasn't long before Gnipa came to them and greeted them lovingly.

"Where do you intend to wander, man?" she said.

Jokul said, "To your father's cave, and I want you to show me the way."

"So be it," said Gnipa. She went ahead of them and didn't stop until they had all come to a huge cave.

Gnipa said, "I won't go any farther, but here is the cave of my father Surt. I want to let you know, Jokul, that my brothers Sam, Snidil and Eitil aren't at home. Eitil is the worst of the brothers to deal with. They've gone to your hut and intend to kill all your men and steal your goods. I'm going now to help your men. Farewell."

So she went on her way, and they went into the cave. By that time it was getting dark. They saw that three ogresses were sitting by the fire, and there was a kettle over the fire. Jokul wasn't afraid. He drew his sword and struck at the giant's neck, so that the head flew off and landed in the kettle. The ogre-women were startled and leaped up. At that instant, Ulf ran one of them through with a spear, but the other rushed at Jokul, so that he almost fell and quickly gave way. They attacked each other and wrestled for a long time and shoved each other all around the cave and towards the fire. They gripped each other strongly, because each wanted to throw the other down into the fire. The troll-woman began panting. At that moment, Jokul got his arm free and ducked under her, and picked her up over his head and plunged her into the kettle headfirst. There she lost her life.

Then they went towards the back of the cave and came to a side passage. There they heard voices and realized that the couple, Surt and his woman Syrpa, must be inside.

Surt said, "I think our sons are slow coming home."

Syrpa said, "Where are they going, my husband?"

"Are you asking about that, old woman?" he said. "I sent the brothers Sam, Snidil and Eitil to the hut of Jokul and Ulf, intending to kill them all and bring their goods here. But that won't be much compensation for our daughters, Geit and Gnipa, whom Jokul killed."

"You speak truly, my beloved husband," said Syrpa. "Let's go find them right now and find out what's delaying them."

They did so, and Surt rushed out of the cave with Syrpa behind him. Jokul saw that, and he swung the sword at Surt and struck his arm, cutting it off at the elbow. Surt let out a loud shriek and charged at Jokul. Their fighting was hard and fierce. Jokul was battered all about by Surt's strength, but he was so nimble that Surt never could get him off his feet. Exhaustion crept up on Surt because he was suffering from a terrible loss of blood. Jokul took advantage of this: he caught Surt in a heel-hook so that he fell, and Jokul wrung his neck. At once he went to help Ulf, and he came to where he and Syrpa were fighting. She had brought Ulf down and was crouching over him, intending to bite out his windpipe. Jokul put both hands under the crone's chin and set his knees on her back.

Syrpa said, "Are you going to play such a spiteful trick on me, Jokul?"

"That's how it has to be," he said. Then he broke her neck, and she died at once. Ulf got to his feet and was very stiff. They searched the cave and found a great abundance of goods: gold and silver and fine clothes, and many costly treasures.

When they had searched the cave as much as they wanted, they went away, wanting to check on their men. They hadn't gone far when they heard shouts and a great commotion, and loud roars of laughter. Jokul and Ulf saw that the brothers had come, carrying huge loads on their shoulders and rushing one after another. But when the brothers least expected it, Jokul came at them and struck at Sam's head and split it down to the shoulders. Then Ulf charged Snidil with his spear and struck him in the back of the neck, so that he lay there thrashing his legs.

Eitil saw that and threw away his load. He had a sharp knife in his hand and furiously charged at them with great giantish rage, and struck at Jokul. The blow landed on his thigh and caused a great wound. Then Ulf came up, and they both attacked Eitil, but he defended himself most bravely. In the end, they managed to kill him, but they were both weary and wounded.

Then Gnipa came up and said, "Are you lads hurt?"

"Not very much," said Jokul.

"It's time to go home," said Gnipa. They did so, and when they had come into the hut, Jokul told Gnipa everything that had happened.

Gnipa said, "This is weighty news that you have killed my father and mother, and my sisters. But I have helped your men, because my brothers would have killed them all if I had not been here. Six are dead and twelve are living. You have now completely avenged your men, Jokul. But as you can see, it appears that you've killed many of my kin. Yet I expect that you will grant me compensation for that before we part."

"I will," said Jokul. He bandaged his men's wounds, and Gnipa worked with him, and soon they were healed and cured. They lacked for nothing that they needed, and Gnipa was always there. Time passed. Several days before Yule, Gnipa didn't come to them, and they didn't know what had become of her.

CHAPTER III

On the evening before Yule, Jokul went out late. He saw Gnipa walking and greeted her. He asked where she had been, and what news she could tell him.

Gnipa said, "I've been wandering far and wide. I've been invited to a Yule feast, and I want you to come with me."

"That's your decision," said Jokul, "but who invited you?"

"Skram did. He is the king over all the wilderness, and all giants are afraid of him. He has a son named Grimnir, a very promising young lad, in no way inferior to his father. He's so far above the young men that each of us maidens eagerly wants to have him for herself. He's twelve years old now. And you would do me a good turn, my friend Jokul, if I could have him."

"I'll arrange something," said Jokul.

"It's time for us to go," said Gnipa.

"Nothing's holding me back," said Jokul.

They went on their way. Gnipa walked in front, and Jokul behind. She walked at a very brisk pace. They went up along the fjord, to the point where it came to an end. It was very late at night. They came to great crags and steep cliffs. She turned and went up along a path only wide enough for one person,[3] and they came to a great cave.

Gnipa said, "Here is the cave of King Skram. He has invited all giants and ogre-women who live in the wilderness. They would send you to Hel if they saw you, which I don't want to have happen. Here is a gold ring that I will give you. It is set with a stone that has this power: if you put the ring on your finger, no one will see you, any more than you want."

Jokul thanked her for the gift, and they went into the cave. Jokul saw that there were trolls seated on both benches, and they all greeted Gnipa. Skram ordered her to wait on the guests. She said that she would. Then she had the most intoxicating ale brought in, which they gulped down in great draughts and guzzled without restraint, so that they became drunk very quickly. Then one could hear plenty of foul language and abuse, and see many punches being thrown and hair being pulled. Jokul couldn't stand this, and he rushed into the mob and killed one after another, laying one on top of another. Each giant mistrusted and blamed the others for this strange omen, but no one saw Jokul. There was an uproar in the cave. Each giant beat another giant senseless and killed him, until in the end they had all fallen, both females and males, except for Skram and his son.

Jokul went up to Skram and ran his sword through him, and he fell forward onto the floor with a great crash. Grimnir was astonished at how it could have happened that his father was killed, but he didn't see anyone. He jumped up and swept with his hands through the entire hall. Jokul thought that this was the best sport. He took off the gold ring and didn't want to hide himself any longer. Grimnir saw that and charged at him, and they grappled each other and began wrestling so fiercely that most things were knocked out of place. In the end, Grimnir fell.

Gnipa saw that. She burst out with roaring laughter and said, "Now the better man has had better luck. Remember what you promised, my dear Jokul."

Jokul said, "You deserve kindness from me. Now you have two choices, Grimnir. One is for me to kill you on the spot. The other is for you to marry Gnipa, my lady friend.[4] You shall be king over Jotunheim, as your father was, and I will grant you all the riches that your father had."

Grimnir agreed. Now Jokul let him stand up, and they went into the back of the cave. There was plenty of gold and silver and fine clothing, fair to be seen. Jokul searched all through the cave, and he saw that there were two people, not in good shape—a man and a woman. They were both sitting on one chair, and were bound to the chair with strong iron chains. They were both thin, yet handsome in appearance.

Jokul went up to the chair and asked them their names. The man said, "I am called Hvitserk, the son of King Soldan of Serkland,[5] and my sister is Marsibilla. The giant Skram drew us here by magic, and he meant for my sister to marry his son Grimnir. We two have been here for five winters, and I am now fifteen and my sister is thirteen. She has seen to it that I have lived so long: she told Skram and his son that Norns[6] had foretold that she would die on the spot if I were sent to Hel, and they believed it. If Skram knew that you were here, he would have you killed and chopped into stewing meat, as he has done to many others."

Jokul replied, "There's no need for us to be afraid of him, because he and all his household are now dead—except for Grimnir, because I spared his life."

"This is good news," said Hvitserk, "and you must do the right thing and give us life."

"I will," said Jokul. He released them and gave them wine to drink. They stayed there for three nights, and on the fourth day, Jokul prepared to go home. Grimnir and Gnipa gave him good gifts: a handsome game board, fine clothes of precious fabric, and thirdly, a sword which Jokul carried for the rest of his life and called Grimnir's Gift. They gave him many other rare treasures, whatever he wanted to keep and take away. Each bade the other farewell. Grimnir and Gnipa stayed behind, but the brother and sister went with Jokul and came to the hut. Everyone welcomed Jokul and his companions.

And so the winter passed. On the first day of summer Grimnir and Gnipa visited Jokul, and each greeted the other warmly. Grimnir asked Jokul to go with him down to the sea, and he did. When they got there, Jokul saw a fully rigged ship floating by the shore, laden with goods.

Grimnir said, "Here's a boat that your lady-friend Gnipa and I want to give you. We assembled it over the winter."

Jokul thanked them very much, and he said, "In exchange, Gnipa, I will give you all the goods that were in your father's cave."

They both thanked him, and told him to call on them if he needed any little thing. "If we don't come, it will be because it's impossible for us. Here, for now, we will separate—to the sight, but not in our friendship."

Then they went home, and Jokul ordered his men to hurry up. They did so; they boarded the ship and set sail out to sea. Jokul said, "Where should we set our course?"

Hvitserk answered, "If I might make the decision, we should go to Serkland."

Jokul said that he should decide. "Come and tell us where to steer."

He said that he would do it. They got a favorable wind at once, and came to Serkland, to the harbor that they had chosen, in front of the capital city of King Soldan. The king sent a message to the ship, and as soon as he found out who had arrived in his land, he himself went to the shore. Hvitserk and Marsibilla ran to meet him, and there was a joyous reunion.

The king invited Jokul and all his men home to feast with him, and he accepted. They went straight to his hall. The king sat in the high seat, and Jokul sat on one side of him and his son sat on the other side. Jokul was held in the highest honor. The king asked Hvitserk what had happened in his life since they had parted. He told him everything as clearly as he could, and explained how Jokul had aided them and what a valiant man he was. The king was pleased, and called him the finest of all men. Now there was great cheer and merriment in the hall, and spiced and honeyed wines[7] were drunk. There was song, and music was played on bassoons and every sort of musical instrument that could be had.

On the next day of the feast, Jokul brought forth his suit and asked for the hand of the king's daughter Marsibilla in marriage. The king welcomed this, and said that it would be most fitting that he should enjoy her love. The agreement was made and the wedding feast was arranged, and Marsibilla was led into the hall with all the pomp and splendor that could be had in the land. Now the feasting was redoubled. The king gave his daughter half of Serkland. The feast lasted for half a month. When it was over, the king and Jokul sent every man away with good gifts, and they returned to their homes.

Jokul gave Hvitserk the fine board-game and the splendid clothes that Grimnir gave him. Those were excellent treasures, and they swore blood-brotherhood with each other. They set out raiding and sought fame and fortune for themselves: they killed berserks and robbers, but granted safe passage to merchants,[8] and set sail for home in the autumn. They did this for six summers all together. And when they tired of raiding, they settled down on land.

Then Hvitserk's father King Soldan died, and Hvitserk was raised to the kingship over all Serkland. He wedded a queen, the daughter of a king in Africa.[9] Then he gave the kingdom to his blood-brother Jokul to rule, and the title of king along with it. Jokul governed all his kingdom until the day he died. He had many children with his queen Marsibilla, and some took the kingship and kingdom after him. And so ends his story.

THE TALE OF BRINDLE-CROSS

Brandkrossa þáttr

CHAPTER I

We begin the saga of the two Helgis[1] with Ketil Thrym, because we know that of all the men whom this saga tells of, he was the most blessed with descendants. From him are descended the men of Sida and the men of Krossvik, and also the Droplaugarsons. We would also like to tell how Helgi Asbjarnarson, who is the most excellent man in this saga in the estimation of wise men, is descended from the first settlers of Iceland.

There was a man named Hrafnkel, the son of Hrafn. He came to Iceland late in the time of settlement and lived in Skridudal. He fell asleep there, and he dreamed that a man came to him and told him to get up and go away quickly, taking all his belongings. Hrafnkel awoke and got away from there at once. Just then, the entire mountainside broke loose in a landslide. A boar and a bull that Hrafnkel had owned were buried underneath; they had stayed behind.[2] Hrafnkel went to Hrafnkelsdal and settled all the valley with his own men, nearly twenty farms. He himself lived at Steirodarstad. He soon became a great and powerful chieftain with a large following. His sons were Asbjorn and Thorir.

When Hrafnkell died, his sons divided their inheritance equally. Thorir was allotted the farm which his father had owned. Asbjorn settled at the farm that was called Lokhilla but is now called Hrafnkelsstad, and he ran his farm well.[3]

Asbjorn married a woman named Hallbera. She was the daughter of Hrollaug, the son of Jarl Rognvald of Mære. They had a son named Helgi. Helgi grew up to be taciturn and reserved in his speech. People talked about how he had matured.

Asbjorn didn't live to be old. When he died, Helgi took over his inheritance and lived at Lokhilla for several years. Later, Helgi moved away and sold his farm to his cousin Hrafnkel Thorisson, but he left Iceland and went raiding with his kinsmen for many years, both in Orkney and in Norway. Helgi spent several summers raiding, and he was the bravest of men, but not exceptionally strong or skilled in combat. When his raiding was over, Helgi returned to Iceland with plenty of wealth and honor. Spak-Bersi invited Helgi to live with him, and he went home with him to Bersastad. In the same half of the year, Helgi married Oddlaug, Bersi's sister, and soon they had a good marriage with much love. Helgi had no home at the time, and no one was eager to give up his own land for Helgi.

There was a man named Odd, who was called Cinder. He was wealthy and difficult to deal with. He had chosen to settle on the other side of the river Lagarfljót from Bersastad, and he ran his farm well. Odd was married and had a son named Osvif.[4] It was said that his temperament matched his name. He was a seafarer and a swaggerer, a great man at games, given to scoffing and boasting.

On one occasion, Bersi and his brother-in-law Helgi were talking matters over. Helgi asked Bersi where he might have seen a place where he could settle, and what advice he might give him. Bersi suggested a good plan, which they soon tried.

As soon as the river was frozen over, Helgi went to Oddstad and made merry with Osvif, and soon games started up between Oddstad and Bersastad. There was a man named Otrygg[5] who was lodging at Oddstad. He began to harass Osvif in the games, and he boasted of his own prowess and called Osvif more of a braggart than a tough player. But then Odd killed Otrygg. Helgi Asbjarnarson took up the prosecution for the killing. Men tried to find someone to settle the case, but no one else but Bersi would do it, and so the settlement was that Bersi imposed a small fine, but made Odd leave his farm and get out of the district. Odd was not at all pleased with the verdict in the case, but it had to be so, since many were hoping to see him defeated.

Helgi Asbjarnarson recovered Oddstad for himself, much to Odd's disgust. Nonetheless, in the end, Odd had to go away, and nothing more is said about him in this saga, although he had been called a great man.

Helgi established his farm at Oddstad and meant to move his entire household there on the first Moving Day.[6] But as Odd was preparing to leave, he had a bull slaughtered and boiled. On the first Moving Day, when Odd was ready to leave, he had the table set from one end of the benches to the other, and all the bull's meat was brought to the table. Then Odd came to the table, saying, "The table is now completely set, as if for our dearest friends. I give all this feast to Frey, so that he may not let the one who is taking my place leave Oddstad with less grief than I leave with now."[7]

After that, Odd went away with all his household.

CHAPTER II

This is a story that some men tell about lesser-known relatives of the Droplaugarsons. Though it seems doubtful to some, it's still enjoyable to hear.

There was a man named Grim who lived on Vapnafjord, at Inner Krossavik.[8] He was a young man, married and well-off. He reared an ox that was brindled, with a cross-shaped blaze on its forehead. It was an excellent beast in form and size. Grim felt that the ox was better than all the livestock he owned. The ox went into the fields in summer, and drank milk both in winter and in summer.

It so happened one summer, when the ox was ten years old, and the hay was piled up in large stacks all around the house, that the ox charged in and out of the hayfield and tossed the haystacks every which way. Men wanted to catch him but couldn't manage to do it, and it made no difference. A great many men came at him, but he rushed ahead of them, and in the end he ran all the way to Outer Krossavik, and swam out to sea as far as men could see.[9] Grim took the loss of his ox very hard.

He had a brother at Oxarfjord[10] who was named Thorstein. He was a good farmer, a wise and well-liked man. The brothers loved each other very much. Now word was sent to Thorstein that he should come to meet his brother Grim at Krossavik. And when the brothers met, Thorstein tried to persuade him not to take his loss so hard. He said that it was still a great consolation that he had enough livestock, and it wasn't out of the question that he might raise up another ox no worse. And he said that it would be a great honor that both the bays there would later be named after his ox. Nearly everything that Thorstein said went in one ear and out the other. Thorstein was there all winter, consoling his brother, yet Grim wasted away. He slept little and took little food.

When half a year had passed, Thorstein asked whether Grim might feel like traveling out of the country for a while. He said that that way, a man's grief is stemmed, and the mind rids itself of those thoughts that stand in the way of happiness and contentment. Grim said that he wanted to go if Thorstein would go with him. Thorstein said that he was quite willing, if it would help ease Grim's mind somewhat.

They set men over their farm to guard it, and then both brothers set out for Unaos.[11] They didn't have much money. It was usual back then to use shaggy cloaks[12] as trade goods, and that's what they had. They had a good sea voyage, and the ship that they were on came to Trondheim. They pitched their tent on land. Each of the other men left the ship for his own household, but the brothers stayed behind in their tent.

Early one morning, a man came to the brothers' tent. The man was tall and strong. They asked him his name. He said that he was called Karhofdi.[13] They asked him where he was going and where he came from. He said that he lived with a farmer named Geitir. He also said that he had to purchase twenty-four shaggy cloaks on behalf of Geitir, who was quite wealthy and the best at paying off debts. They gave him the cloaks, as he wanted, and agreed to trade them for flour. He threw them over his shoulder and left quickly.

After that, a man named Thorir, who lived inland from Trondheim, came to them and invited them to lodge with him. He was a good farmer. They accepted and went to his house. They were given good lodgings. They kept asking farmer Thorir about Geitir, but he claimed to know nothing about him.

They hadn't stayed there for long before they wanted to go out and search for Geitir. Thorir discouraged them, but to no avail. They went up along the valley and always asked for Geitir, but no one could tell them anything. In the end, they came to an old man in a side valley and asked him about Geitir, but he said that he didn't know him. Then Thorstein asked if he knew of any old place names that might be named after Geitir. He said that there was a place called Geitishamrar,[14] and told them how to get there. They went straight there the next day.

They came to the entrance to a cave. A fire was burning in the cave, and a man was sitting by the fire. They recognized their companion Karhofdi. He leaped to his feet and gave them a warm welcome. They sat down by the fire and looked around. They thought they saw Grim's ox Brindle-Cross standing alive and well on the other side of the fire, under a rocky ledge. Karhofdi took their outer clothes and kept them, and when he came back he invited them to come into the main room. And when they came there, men were sitting on both benches, and they recognized their shaggy cloaks on them.

A man in a red cloak, tall and noble, sat on the high seat. This man greeted them first and invited them to stay there as long as they wanted. He seated them next to himself. There was good food and good drink. Two women were close by Geitir, both beautiful, and the older one sat nearer to him. She was his wife, and the younger one was his daughter.

They stayed there only a short while before Grim became unhappy. Geitir soon noticed, and he spoke with Grim about it one day. "I have wronged you, Grim," he said. "I sent my slave Karhofdi after your ox Brindle-Cross, the best ox in all of Iceland. Where you thought you saw your ox on that first evening, that was its skin stuffed with flour. I intend for you to have that as the price of the ox. And it seems to me as if you have set your eyes on my daughter Droplaug. I will betroth her to you, if you want to bring her out to Iceland, with a great share of wealth for her dowry. She is well-born on her mother's side, yet not low-born on her father's side. My mother was well-born, but I had a rather huge father."

Grim accepted this proposal, and right away Grim and Droplaug were betrothed. There was the most magnificent feast. The three of them slept in the same bed in one side cave all winter long: Grim, Droplaug, and Thorstein. The love between Grim and Droplaug grew strong. Grim was well content with his his marriage.

When spring came, Geitir asked Grim what he had decided to do. He said that he wanted to return to Iceland to live out his life. Geitir told the brothers to buy themselves a ship and prepare to sail. He said that Grim and his wife wouldn't be short of money, and said that he and Karhofdi would bring everything that the brothers owned to the ship, both money and cargo.

CHAPTER III

The brothers did as Geitir advised them, and prepared to sail away. Grim and his father-in-law praised each other before they parted. Geitir asked Grim to accept his advice for both him and his wife, and told them that they would do well.

When the brothers were almost ready to set sail, Karhofdi came down to the shore. He carried Brindle-Cross's skin on his back, stuffed with flour. He boarded the ship and laid it down gently, as they wanted it. He came down a second time with their cloaks. He came down a third time with two chests. In one were Droplaug's clothes and belongings, and in the other there was gold and silver and treasures, and that was Droplaug's dowry.

Then they sailed out to sea, and they had a good voyage and landed at Inner Krossavik. That's where Brindle-Cross's skin was brought from the ship, and both bays are named after it. The brothers sold their ship, and each went home to his own farm.

Thorstein married and was thought to be the most capable farmer. He raised his family in Oxarfjord. Grim lived at Krossavik and was well content with his marriage for as long as he and Droplaug lived, and he was considered the most valiant of men. Droplaug was a beautiful and splendid woman, a busy worker, high-minded and not an excessive talker. She insisted on having her due if any offense was done to her; she was reserved and generous and steadfast to her friends, but quite hard-hearted towards her enemies. She didn't live to be a very old woman, and she died of a sickness. Grim felt that it was a terrible thing to lose her. He grieved for her strongly and wasn't very content.

They had a daughter named Mardoll.[15] She was a lovely and worthy maiden very much like her mother: a hard worker, well-liked, and friendly, when she came of age. First she kept house for her father after her mother's death. Everything that she planned seemed to turn out well. Then she went east to Heradsdal to be married to Gilsar, and she was the mother of Grim Mardallarson, the father of Droplaug, the mother of Grim and Helgi Droplaugarsson.

THE SAGA OF THE PEOPLE OF FLJOTSDAL (excerpt)

Fljótsdæla saga

CHAPTER III

There was a man named Thidrandi. He lived at the farm called Njardvik; it lies in between the Fljotsdal and Borgarfjord districts. Thidrandi held the chieftainship of the Njardvik region as far as the river Selfljot. The Selfljot lies to the east, flowing out of the mountains between Gilsarteig and Ormstad, and down to the river Lagarfljot.[1] The Selfljot marks one boundary of the district, and Lagarfljot lies to the west, and the area in between is called Utmannasveit.[2] At the time, a hundred and seventy farmers held lands there.

Thidrandi was a powerful man, yet well-liked, because he was on good terms with his subordinates. He was strong and very tall, with a mind as keen as a hawk. He lived a long time and was most generous. When he was an old man, he was called Thidrandi the Old. And that was the truth, because men say that he had lived to be a hundred and thirty-six. Yet he was a vigorous man. He cared for his livestock, and he always set about doing what his servants neglected to do.

One winter, around the time when the ewes were in heat, when some of his servants had rowed out to sea to fish, and some were feeding hay to the animals, Thidrandi went to the shed where he kept his rams, inside his home field. That evening, everyone came home but Thidrandi. People asked where he might be. The women said that he had gone to his rams' shed. They looked for him there; he was sitting outside the fence next to the shed. People asked why he hadn't come home. He said that walking had become impossible and hadn't gotten much better, and he said that a ram had broken his thigh. He was carried home at once and put to bed. But afterwards he was wracked with pain and his thigh swelled up severely, and this brought about his death.

He left two sons after him. The older one was Ketil, and Thorvald was the younger. Both of the brothers were tall. Thorvald was the most handsome of men, attentive and quiet, and he was the most peaceable man in most respects. But Ketil was the strongest man in those days; he was an ugly man, yet with a chieftain's bearing, dark and imposing. He was the most placid of men every day, but he was silent and taciturn from an early age, and he was called Thrum-Ketil.[3] There were serious faults in his temperament; some called it a disease. It came over him every half-month: his flesh would start trembling so much that every tooth in his head chattered, and he would jump out of bed. A great fire had to be made before him, and all the comforts that could be found had to be sought for him. Outbursts of rage followed these chills and shivering fits, and he didn't spare anything in his way, neither planks nor posts nor men. Even if there were fires in front of him, he would wade right through them. Then he would smash through houses' planks or doorframes, if they were in his way. He did this on every day that the fit came over him, and men had to stay out of his way as best they could. But when the fit left him, he was calm and self-controlled. It was a great relief to him and many others when his fury had passed.

The brothers' sister was named Hallkatla, the daughter of Thidrandi the Old. She was betrothed to Geitir Lytingsson, who lived to the north, at Krossavik in Vapnfjord. Geitir was well-liked, and Hallkatla managed the house very well. They had two sons: the older one was named Thorkel, and the younger was Thidrandi, who was named for his grandfather. These brothers were both accomplished men, each in his own way. Thorkell had brown hair and a dark complexion; he was short and stocky, and said to be the smallest of the men who lived there at the time. He was the quickest and most vigorous of men, as it turned out, because he often had to deal with difficulties, and he bore up well every time.

Thidrandi Geitisson was the tallest and strongest of men. There was no one to be found at that time who was his equal. And it's said that he was one of the four most accomplished men in all of Iceland. The second man who is named was Kjartan Olafsson[4]; the third was Hoskuld Thorgeirsson, the godi of Ljosvetning[5]; and the fourth was Ingolf Thorsteinsson, called Ingolf the Handsome.[6] Well-informed men say that no one in all Iceland had been gifted with accomplishments like these four men. These men's looks were said to be so fine that many women lost their minds if they saw their handsomeness. And everyone said that their other accomplishments were equally great.

CHAPTER V

The brothers in Njardvik couldn't agree on all their financial matters. Ketil wanted to decide everything himself, without consulting Thorvald. Thorvald soon got tired of that, and he asked that they divide their wealth and the chieftainship. Ketil told him to divide it whenever he wanted, and said that he would grant him half of all the wealth—"but the chieftainship is small, and I refuse to share it, because I will not grant this to anyone but myself."

Thorvald thought that he should share in both equally, even though he might not get them. "I have seen for a long time that you want to deprive me of most things. It seems that soon my only option will be to make do with whatever portion of money you scrape up for me. Still, we should separate for now, even though you're treating me harshly. You should know that I think I should have half, though as it is I may not get it."

Then Ketil went and got the valuables and divided them all evenly with Thorvald, both the livestock and the movable wealth, and everything within the fences—except for the chieftainship; he didn't divide that. After that, Thorvald left and went up over the mountains with all his belongings. He rented out the lands that he had been allotted, and loaned out his livestock at interest.

A ship was anchored in the Fljotsdal district, along the mountains to the east at a place called Unaos. Thorvald got some wares for trading, boarded that ship and left Iceland. When they got out to sea, they didn't get very favorable winds, and they were adrift all summer. And when summer was over, they encountered a strong gale and a fierce blizzard. The gale forced them from the ocean and drove them to Shetland in the night. The tide was very low, and they sailed onto hidden rocks and broke the ship to splinters. All their goods were lost, but the men reached land alive. Thorvald came to land like the other men. He was wearing Icelandic clothing.[7] None of Thorvald's belongings washed up, except for one great spear; he took that in his hand. He spent two nights on the shore, waiting for any of his goods to wash up, but nothing bearing Thorvald's mark was to be found. He felt it was best not to stay there any longer, without any provisions, and one day he went away.

A jarl named Bjorgolf ruled over Shetland.[8] At that time he was an old man. Thorvald thought that he should head for where the jarl had his seat. He sat by the wall in the evening, and in the morning he went before the jarl. This jarl was well-liked by all his people, yet he was unhappy. Thorvald greeted the jarl warmly. The jarl accepted his greeting and asked who he was. He said that he was an Icelander, a freed slave of humble family who had just escaped from a shipwreck, a penniless man. "Grant me lodging for the winter, lord, for I would gladly stay with you."

The jarl said, "You look to me as if you need it."

Thorvald asked him to show him where to sit.

The jarl said, "Sit on the lower bench, where the slaves and freedmen are eating. Don't be meddlesome, and be cheerful about your hardships with everyone."

Thorvald went to his seat, and stayed there over the winter. He behaved as the jarl had said: he was cheerful with his benchmates, while they readily answered all his questions, and he always asked many questions. And so the winter passed until Yule. Then the people became very sad, and the jarl became very glum. The jarl had a young wife and two sons by her, young but handsome. One evening, Thorvald asked the men next to him what was making people unhappy. None of them wanted to tell him, and Yule was approaching.

One night, the men lying next to Thorvald heard him tossing and turning in his sleep. They wanted to wake him, but the jarl ordered them to let him enjoy his dreams. Then he awoke, and people asked what he had dreamed, but he didn't want to say anything about it.

It was two nights before men held their Yule feast when Thorvald went before the jarl and greeted him well and respectfully. The jarl gladly accepted his greeting.

Thorvald said, "I've come here because I want to ask you about what no one else will tell me. I want to know what's causing the unhappiness of the men here, because the men are enjoying neither sleep nor food, and that causes me some grief. You seem to be the likeliest to tell me about this, since you are the leader of them all."

The jarl told him that there was no need for him to be curious—"because it's not your concern. You can't do anything about it. You'll get no thanks for asking. You've become curious about many things that you don't need to know, and it would be fitting if someone paid dearly."

Thorvald said that he would not have asked if he had known that the jarl would take offense. "I'll leave off asking. But I would ask you to interpret my dream."

The jarl said, "I am no dream-man, and I can't interpret them, because I don't take any notice of them. But you can still tell it if you want to."

Thorvald said, "I seemed to be going to the shore, in the same outfit that I usually wear every day. The path seemed to shine, so that I could see where I was going. I had my spear in my hand. It seemed that the tide was low when I came to the sea, not high. I thought that I walked along the shore to where a great sandbar was exposed. When that came to an end, there was a flat rock in front of me. When I walked across the divide, the seaweed had grown thickly there.[9] Then I saw a great hill or mountain up on the land, and on the front of this mountain were sea crags and a huge high cliff. I seemed to be heading for this cliff, until I came to a stretch of shoals. I thought I was wading forward through the water, and it was deep. And then I came to a pebble beach, and I walked for a long time along the shore, between the sea and the cliffs. Then there was a great cave in front of me, and I went in. I saw a light burning there, so that there were no shadows anywhere. I saw a single iron pillar standing under the roof of the cave, and there was a woman bound to this pillar. Her hands were tied behind her back, and her hair was wound around the pillar.[10] There were iron chains around her with a padlock on one end, and there she was locked up. I thought I started to free her and managed to accomplish it. I saw no other living beings there, except for her alone. Then I went away with her. I thought I was going ahead of the returning tide, and I managed to get across. Then it seemed as if I were being pursued by some being; that made me very afraid. The two of us met, but I don't remember how it went with us. I must have been tossing in my sleep, and at that moment I awoke."

The jarl turned so red when he heard this, that one touch of a finger would almost have drawn blood from him. He drew himself up and said, "You've done a strange thing, saying that you dreamed what men are telling you. It causes me quite enough grief even if I'm not reminded, because I still remember when my daughter disappeared. It would be fitting for whoever told you this to get what's coming to him, since I had forbidden it to everyone."

Thorvald replied, "You should know this, lord: none of your men has told me these events. This has been shown to me in a dream. I will talk about this as much as you want."

The jarl fell silent, and after a while answered, "Your affairs could go one of two ways: either you're a man with second sight, or else you'll soon be a dead man."

Thorvald answered, "I want you to tell me what has happened here in your household. I realize that it must have been terrible."

The jarl answered, "Why not? Before I had these two boys, I had a daughter named Droplaug. It was said that she was quite accomplished. I loved her very much. Last Yule, she disappeared from here. The giant named Geitir took her. He has his home where you were dreaming that you went. It's called Geitishamar, and that mountain is called Geitissulur.[11] Many have suffered because of him. He hurts both men and cattle, and he's the most harmful being in all Shetland. I have stated that I will betroth her to the man who can fetch her away, if anyone is so brave."

Thorvald said that it seemed unlikely that she could be rescued.

The jarl answered, "I would not have let her go away without any dowry, if I had a choice.[12] I think you should risk it, since you were the first to ask about it."

Thorvald replied, "I wish I'd never asked." He turned away and went back to his seat.

After the evening meal, the men went to bed. When Thorvald found that the men were asleep, he got up and took his spear in his hand. He went outside and down to the shore, and the tide was low, not high. He went down an exposed sandbar and headed north, along much the same path that had appeared to him in his dream. He went past the flat rock and the divide and the thick seaweed, and then a pebble beach lay before him. He kept going to where the tidal shoal was, and waded through the tide. He came to the place that had appeared to him in his dream, reached the cave, and entered it. He saw a light burning. On one side of the cave he saw a single bed far larger than any bed he had ever seen before, and he supposed that even if he lay down on the bed with another man just as tall, and they put the soles of their feet together, the bed would still be long enough for them, even though Thorvald was the tallest of men.[13] This bed was no less wide than it was long. It had no hangings that were not embroidered tapestries, and fine velvet was spread over the bed. The mattresses were so thick that they stood up high from the bed.

Over the bed he saw a great sword hanging. He took it down, and a large rockfall followed. The sword was fitted with a fine scabbard; it had an iron hilt and pommel but no further decorations. He drew the sword, and it was green in color, but brown along the edges, with no flecks of rust anywhere on the blade. He had never seen such a desirable weapon.[14] On the other side of the cave he saw a pile of cargo. He saw all sorts of goods from Iceland, and linen cloth, and many sorts of wares lying there, every kind that could be named, along with food of the best quality and plenty of drink. There were all sorts of goods that would be better to have than to lack.

He saw an iron pillar in the middle of the cave, and a woman tied to it in just the way that he had seen in the dream. She sat wearing a red tunic[15]—and as fair as she had appeared to him in the dream, she seemed much more beautiful now. He went to her and she greeted him. He accepted her greeting and asked who she was. She said that she was named Droplaug, the daughter of Jarl Bjorgolf. She begged him not to talk with her for long. "You must save your own life, because you're in a worse situation than you think. This place is ruled by a troll so large that there's not another one like him to be found. I am held much too strongly for you to be able to get me out of here."

He said that she would go with him.

She said that he wouldn't be able to do that—"because he is a much greater troll than humans can shield themselves against. He will soon come home, because he goes out fishing at night and binds me to the pillar while he is away. But by day he lies on his bed and plays with me, tosses me from hand to hand and catches me. When he wants to sleep, he brings me gold and treasures to play with. He also never brings me any food that I can't enjoy, and he doesn't think that anything he can do for me is the least bit too good."

Thorvald answered, "Either both of us will escape, or neither one of us will."

He drew the sword and cut the iron chains from her, and the sword cut so well that it severed them at once. Then he led her out of the cave. He took none of the riches away, except for the sword. They went along the pebble beach and towards the tidal channel. He found that she was quite worn out because she was pregnant.[16] He picked her up in his arms and waded through the tidal channel, and it was notably deeper than the first time because the tide was coming in. He could see that there was a cleft on the cliff, a little way up above him, that had been carved out as if it had been quarried, but he couldn't reach it. He saw the moon, but day was coming on quickly. By then he had gone most of the way to the flat rock; it took a long time to cross—and then he heard a loud scream from the cave behind him.

The woman was startled at this cry, and begged Thorvald to put her down—"and I told you before that you wouldn't be able to look after me. Save yourself! Now he has come home. He'll be glad to see me, but he won't come after you if he can find his way to me."

Thorvald replied, "That will never happen, because the same fate shall befall both of us, as long as I can hold on to you." He took off his shaggy cape and put it on her, and then set her down in the cleft with the spear next to her, but he turned back the way he had come. He saw the giant's head against the sky, much higher than the cliff. He set such large boulders over her that she couldn't get away. Then he took his sword and went up against the giant.

The giant called out in a loud voice and ordered him to drop his concubine. "You must think that you can handle a great deal, you wretch, if you want to take the one away from me whom I have kept for a long time."

At that, the giant stepped up into the cleft that Thorvald had seen, and he stepped with his other foot onto the flat rock, and he didn't get his shoes wet. Thorvald saw that the cleft was there because the giant didn't want to wade. At that moment Thorvald came up and dashed in under him, but the giant reached out in front of him with his paws and meant to catch Thorvald. But just then Thorvald struck at him. The sword landed in the middle of the giant's thigh and cut off his left leg above the knee and his right leg below the knee and plunged down into the sand. The giant fell down and cried out in pain and said, "You've deceived me wickedly and worse than I expected, by taking the only weapon that might do me harm. I went after you without fear because I didn't imagine that little men might be the death of me. Now you must think that you've won a great victory. You must think that you'll bear that weapon, you and your descendants. But I pronounce that it will be least helpful to them when their need is greatest."[17]

Thorvald tried to ensure that he should speak no more words to cause them harm. He struck at the giant's neck so that he cut off his head, and he stuck the head between the giant's thighs.[18] He couldn't do that at first because the giant was flailing his arms, and Thorvald couldn't manage to put the head on him until he grew still. Then he left him and went to where the girl was lying, and he found that she was in a swoon or a faint. He picked her up, and her fainting quickly passed like a dream. He walked with her until he came back to the hall. Men were at their daytime drinking; they had noticed Thorvald's absence but paid it little mind. Now he entered the hall, and he had Droplaug on his arm and the sword in his other hand. He went before the jarl and greeted him and said that he had brought him his daughter. The jarl was very glad to see her, and so were many others. The jarl asked how he had managed to get her. He told the whole story, and said that it had mostly gone according to his dream.

The jarl answered, "Great is your fortune and luck, since you've beaten the worst enemy in our lands. Still, we will go and see it soon."

The jarl's retainers said that it couldn't be as huge a troll as everyone had said, "if he beat it single-handedly. This can only be a lie."

Thorvald meant to return to his seat. The jarl called to him and told him to sit on the front bench before the high seat. "Your position will be one of two things: You will either be found worthy of more honors than what I've done for you, or else you won't live much longer. But everyone can see that you have offered us a fine gift. Your journey has turned out well, and it is still fresh in our mind that no one else went out to run this risk. Yet I will never be sure that we can celebrate this woman's return until I am certain that this fiend has been killed."

After that, men drank up quickly, and then the tables were take down. Jarl Bjorgolf ordered his men to arm themeslves and go to see what had happened. They went out, and Thorvald went with them. They came to where the monster lay, and now they all saw how it had been defeated. Many who had formerly called it a deed of little bravery could scarcely approach the corpse now. The jarl had a forest felled and the logs brought together. He had the logs stacked into a pyre, and then had the giant dragged to the pyre, and burned him to cold ashes. Then they carried the ashes out to sea.[19]

They went to the cave in ships and carried off much wealth and everything valuable, and brought it home. The place has been called Geitishellir or Geitishamrar ever after. And it isn't said that it's been settled by trolls since then.

CHAPTER VI

When the men came home, the wares were picked through, and it's said that most of the wares that had been on the ship with Thorvald were there, and Thorvald recognized all his property. Thorvald and the jarl let every man have what he recognized as his own, but there was much more that no one could recognize. The wares from Iceland were worth little compared to what was left, because it was the wealth of many men. Thorvald rewarded the men well who had worked hard on his behalf.

Thorvald stayed in Shetland, held in high honor. What he had accomplished was thought to be an outstanding feat. The jarl valued no man more than Thorvald, and other men did likewise. He stayed there for the next half year. That same summer, the honor that Thorvald had won in Shetland was heard about in Iceland. Many men in the Eastfjords were glad when they heard that things had turned out that way—except for his brother Ketil, who acted as if he didn't know. People felt that Thorvald had been blessed with great good fortune, considering how Ketil had cut him off.

Thorvald stayed on in Shetland until Yule, and then he went before the jarl and greeted him, and asked him whether he remembered anything from the previous Yule. The jarl said that he certainly did remember.

Thorvald said, "Then I will claim the reward that you yourself declared when I told you my dream. You swore to give your daughter to the man who could get her free. Now I want to know the answer to my request. I don't want to stay here if there's nothing to keep me."

The jarl said, "I am of the same mind now as then: you seem to be the most fitting man to enjoy her, if there's any enjoyment in it.

But I don't feel that she's as good of a match as when she went away, because this woman is not well suited for everyone, on account of her temperament. But you yourself must be responsible for your marriage. I will hold to all that I have promised, but you're the one who'll have to pay if something goes wrong. It's likely that it will turn out well, because she thinks very highly of you. Every time that you are mentioned, she says that no one can equal you. And I want to give you the jarldom until my sons are quite capable of assuming power."

Thorvald said that he didn't want that—"because it seems best for you to guard it until they claim it. That isn't suitable for me, since I am not of noble stock."

After that, Droplaug's mother was sent for; she was called Arneid. Arneid's brother was named Grim; her father was Helgi, a Danish man, and her mother was Hallerna. Grim and Arneid arrived, and the proposal was put to them. They said that they supposed that there could not be anyone else more suited to enjoy this woman than this man, and they said that they would consent to the betrothal. And with that, Droplaug was betrothed to Thorvald with a large dowry. A fine feast was laid on; there was no lack of plentiful provisions, nor of great crowds, and the feasting went on in splendor. When it was ended, Thorvald gave every man good gifts. He gained such popularity in this way that almost everyone wished him well, and he stayed there for the winter until spring came.

Then Thorvald bought a ship that was anchored in the river Thorsa,[20] and brought his great riches and his wife Droplaug there. Their marriage was good, because each of them suited the other well, but she was rather proud-minded, and somewhat reserved and haughty with other men. Yet she excelled other women both in appearance and acomplishments. Her mother Arneid had many children from her marriage, and she had been a widow when she had her daughter Droplaug. That spring, she gave her farm over to her sons, but married off her daughter, named Groa. Arneid arranged for passage on Thorvald's ship, and wanted to go with her daughter to Iceland. Grim Hallernuson went with them as well.

When they were ready, they sailed out to sea and had good weather and favorable winds. They reached Iceland early in the summer. They landed at the place called Hofn in Borgarfjord, south of Njardvik. Many of Thorvald's kinsmen rode to the ship as soon as they heard of his arrival, and they welcomed him warmly and invited him to stay with them in honor, along with as many men as he wanted to bring. But Ketil his brother didn't come to the ship, and Thorvald sent no word to him.

At the time, Ketil was married and had a son who was named Thorkell and called "the Fully-Wise." He has little to do with this saga, though he comes into it later.

THE SAGA OF HALFDAN, BRANA'S FOSTERLING

Hálfdanar saga Brönufóstra

CHAPTER I

There was a king named Hring who ruled over Denmark. He was wise and well-beloved. He was married to a queen named Signy, the daughter of Ulfhedin, king of Reidgotaland.[1] She was the loveliest and wisest of all women. King Hring soon had three children with her: two sons, and one daughter named Ingibjorg. She was adorned with all womanly accomplishments. Her appearance was as bright as shining gold, and in all her features she was shaped in just the way that every woman would wish for herself. The sons of King Hring were named Halfdan and Asmund. They were handsome; however, Halfdan was foremost in every respect. Asmund was ten years old, and Halfdan was nine, when this saga begins.

The king had a bower built for his daughter. That house was made with great craftsmanship. Twelve ladies-in-waiting served the king's daughter, and they were the daughters of jarls and dukes. The king loved his daughter very much. She continued to flourish, as was said before. The king was quite elderly.

There was a jarl named Thorfid. He lived in the king's realm and was his greatest friend, faithful and true to him in all his counsels. The jarl was the wisest of men, and for that reason the king always had him in his household. He fostered the king's children and loved them very much.

A jarl named Thorir was with the king; he was called Thorir the Strong. He was so strong that no one in the kingdom was stronger. The jarl was in charge of the kingdom's defenses. A troll-woman had laid a curse on Jarl Thorir, so that he could not stand the sight of human blood.[2] Nonetheless, he was highly valued by the king. He usually stayed at an estate on the island of Fyn.

One night, as Ingibjorg lay in bed in her bower and slept, it happened that she tossed and turned in her sleep, and after a long time she woke the household. Her ladies-in-waiting asked her what she had dreamed, but she would not tell them.

The next day, Jarl Thorfid came to the bower and sat down beside the king's daughter. They began to talk amongst themselves. Ingibjorg said, "I want to tell you my dream, foster-father."

"What sort of dream was it?" said the jarl.

She answered, "At the beginning of my dream, I thought I saw something. At first it was far away from me, but it came nearer and nearer. Then I saw that it was a fleet of many ships, and they made landfall here. Countless wolves rushed out of them and gathered here at the fortress. Two white foxes ran ahead of the wolves, and both of them were horrible. All these beasts were fierce. They left nothing undamaged, and they tore both men and horses and everything they caught. And at last they attacked you, my foster-father, and they attacked my father. At that moment I awoke. Now interpret the dream, foster-father."[3]

The jarl began to speak. "This dream is easy to interpret", he said. "Tidings of war will come to us soon. But I will not interpret it any longer." Their conversation came to an end, and the jarl went away.

One evening, it so happened that the king was sitting at his feasting-table when the hall-doors opened. Ten men came in. The king recognized Jarl Thorir and his company. The king asked for news. The jarl said that vikings had invaded the land and left nothing undamaged. The king asked what their names were. The jarl said that one of them was called Soti, and the other was Snaekoll. "Soti has come on a mission to ask for your daughter in marriage."

The king asked what Soti looked like.

The jarl relied, "Soti is an accursed berserk. He is two-colored. On one side he is black, and on the other side he is red. He wears no clothes on his torso. His entire head is bald, except for one hair that stands up in the middle of his skull."

The king said, "Then we must fight, rather than give these men our daughter." Everyone strongly encouraged this, although the king had no forces with him. The vikings had a two-day advantage over the king in mustering forces, and the king got only a small host, since time was short. He got three hundred men in all.

On the evening of the battle, Halfdan said to his brother Asmund: "Brother, I want the two of us to go down to the shore and find the vikings, because I have the greatest curiosity to meet them and see Soti."

Asmund said, "I'll never go there, because I know that I'll be killed immediately if I go."

Halfdan said, "I knew you'd be a sissy,[4] because you never dare to rouse yourself."

Asmund said, "I will follow you, if you're so intent on going."

Halfdan said, "Now you're doing better. Let's go to this place."

CHAPTER II

After that, the brothers left, and they didn't stop until they came to Soti's tent. Halfdan went before Soti and addressed him graciously. Soti gave him a warm welcome.

Halfdan said, "It is quite true to say that you are a princely man, Soti, and you are just the sort of person that I would most wish to have as my brother-in-law."

"You're a lad born with sharp wits", said Soti, "and clearly you seem to be a clever fellow. You would not be lacking in good fortune if you were to join up with my company."

Halfdan answered, "I'll have no good fortune until I can serve such a great chieftain as you are, my dear Soti."

Soti said, "I don't want you to go on your way without a gift. Where is Hundi, my treasurer?"

"Here I am," said Hundi.

"Give this lad three marks of silver."[5]

Hundi did so. Halfdan thanked Soti and then went out of the tent. Asmund, his brother, had stayed outside the tent while Halfdan had been inside. Now they went home to the hall. Halfdan told Jarl Thorfid everything about their journey and delivered the money into his hands. The jarl approved of this journey.

The next morning, the king prepared for battle. The fortress had three gates, and the king intended to defend it. He assigned Jarl Thorfid to defend one gate of the fort. Jarl Thorir the Strong defended another gate, and the king himself held the third. Each one had a hundred men. Both the king's sons were beside Jarl Thorfid in the battle.

Now concerning Soti and Snaekoll, it should be told how they divided their forces so that Soti would fight against the king, Snaekoll against Jarl Thorir, and the remaining third of their forces against Jarl Thorfid. The vikings now swarmed from their ships, biting their shield rims.[6] A fierce battle broke out there.

Soki pressed forward to where the king was. Snaekoll made a fierce attack against Jarl Thorir, striking with both hands. Jarl Thorir pressed forward at the head of his men. Just then, Snaekoll struck at a retainer of Jarl Thorir. He was killed at once. And as soon as the jarl saw the blood, he fled from the gate and rushed into the fortress. Snækoll and his men rushed through the gate and into the fortress at once, and there he killed Jarl Thorir. Jarl Thorfid saw that and immediately turned to attack Snaekoll, with some men. Meanwhile, Halfdan defended the gate which the jarl had defended previously.

Now the battle was harshest. Jarl Thorfid saw that Soti was attacking the king fiercely, and he rushed to his side. Just then, Soti struck at the king. The jarl blocked the blow with his shield, but Soti cleaved completely through it, and his sword struck the king's leg and cut it off. Then the king fell. The jarl was both wounded and weary, and at last he fell among the slain.

By then the night was so dark that no one could see a thing in front of him. None of the king's men were left standing. The vikings went to the ships, weary and wounded. They drank for a long time into the evening, and then went to sleep and took their rest.

CHAPTER III

Now there is this to be told about Jarl Thorfid: He got up from among the corpses. He first touched the breast of the king and found that he was dead. Then he went to where Halfdan and Asmund lay. He saw that Asmund was dead. He asked whether Halfdan could say anything. Halfdan said there was no reason why not.

The jarl asked whether he was wounded. Halfdan said that he wasn't wounded, "but I collapsed from exhaustion. But what can you tell me about Asmund, my brother?"

The jarl replied, "He is dead now."

"I knew he was worthless," said Halfdan.

The jarl carried Halfdan out from among the slain, because he was so very stiff that he could not walk. The jarl went to Ingibjorg's bower, and when she saw the jarl, she welcomed him warmly and asked for news. The jarl said that the king and her brother Asmund were dead, and so were all the men of the fortress. Ingibjorg became very grieved at this and wept. The jarl said that there was something better than weeping. Then he said that her serving maidens had to part from her. He took Ingibjorg and carried her on his arm, with Halfdan on the other side. They went to the forest and found themselves before a little house and knocked on the doors. A woman came out and greeted the jarl. He accepted her greeting. This woman was named Grima.

The jarl said, "Grima, I want you to accept these children and take care of them until I come for them, for I know that they will be safe here from the vikings. Here are three marks of silver which I will give you."

She accepted both the money and the children. The jarl went back to the fort and lay down among the corpses. No one knew about his trip.

Soti and his men woke early in the morning and thought it would be good to find the king's daughter. He and all his men went from the ships straight to the fort. When they arrived, they ransacked the corpses but didn't find the king's other son. They saw Jarl Thorfid and asked whether he knew anything about the king's other son, but he said he knew nothing about him. Soti had gone to Ingibjorg's bower and come back, and he said that she was gone. He asked the jarl if he knew about the children. The jarl said that he knew nothing about them, and Soti promised to tear him limb from limb if he would not tell them about the children. The jarl said that he would not talk. But Soti no longer felt like killing the jarl.

Soti took both the kingdom and its subjects for himself. He made himself king over Denmark, even though it was a wrongful gain. Men served him more out of fear than good will. The jarl was silent that winter. Soti ordered a search for the brother and sister, but they weren't found: as soon as anyone came into the neighborhood of Grima's hut, a blizzard always blew up, and Soti's men had to turn back.[7]

Early one morning, without anyone knowing, the jarl went to Grima's house. When he arrived, she was standing outside with both children beside her. She welcomed the jarl cheerfully. He took this well. The brother and sister were very happy to see their foster-father, and they kissed him. The jarl now said that the children must part from Grima, and they bid her farewell.

He went away with the children until he came to the beach. There Halfdan saw a fleet of ships. The jarl owned one ship there, and said that Halfdan should have it, along with a sum of money—"and you must travel to Bjarmaland[8], to Jarl Ottar, my brother. Say that he should receive you because of my word. If he is unwilling, give him this gold ring as a token, and then he will receive you."

Halfdan said: "What I want now, my foster-father, is for you to come with me."

The jarl refused. He kissed the brother and sister, and went straight home. Halfdan boarded the ship with Ingibjorg and put to sea, and they got a favorable wind and reached Bjarmaland. He went with all his men from the ship to the jarl's hall.

Halfdan came before the jarl and greeted him. The jarl welcomed him and asked for news. Halfdan told what had happened: King Hring was deceased, and Jarl Thorfid had sent him there to gain his help and support. The jarl received this news with reluctance.

Then Halfdan gave the jarl the gold ring. The jarl said: "My brother felt it to be of great importance that I receive you, and of course I shall do so willingly."

The jarl seated Halfdan next to himself. Ingibjorg was led to the bower of the jarl's daughter, who was called Thora. She was both beautiful and wise.

CHAPTER IV

One day, Halfdan went before the jarl and greeted him. The jarl welcomed him and asked what the greeting was about. Halfdan said that he wished to sail away from the land. The jarl gave him three ships and a great dragon-ship in the fjord. These ships were well equipped with men and weapons. Halfdan thanked the jarl for this deed and took leave of him. He went to the ship at once, and his sister Ingibjorg went with him.

Halfdan was twelve years old when he set out from land into the open ocean. He sailed far and wide throughout the summer.

When it was autumn, he wished to sail back to Bjarmaland. Then mists and fogs rose up before him, and he lost his bearings and drifted all over the ocean. Huge gales came upon them, so great that all the ships were lost except for Halfdan's dragon-ship; he drove in many pegs to tighten the cross-rope under the ship.[9] But no sooner was this done than the dragon-ship drifted towards huge cliffs and ran aground on sandflats. Halfdan said that they would camp there, and his men asked him to oversee it. They hauled the dragon-ship up on shore. Plenty of flotsam and jetsam was strewn all over the sand. There they began building a hut, and it was soon finished.

Halfdan usually went out onto the ice, and some men went with him, while others stayed with Ingibjorg at the hut. The men asked Halfdan what country this was. Halfdan said that they must have come to uninhabited Helluland.[10]

One day Halfdan went onto the ice alone to catch fish. He traveled all day. At last he came to a path, wide enough for only one person.[11] He had an axe in hand, which Jarl Ottar had given him. Halfdan went up the narrow path. Steps were carved in the cliff, and the height of each step was no less than four ells.[12] Halfdan hooked the horns of his axe up over the steps and pulled himself up by the handle until he reached the top of the cliff. There he saw a great cave, and a bright fire inside. He went to the cave entrance and saw that two trolls were sitting by the fire, one shaped like a woman and the other shaped like a man. They had a cooking kettle between them. There was both horseflesh and human flesh in the kettle.[13] The male had a hook in his nose, and the female had a ring. This was their game: he would hook his hook in the ring, and they turned somersaults so that each of their behinds went up in the air by turns. But when the hook slipped out of the ring, the female took a fall backwards. She said, "I don't want to play that game, Jarnnef my love."

"So be it, my dear Sleggja,"[14] he said, and they heaved the lid off the kettle.

Jarnnef then spoke up. "Are there any left, Sleggja", he said, "of those twenty-five men whom I bewitched to come here[15] last winter?"

She said very little about that. She went deeper into the cave and came out with a man under each arm. She laid them down by the fire and said that there were no more left. Halfdan saw that these were grown men, so much alike that either might be taken for the other, and he supposed that they were twins.

Halfdan then dashed into the cave and rushed at the male troll. He struck at his neck with the axe so that he cut off his head, but his body remained sitting. The female leaped to her feet and said, "It's a good thing that we two have met, Halfdan." He got away from her, but she pursued him until she picked up a knife. She attacked him fiercely, but he defended himself well. Sleggja flung the knife away and rushed at him. Their wrestling was hard and long, and Sleggja shoved him all over the cave, but so agile was he that she never knocked him off his feet. He was driven until they came to a chasm, both deep and wide. Sleggja was right on the brink of the chasm. At that very moment, her feet were snatched out from under her, and she dropped down into the chasm.

Halfdan held onto her hair. He saw a knife lying next to him, ornamented with gold. He quickly drew it and cut off Sleggja's head. Halfdan asked who had helped him and given him the knife, but no one answered him at all.

CHAPTER V

When Halfdan had won this battle, he went further into the cave, until he came to a side cave. There he saw a woman sitting on a chair. Her hair was bound to the chair-posts.[16] Her legs were in icy cold water.

When she saw the man, she said, "Jarnnef will swiftly kill you, man, if he knows that you are here."

Halfdan said: "I have killed him, and Sleggja too. But what is your name?"

She said that she was called Hild, the daughter of Jarl Angantyr of Scotland. "My brothers are called Sigmund and Sigurd. They are twins. We set sail from our land last summer. Jarnnef bewitched me and all of us here. He intended to marry me himself and kill his own woman, but I didn't want that."

Then Halfdan freed her, and they went towards the front of the cave. There were the brothers, and they were very weak. They were so thin that their skin was shrivelled down against their bones. She supported Sigurd's shoulders, and Halfdan supported Sigmund's, and they dripped wine between their lips. The brothers swiftly revived so that they could speak. They asked who had saved their lives. Hild said that he was called Halfdan, the son of King Hring of Denmark. They were very glad to see their sister unhurt, and they all thanked Halfdan, and they stayed there for five nights.

But on the other hand, there is this to be told about Halfdan's men: they were very anxious about him. His sister Ingibjorg stayed awake both night and day, and enjoyed neither sleep nor food.

After five nights had passed, they all prepared to leave the caves. Halfdan carried off gold and silver and many treasures, and came safely to his men. They were happy to see him, and his sister most of all. He told them all about his journeys. There was great affection between Hild and Ingibjorg. Halfdan stayed there that winter, and everything was uneventful.

CHAPTER VI

In the spring, Halfdan had his dragon-ship made ready and launched, and he set out on his way towards the end of summer. Then a gale blew up before Halfdan, and he had to steer for the cliffs on the other side of the fjord. Halfdan said that they had to camp there, and they stayed there for another winter. Halfdan, Sigmund and Sigurd went over the ice every day to get provisions. Not a thing was lacking in their huts.

One day, as the sworn brothers[17] traveled over the ice in the evening, they heard great roaring laughter. Then they saw three troll-women, and the one who was walking in front was wearing a red tunic.[18] Halfdan saw that she had the likeness of a human being, but not the others.

As soon as they met, the one in the red tunic said, "Here's a good chance to have some fun. I mean to have a king's son for myself."

Halfdan asked their names.

"I am called Brana", said the one in the red tunic, "and my sisters are Molda and Mana."[19]

"Shame on your sisters," said Halfdan.

Brana attacked Halfdan right away, and they wrestled for a long time. Mana rushed at Sigurd, and Molda at Sigmund. They got wrapped around each other, but could not knock each other down. Halfdan and Brana had a long struggle.

Brana said, "Are you an old man, Halfdan?"

"Sixteen years old," he said.

"And yet you're no match for a woman," she said.

"Why not put that to the test right now?" said Halfdan. He caught her with a hip-throw, so that she fell.

Halfdan asked what she would do to him, if he were in the same situation as she.

Brana said, "I'm neither a blood-drinker nor a man-eater. I wouldn't kill you, for I saved your life in Sleggja's caves. I pulled her feet out from under her, and I gave you the knife which you struck her with."

"Why did you tell me this so late?" said Haldfan. "Surely you should stand up."

Then they began to talk among themselves. Brana said: "You should know, Halfdan, that I am human on one side, because my mother was the daughter of King William of Normandy.[20] Jarnhaus,[21] my father, took her away. He begat me on her, and I take more after her, but somewhat after him. I have to serve a hundred ogresses."

Halfdan said, "I believe you're in a bad situation. But now you must grovel on your belly, while I play with your sisters."

She said that it should be so.

Halfdan went to where Sigurd and Mana were wrestling. He pushed her headfirst over the cliff, and did the same to Molda, and got a good look right up her behind.[22] Brana then looked up and asked where her sisters were.

"I pushed them over the cliff," said Halfdan.

"That brought you little honor," she said, "because one of them was five years old, and the other was six. I will gain good from you, and you from me as well. In six nights I want your band to come to my cave. It's a short distance from here."

Halfdan said that it should be so. Brana then went to her cave, and the companions returned home to their hut.

CHAPTER VII

When the six days had passed, the sworn brothers prepared to leave their huts. They were well armed, and they didn't stop until they came to Brana. Brana came to meet them and greeted them gladly.

She said, "Now I want you to help me, Halfdan. Let's kill all the ogres, since I have already killed some this way: I got them all drunk, so that they killed each other themselves. My father is lying in a cart. He has three heads, and they're all hideous. The cart stands in the middle of the cave floor. It is huge, but nothing takes him unawares. Even if you should manage to kill him, I don't want to see that—but I will have to come help you if it's to go well, and I think that will be difficult for me. No weapon can cut him except for your knife, and I want to have that."

Halfdan said that it should be so, and he gave her the knife. She gave large clubs to each of the sworn brothers, plated all over with iron.

They went into the cave. Brana went first. She extinguished the light. The companions then struck the ogres, both hard and often. Many a two-headed giant fell there.

Then Halfdan saw Jarnhaus lying in the cart. He dragged himself to his feet at once. Halfdan aimed for what he could most easily reach and bashed the side of his head with the club, but Jarnhaus didn't react. He said, "You've betrayed me now, daughter Brana. I know that Halfdan Hringsson, Sigmund, and Sigurd have come here."

Both brothers then struck him with clubs at the same time, but he stayed on his feet. By then all the other ogres had been killed. Jarnhaus grabbed Sigurd and brandished him in the air. At that very moment, Halfdan struck the back of his knees, so that he fell and Sigurd ended up underneath him. Halfdan didn't know what to do.

Then Brana came up and said, "I must kill my father myself, because I see that you can't be his killer. My reputation will suffer if I have to kill him, yet I shall do it now."

Brana sprang at him and struck at his neck with the knife, and so he lost his life. Then Halfdan rolled him off of Sigurd.

At that moment, day came over the cave mouth. Brana wasn't troubled about that.[23] She pulled up a trapdoor in the cave floor. Beneath it was the deep sea.[24] There she dumped the ogres. When they had done that, she thanked them for this work and asked them to stay with her for the winter. Halfdan said that they would do so, and then Brana was in good humor. Hild and Ingibjorg came into the cave.

Halfdan lay next to Brana every night, and the sworn brothers played board-games by day.

CHAPTER VIII

Brana went out every morning and didn't come back until nightfall. One time Brana asked Halfdan how long it would be until summer.

"Six weeks," he said.

"Then it's a good thing," she said, "that it hasn't seemed any longer than that to you in the caves, because tomorrow is the first day of summer. You must want to sail away from here, and it must be so—although there's something else that I would like better, and I'm not alone[25], for I am pregnant, and you are the father of my child."

Halfdan said that he wouldn't argue. "I want you to send it to me if it's a boy," he said, "but do as you like if it's a girl."[26]

She said that she would do so—"and you must sail from here to England. A king named Olaf rules there. He has a daughter named Marsibil. She is said to be the loveliest of all the maidens in the world. She knows all womanly accomplishments, and I want you to have her. You should call yourself a merchant there. Here are some herbs which I'll give you. You should give them to the king's daughter, and then you will win her love. They have this nature: if she lays them under her head and sleeps on them, she will love you as she loves her own life.[27] And here is a mailcoat[28] that I want to give you. No iron can cut it, except for this knife. You will never become exhausted when swimming, if you are wearing it, and fire cannot hurt you. A ring is the third treasure which you shall have. Its name is Hnitud. It can be taken apart into three parts[29]. If your enemy is next to you, and you have the ring, then you can know what means of death he's planning for you. If he wishes to slay you with weapons, the ring turns red as blood, and if he wishes to poison you deceitfully, it turns as black as pitch."

Now they went to the shore. There stood a ship on the sand. Brana said: "Here is the ship which I want to give you, Halfdan. I built it this winter. It will have a fair wind wherever you want to sail. The ship is named Skrauti."[30]

Halfdan thanked Brana for the gifts. She said, "From now on you shall be called Halfdan Brana's Fosterling. Aki is the name of the man in charge of King Olaf's defenses. He is a wicked and treacherous man. He's called Aki the Evil, a highly skilled man at sports. Don't let him betray you."

Halfdan promised her this. They then went home to the cave and slept for the night.

CHAPTER IX

In the morning, Halfdan got up early and dressed. Brana had completely readied his ship, and his men had arrived. He asked Brana to go with him, but she answered that she had to stay there. But she asked the sworn brothers to carry their loads of gold to the ship, and they did. Brana took a load herself, and it was heavier than all of theirs, and they went over to the ship with it. Halfdan went on board, and his parting from Brana was both hard and long. And Brana pushed the warship away from land.

Halfdan sailed out to sea and had a fair wind. Brana kept Halfdan's old dragon-ship with her. He sailed until he came to those islands which are called the Hladir Islands. A woman named Hladgerd ruled over them.[31] Halfdan stayed there for a while and gave her much wealth. She asked him to visit her again, if he should need any little thing. He agreed to that and sailed straight away from the islands, and he didn't stop until he came to King Olaf's fortress in England.

Halfdan came before the king and greeted him. The king welcomed him and asked who he was. He replied that his name was Halfdan and that he was a merchant, "and I would like to ask you for lodging over the winter."

The king granted him that. Halfdan took an outbuilding to store his goods and set his men to watch over it. Sigurd and Sigmund went with him wherever he went.

One day they all went walking together and came to an enclosure, fenced off with planks. In the enclosure they saw a very beautiful bower. The fence was so high that none of the local men could get over it. In the enclosure was a most fair grove. Halfdan asked the brothers whether they could manage to get over the fence. Sigurd made an attempt, and got a third of the way up. Sigmund made it halfway up, but Halfdan climbed up over the fence and got into the grove. There he saw a maiden. She was playing with a gold ring, throwing it up and catching it. Once, she missed what she wanted to catch, and it fell down in the enclosure. She looked for the ring. Halfan went over to her and gave her another gold ring that was larger. She thanked him very much and said, "I have never seen a more handsome man than you. I want you and my kinswoman Marsibil to meet, because you are very much alike."

CHAPTER X

After that, the girl went into the bower, but Halfdan went back to the brothers. This maiden to whom Halfdan had given the ring was named Alfifa.[32] She was the daughter of King Sigurd of Scarborough, who was the uncle of King Olaf.

Alfifa handed over the gold ring to Marsibil. Marsibil said that that wasn't the ring that she had given her. "But this one is even better. Who gave it to you?"

She said that she had found a man outside in the enclosure—"and he gave me the ring. I have never seen a more handsome and courteous person, aside from you alone. It seemed to me that you two could be man and wife."

Marsibil was so angry with her that she boxed her ears and made her cry. Thus ended their conversation.

One day, Halfdan went to the princess's bower by himself. The gate was open. He entered the enclosure and went to the grove which he had seen before. There sat Marsibil the princess. He thought that he had never seen any maiden more lovely. She was combing her hair with a golden comb. When she saw Halfdan, she said "Go away, man, if you don't want to be killed. You're quite brash to come in here without leave."

Halfdan pretended not to hear. He sat down next to her and untied a knotted kerchief. Inside were the herbs which Brana had gotten for him. He asked the king's daughter to have them, but she didn't want them. He laid them on her knee and went away. She picked up the herbs and went into her bower, and laid the kerchief under her head, and slept that night.

In the morning, she called Alfifa to talk with her, and said: "Kinswoman, you shall go to this merchant whom you found in the enclosure. Tell him to come to meet me as quickly as possible, and do it in secret."

Alfifa said: "It must be that now he seems no worse to you than to me—and now I shall go."

She hurried on her way and found Halfdan, and spoke to him and told him to make haste. He did so; he went with her and met the princess Marsibil. She said, "There is a great power in those herbs that you laid on my knee yesterday, because I love you so much that I can't take my eyes from you. I want each of us to pledge to be faithful to the other, right now."

Halfdan said that it would be so, and so it happened. The princess asked him to come there often and converse with her. He agreed to this, and then went away.

So time passed, until Aki, the guardian of the king's lands, came home. Halfdan had become so highly valued by the king that he sat by his side. Aki brought the king many treasures, and he was accustomed to sit next to the king. He envied Halfdan strongly, and he eagerly wanted him dead. He set men to kill him, but that was never successful. Aki often slandered Halfdan to the king, but the king did not want to listen.

CHAPTER XI

One evening, Aki and Halfdan were drinking in the hall, but the king had gone to bed. Aki said: "Are you much of a man for sports, Halfdan?"

"I'm not," he said.

"Will you have a swimming match with me?" said Aki.

"I might," he said.

Aki was happy to hear that, for he was a great swimmer. Then the men went to sleep.

In the morning, Aki arose early and thought it would be good to compete in swimming with Halfdan. He went before the king and told him of his conversation with Halfdan, and asked him to come with all his retainers and watch their contest. The king agreed. He summoned all his guardsmen with a signal on the trumpet, and the king himself went to see this contest.

There was a lake not far from the town. There they meant to hold their swimming contest, and so they did. They threw themselves into the water. Halfdan was wearing the mailcoat Brana's Gift. Aki came at him, and Halfdan dunked him and held him underwater for more than three hours.[33] Then Aki bobbed up and wallowed there in the chilly water. His retainers got him to land and brought him to his lodgings, but he was so chilled that he could not speak. Halfdan continued to play at yet more swimming games, and then came onto land and went back to the hall with the king. The king valued Halfdan more than before.[34]

The next morning, Halfdan went to the princess's bower and told her about the swimming contest. She approved of what he had done, but begged him to beware of Aki. She said that he would deceive him, but Halfdan said that it had to be that way, and left. Aki felt that he had been suffered a worse shame, and now he eagerly wanted to betray Halfdan in every way.

On one occasion Aki invited Halfdan to joust, and Halfdan quickly agreed. Aki had such a good steed that there was none better in England, except for the princess's steed. Aki's steed was named Longant, and the princess's steed was named Spoliant.[35]

Halfdan now went to the princess's bower and told her about his conversation with Aki. She said little about it. He asked her to lend him her steed. She said that she was willing to do that, but begged him to conceal it, so that it would not be obvious to everyone. He agreed to this and went away.

The princess went to speak with Alfifa, and said, "I will send you to a farmer who lives not far from here. His name is Ulf, and he takes care of my steed. You must fetch the horse in secret and get him into Halfdan's hands."

Alfifa hurried on her way, and came to Ulf and told him of her lady's errand. He got the steed for her, and she brought it to Halfdan.

CHAPTER XII

Now that day came when Aki and Halfdan were to joust. Aki took his steed and rode to the woods, where Halfdan came against him. They rode alongside a ditch. Halfdan thrust at Aki with his lance, and he heaved him right out of the saddle and cast him down into the ditch, so that he stuck fast in the mud and could not get out. His followers rushed to him and pulled him out. Now his fortunes were worse than before, but Halfdan won great fame from this deed. Aki plotted all night and day to betray Halfdan.

Aki had found out that Halfdan had one sister, and he intended to rape her to dishonor Halfdan. He got up out of his bed one night, and went to the bower where Ingibjorg and Hild were lying. He was wearing a shirt and linen breeches. No one else was in the bower. When Aki pounded his palm against the door and whispered that they should open it, and said that it was Halfdan, Ingibjorg asked Hild to go to the door. Hild went to the doorway and opened up the door and saw that it was Aki. They were so terrified that they didn't know what to do, but Aki was too startled to come in, and was leaning against the doorpost.

Ingibjorg said, "I wish Halfdan's fosterer Brana would help me."

And when she had said that, Aki became stuck fast to the door, so that he couldn't get away.[36] The wind began to blow, sharp and icy, and Aki began to freeze, so that he shivered from the chill. There he had to stand all night long.

In the morning, when Halfdan's men came to the bower, they saw Aki where he was standing and told Halfdan. But as soon Halfdan arrived, Aki got loose at once, but he could not speak. Halfdan had Aki carried to his own lodgings.

As soon as Aki could speak, he blamed himself very much and felt that he had suffered a great disgrace. Now he plotted to betray Halfdan in the worst possible way.

CHAPTER XIII

One time Aki invited the king to a feast. The king came with many men, and Halfdan went on the journey with Sigurd and Sigmund. Aki feasted them well and was cheerful to Halfdan. One day during the feast, Halfdan and his fellows were drinking in a certain castle with Aki close by them, and the king and his men were in another place. Aki was very merry and brought them strong drink. And because the drink was intoxicating, they soon fell down asleep. Then Aki summoned his men and had them set fire to the castle, intending to burn them inside. The king did not know of this. The castle began to burn, and so did the sworn brothers' clothes.

At that moment, a woman came out of the forest. She was very large, and she waded right through the fire. She took all the sworn brothers into her arms and carried them out of the flames into the forest.

Halfdan woke up there, and he saw that Brana had come. She said, "There is an old saying and it's true, 'slowly does a fool become wise', and it applies to you. I warned you that you must never let Aki deceive you. I have now left my week-old girl, and I believe that she has gone crazy. I can't stay here any longer."

Then they parted—to the sight, but not in their friendship. The brothers woke up and went home with Halfdan and told the king what Aki had done. But the king received the news coolly, because he was Aki's friend.

Now concerning Aki and his men, it must be said that as soon as they saw the woman, they rushed into the forest in terror. Aki is out of the saga for now. The king went home after this occurred.

CHAPTER XIV

Next we must tell how the king prepared a great Yule feast. King Sigurd came there from Scarborough, as well as many other powerful men. And the first night, when men had taken their seats, Marsibil the king's daughter entered with her attendants. Hild and Ingibjorg were there in her retinue. They sat on each side of her, and next to them sat her chamber-maids.

Alfifa was playing on the floor. King Sigurd, her father, called her over and sat her on his knee and said, "Tell me, what woman is that who sits on the right hand of your lady?"

"Her name is Ingibjorg," said Alfifa, "and she is the sister of that merchant who came here this summer."

The king said, "You shall go to Princess Marsibil and tell her to arrange it so that I marry that woman."

Alfifa left him and came before her lady, and brought her father's orders. The princess asked her to discuss that with Halfdan.

The night passed, and on the morning of the next day, the princess and Halfdan and King Sigurd went to confer together. King Sigurd asked them for Halfdan's sister. The king's daughter urged him to accept the arrangement.

Halfdan said, "It would seem to me to be a good match for the king if he were to marry Hild."

The king then began his courtship anew. Halfdan accepted this, and it was agreed upon with the consent of her brothers. Then the Yule feast was turned into a wedding, and people stayed for half a month. After the feast, King Sigurd gave good gifts to many people, and went home to Scarborough with his queen. Sigurd went with them, but Sigmund stayed behind, close to Halfdan.

CHAPTER XV

When summer came, Halfdan hoped to leave England. One day, he went to the princess's bower, and told her that he intended to go away and avenge his father.

The princess said, "There are twenty ships that I will give you, here in the harbor."

Halfdan thanked her, and told his sister that she should stay behind with the princess. She agreed. He took leave of the princess and of his sister. He left them and went before the king and thanked him for his winter accommodations, and took leave of him. He and Sigmund went off to the ships.

But when Halfdan had gone away, Aki came to speak with the king, and said "Did you know, my lord, that Halfdan has gotten your daughter pregnant?"

"I didn't know that," said the king, and he asked Aki to pursue him at once, with many men. He was quite willing to go on that journey, and he went after Halfdan with nine other men.

Now there is this to say about Halfdan's men: They took a road through the forest. Halfdan was able to see Aki coming. He was wearing the mailcoat Brana's Gift. Suddenly Aki came upon them, and at once he got down off his horse and attacked Halfdan. Halfdan and Sigmund turned back to back and defended themselves most manfully. Yet it happened that Aki killed Sigmund by cutting both feet out from under him. After Sigmund's fall, Halfdan became so furiously angry that he killed all of Aki's men. But he captured Aki himself, and he cut off his nose, gouged both eyes out of his head, cut off both his ears, and castrated him. Then he broke both of his legs and twisted his toes to face backwards and his heels forwards. And then he set him on his steed's back, and pointed the horse back towards the king's hall. Halfdan was neither weary nor wounded. He buried Sigmund in a mound, and after that went to the ships and told the men what he had done to Aki. They approved.

Halfdan now sailed from England with twenty ships, and his dragon-ship was at the forefront. He came to the Hladir Islands, and Hladgerd received him warmly and gave him twenty ships with men and money. Halfdan thanked her for this gift.

Now it must be said about Aki that he came home, and he wasn't at all puffed up. The king's men saw him and told the king that he had come home. The king saw how Aki had been treated. The king drove him away, and Aki no longer enters into this saga.

CHAPTER XVI

Now we shall return to Halfdan. He sailed away from the Hladir Islands with forty ships and headed home to Denmark. When the vikings knew that an attack had come, they hurried to the battle. None of the people of the land wanted to fight alongside them. The vikings went in search of Halfdan, and they encountered each other on a level field. A fierce battle broke out.

The vikings came on savagely. Soon there was great slaughter among Halfdan's forces. He told his men that they should defend themselves and not expose themselves so much to injury from the vikings. Halfdan's forces then advanced fiercely. Snaekoll and Halfdan faced each other in the battle, and their encounter ended when Snaekoll fell dead to the ground.

When Soti saw the fall of his brother, he charged at Halfdan and struck at him. Halfdan leaped into the air and Soti missed him, but Soti's sword plunged down into the ground. That stroke made him bend over. At that moment Halfdan cut both legs out from under him at the knees. Then he fell, and his death was near.

Soti spoke. "You have now won a great victory, Halfdan", he said, "and you have laid me on the ground. I now pronounce that you will not remember Princess Marsibil, your promised wife."[37]

After that Soti died, and Halfdan killed every man's son who had followed Soti. Halfdan made himself king over Denmark, but he did not remember Princess Marsibil.

CHAPTER XVII

One night, as Halfdan lay in his bed, he was awakened by his fosterer Brana coming in and speaking to him. She said, "Get up, Halfdan, if you want to marry Princess Marsibil. King Eirek has come from Constantinople to England and asked for her hand, but she has shut herself up in her bower, and the king can't reach an agreement with her. Get to Skrauti, your dragon-ship."

Halfdan got up and remembered everything, as if he had awakened from a dream. He went to the dragon-ship by himself and set sail. Right away a favorable wind blew up. Halfdan didn't stop his journey until he came to England, to the harbor where he had docked before. He arrived at evening.

He went up from the ship and came to the princess's fenced enclosure. At once he climbed the fence into the yard, and knocked on the door.

Marsibil and Ingibjorg heard the knock. Ingibjorg said, "I like the sound of that knock, and I want to let him in."

Marsibil asked her to do as she wished. She opened the door and saw that Halfdan her brother had arrived. They were very glad to see him.

As soon as morning came, Halfdan went before King Olaf and asked for Marsibil's hand. The king was so surprised to hear these words that he gave him his daughter, although he had previously intended to kill him. King Eirek now asked for Ingibjorg. Halfdan gave her to him. Sigurd the king of Scarborough had come there, and with him Sigurd, Halfdan's blood-brother. He asked for Alfifa, and she was given to him, and all the weddings were held together. They stayed for half a month in great pomp and splendor. After the feasting was done, each king gave the others goodly gifts.

King Eirek and his queen traveled home to their kingdom, and ruled there until they grew old. Many people are descended from them. Sigurd and Alfifa traveled home to Scotland, and they governed the kingdom until their dying day. Angantyr, his father, was dead by then. Sigurd had a son named Angantyr, who took the kingdom after him and became a great man.

Halfdan and Marsibil went to Denmark and ruled there until King Olaf died. Then they traveled to England and ruled there until they grew old. They had a son named Richard. He became king in England after his father. Some men say that that Richard was the father of Ali Spot.[38]

And here ends the saga of Halfdan, Brana's Fosterling.

THE SAGA OF SORLI THE STRONG

Sörla saga sterka

CHAPTER I

In the days when King Halfdan Brana's-Fosterling ruled over Scythia[1], which he won from Agnar the Rich, but set his son-in-law Astro to rule England and made him its duke, a king named Erling ruled Oppland.[2] He ruled over a third of Norway, but King Harald Valdimarsson ruled the other two-thirds of the realm. King Erling was considered a great and wealthy chieftain, because he had long been with King Knut the Mighty and had gained much wealth, riches, and fine treasures from him. The king's queen was named Dagny, and she was descended from the Æsir. With her he had two sons and one daughter, who was named Ingibjorg. The king had a hall built for her, with stout stone walls and a carefully wrought plank fence. There the king's daughter stayed, with a great retinue of the loveliest maids and lordliest court servants.

The king's elder son was named Sigvald, and the younger was named Sorli. They were both the most accomplished of men, well trained in sports and skills. Yet the king favored Sorli more than Sigvald, because he was a handsome man, and so physically strong that no one could equal him in all Norway and even farther beyond. The king found a man to tutor him. His name was Karmon. He taught Prince Sorli all the arts with which a man might adorn himself most splendidly.

When Sorli was fifteen years old, he was well accomplished in most arts, and so strong that there was no man in Norway whom he would need to fight using more than one hand at a time, whether in armed combat or in any other contest. He was so heavy, on account of his size, that no horse could carry him for more than half a day without collapsing from exhaustion.[3] Thus he was called Sorli the Strong.

CHAPTER II

One day the prince was talking with his father. "I believe", he said, "that I will win little distinction by staying here at home next to you, like a cloistered monk or a betrothed maiden. So be it known to you that I want to sail away from this land, right here and now, with five ships and many bold men. Karmon, my foster-father, will also accompany me, with as much travel gear as may be needed."

When the prince had ended his speech, the king said, "All that you ask shall willingly be granted to you." He now got five ships and many bold companions for his son. Sorli's foster-father Karmon went on the journey with him.

Sorli bid farewell to his father and all the men of the town before he went away. He sailed away from that land, and he won the victory in every battle that he engaged in. When the summer had mostly passed, the prince had taken eight ships, all well laden with gold and precious treasures and everything that he could desire. He had also taken on plenty of brave men.

The prince now wanted to return to Norway. They set their course due east, and they hoisted the sail to the top of the mast on every one of their ships. But when they had sailed this way for several days, such a great fog blew up in front of them that they couldn't see to sail a straight course at all. For several days they sailed on and didn't know in what direction they were sailing.

Finally, they realized that they had come to some land or other. The prince asked whether any of his men had any knowledge of where they had come, but there was no one who could figure it out. The prince ordered them to drop anchor and stay on the ships. He said that he wanted to stay there until they could find out a way to depart. It was done as the prince instructed. And when all was made ready, Sorli said that he wanted to go onto land and discover whether they might find human settlements.

Now the prince went on land with eleven other men. The weather was quite mild. They saw that the land was thickly overgrown with forest. They went onward until they approached the side of a mountain. The prince and his men took up a position in a clearing. He had nothing but his own sword.

At that moment they saw twelve men heading for them, incredibly huge and unlike other human beings. They were swarthy and hideous, with no hair on their heads, brows that hung all the way down to the nose, yellow eyes like a cat's, and teeth like cold iron. They all bore iron-rimmed shields and great cudgels studded with steel. And when they saw the prince and his men, they all began to shriek most fiercely, encouraging one another. The prince told his men not to lose heart at that, but rather to be bold against them. Now each man advanced against the others.

When the prince met these huge black men[4], the fiercest battle broke out, with such mighty attacks that everything seemed to be bursting apart. Each of their blows was so powerful that it sank into the earth, and it wasn't long before the prince's men had all fallen, and the prince himself was so weary that he was at the point of collapsing. The black men then attacked him, inciting each other and savagely howling and roaring, but he defended himself well and bravely and leaped up in the air over their mighty blows. At the same time he switched his sword and shield to opposite hands as he fought, whenever he saw fit. They had no defense against that.[5] Now he cut off their arms and legs and sliced through their mailcoats and bodies, so that their armor was of no more use to them than a burned beanstalk. He played with them like a lion with sheep, and he didn't stop before he had put all of them to death. By then he was terribly weary, but little wounded. And when what has been told was over, it is said that the prince sat down in the clearing and let the weariness pass from him for while. He thought that he would go to his ships.

CHAPTER III

Just then, he heard a rushing noise and loud cracklings very near him, and he wanted to know what the noises meant. Now he went a little farther into the woods along the mountainside, until he came to a great cave. He peered through the window in the cave and looked all around. He saw a fearsome giant lying in his bed. Never had the prince seen a larger man. His body took up all the space between both walls, with such a hideous and monstrous countenance that the prince was much amazed at it. He also saw a most striking old crone. She stood on a raised floor and was hard at work butchering the flesh of men and horses.[6]

Then the prince heard that the crone was speaking with her man—she gave his name as Skrimnir—in this way: "Now there are no more stores of food in our cave," she said, "other than what I have prepared for our next meal."

Skrimnir said that this was not unexpected, and said that things had turned out well. "You should know," he said, "that although I may be lying down now, something will still be accomplished before our lads come home in the evening, because no fewer than eight ships have landed here. This is by my will, for I made a mighty wind and fog for them, so that they should all blunder their way to this place. They will all be lodging in Hel before this day is ended."

The old crone was very happy at this. She went into a side cave.

Now the prince jumped up from the window and entered the cave. He bore his spear in his right hand and his sword in his left hand. He stabbed the spear into the giant's belly with both hands, so that the point protruded from the giant's back. In the next moment, the prince stabbed his sword into the giant's maw with both hands. The giant struggled when he was struck, roaring and howling savagely, until the bed broke and the giant tumbled down on the floor in huge convulsions.

At that moment the old crone came back into the cave, and she saw what was happening all around. She seized a sharp short sword, brandished it, and struck out at the prince, so that she split his shield completely in two. The point lodged in his breast, so that it stuck in the bone. She struck one blow after another, and the prince leaped backwards away from every one, or else she would have been the death of him. She pursued him so doggedly that the longer she attacked, the more savage she got. She was bellowing and screaming so that flames seemed to be burning in her eyes and maw. The prince felt such great terror from this foe that he didn't dare to face the fiery breath that gushed from her jaws, and he couldn't stand her dreadful howling.

Now the prince saw a chasm in the cave floor, so deep that he supposed that death was certain for whomever fell in. He went to the brink of the chasm, and thought he might push the hag in. Then he flung away his sword and rushed under the troll-woman, but she seized him fiercely and sank her claws to the bone. They had a fierce wrestling match, and she shoved the prince all around the cave. But even though she was possessed by trollish strength, she could never get him off his feet. The prince got her in a back-hold, and he saw that nothing was more likely than that both of them would fall into the chasm. The troll-woman sank into the floor up to her knees[7] and pulled the prince towards her, so that he couldn't use his strength against her. Her heels caught on the chasm's edge, and Sorli charged forward to grapple with her so hard that both of them tumbled into the chasm. They fell deep down into the chasm and landed on a ledge, with Sorli on top. The crone had clawed one of her hands into the prince's hair and the other into his chest, and when she was stunned by the impact of the fall, she let slip the hand which she had in his hair. Sorli gripped her around her throat with both hands and didn't let go, and sank his knee into her belly.

Then all the strength went out of her, so that she began to beg for mercy. She said, "Grant me a truce, king's son, and I will do everything you want me to do, as long as I keep my life."

The prince said that he wasn't about to grant her life, and he said that she should die in this chasm without any delay, as soon as possible. But she begged him in many ways for her life, as best she could.

In the end, Sorli said, "I will risk letting you live, on these conditions: that you fetch me armor so good that no sword can ever cut it, and the sword that bites steel as well as stone. You must have this done within a month. You must also lend me your aid when I want it and have need of it."

The old crone said, "All of this shall be done as you ask, and every effort will be made to fulfill it."

Then the prince let her stand up, and they both climbed back into the cave. She asked him to help her drop the dead giant into the chasm, and he helped her. When the work was done, the crone put a cover over the mouth of the chasm. Then she led the prince to a bed, and he thought that that bed was fit for a king's son to sleep in. Now the old crone took a horn and asked him to drink from it, and so he did. He thought that he would hardly suffer harm, and he quickly fell asleep.

CHAPTER IV

In the morning, when the prince awoke, he looked around inside the cave and thought that he saw an abundance of riches. He thought to himself that all the wealth of Arabia piled up together could be no greater than what he saw.

The old crone came to the bed and said, "How did you sleep in my bed last night, prince?"

"Very well," he answered.

Then he asked the old crone what the land to which he had come might be. She told him that it was Africa[8], governed by a king named Estroval the Great,[9] one of the most generous lords in that part of the world. "But my name is Mana", she said. "My husband Skrimnir and I have kept this cave for forty years. There always were some stores of food, because every year, the two of us bewitched[10] three ships and their crews into coming here. We also plundered some villages for horses, camels, and asses most of all. Besides, we have brought many good treasures from various lords here by magic. And now I can show you some noteworthy things here."

Sorli said that she was wise in discerning many things. He dressed quickly. And when he was dressed, he sat down at a table, and the old crone brought out delicacies and all sorts of fragrant drinks. The napkins were made of velvet and purple, and the vessels and bowls were made of gold, set with gemstones.

When Sorli had eaten and drunk as much as he desired, the old crone led him into a side cave and showed him a great store of gold and gemstones. From it, she gave him a game board made of gold, and he thought that he had never seen another one like it. She gave him a cloak[11] worked with lace on the lower edge, and a gold ring which was screwed together in nine places.[12] She said, "Wear this ring on your hand, and you will never be able to get lost, at sea or on land."

Sorli said, "Never before have I received such gifts from anyone," and he thanked her for the treasures with many fine words.

Then he made ready to leave, and she went with him for a long way. The crone said, "Fare well, and do one of two things: stay on the coast of this land until I have procured the treasures, or else set sail for Norway, and come back here to visit when you see fit." The prince answered that he would do so.

The prince headed back to his own men, and they were all glad to see him, but the crone went home to her cave. Sorli told his men all about his journey, and asked Karmon, his foster-father, which option seemed most advisable to him: whether he should sail home to Norway, or stay there on the coast until the crone had gotten the treasures. Karmon felt it was best for Sorli to stay there for the next month, until the old crone had gotten the treasures. So time passed, until the prince decided to fetch the treasures.

CHAPTER V

One day, when the weather was very mild, Prince Sorli summoned twelve men to him and thought that he would meet and speak with the old crone. They all journeyed together until they found the cave.

The prince went in first. When he came through the doors, he heard such a great clashing and crashing in the cave that it looked as if everything all around was swinging on threads. Then he saw that two ogre-women were wrestling violently, and each one was tearing the other's hair and clothes so that they were both bloody all over. He recognized that one of them was the ogre Mana, his lady friend.[13] He realized that she was certain to get the worst of the exchange, and that she was nearly worn out from exhaustion. The flesh all over her body was being pulled from her bones.

Sorli drew his sword as fast as he could, and ordered his men to help Mana. He struck out at the ogress's breast, so that the sword stuck into bone. At that she raged so furiously that she sank her claws into Mana's breast, and Mana fell down in a swoon. Then the troll-woman grabbed a beam and struck all the prince's men dead with one blow. But the prince swung his sword with two hands at the side of the giantess's head, so that he cut off all the flesh of her cheek, and the sword plunged down so that it split the beam with which she was defending herself. With that she raged and sank her claws into Sorli's chest so that he fell down in a faint. Just then, Mana got back on her feet and attacked the ogress. Then Sorli recovered his senses and stabbed his sword through the giantess's belly so that the point came out of her back, and that was the death of her.

Now Mana was very glad, and thanked the prince with many fair words for granting her aid. The crone asked him to go with her, and said that it was time for him to see the treasures.

CHAPTER VI

The old crone picked up a suit of armor and a sharp sword. "This armor," she said, "I fetched from Serkland, from Emperor Maskabert. The great champion Pantiparus, who ruled Greece after Emperor Agamemnon, wore it in former times.[14] It is so good that no sword can ever cut it, whether you fall into the hands of humans or trolls. No venom or fire that spews forth will be hot enough to damage it in the least. And the sword cuts everything, steel just as well as straw."

The prince accepted the treasures and thanked her with many fine words for this advice. The old crone dismissed him with fitting gifts, and they parted in friendship.

The prince boarded his ship and sailed home to Norway as directly as the winds would allow. His father and all his friends met him there, safe and sound. Sorli told the whole story of his journey and the renown which he won in Africa. The prince now stayed home with his father through the winter, and nothing of note happened.

CHAPTER VII

Now the story turns to King Harald Valdimarson, who ruled two-thirds of Norway, with King Erling ruling the rest, as was mentioned before. One day as he sat at the drinking table, twelve men came into the hall and made an eloquent speech before the king, saying: "Two brothers have come to this land all the way from Morland[15], bringing twelve thousand bold fighting men. One of the brothers is named Gardar, and the other is Tofi. Gardar wants to marry your daughter Steinvor, and what all the people are saying is that she would never get a more valiant man. Lord king, answer my speech quickly," said the messenger.

The king replied, "Every man here in Norway shall sink down dead on the battlefield before I would give my daughter to such loathsome trolls and sorcery-strengthened berserks. You tell the brothers that I will come at once to attack them in the morning with all my fighting forces."

The messengers went to their tents and informed the brothers how their errand had turned out. King Harald had the war-token carved,[16] and ordered every man who could wield a shield to come and join him. The king got over four thousand fighting men.

The king and all that host now set out from the town against the brothers. And when the brothers became aware of that, they advanced against them with all their host, and the battle-lines clashed together. Matters quickly took a dire turn. In short, the brothers destroyed the king's forces so quickly that few of his warriors were left standing. As soon as the king saw that, he ordered his surviving men to return to the town. He had no more than three thousand men, and he fled into the town with this force. The brothers chased their fleeing foes all the way to the town gates, and thus the fighting ended.

CHAPTER VIII

King Harald held a council with his men to decide what steps should be taken in the perils and difficulties that had come into their hands. It was decided at their meeting to do what everyone felt was the most advisable: word should be sent to the kingdom of Oppland, with a written summons to King Erling and his sons, so that they should come to help, with as great a host as they could get, as quickly as possible. This was now resolved.

Now the king sent twelve men to the kingdom of Oppland. Their journey went well, and they brought a letter to King Erling and his sons, who set out quickly when they got the summons. They left Oppland and didn't stop until they met King Harald. They received a glad welcome, and all of Harald's men prepared together for battle. Then they rode out from the town against the brothers. At once the brothers came out of their tents against them, with black men and outlawed warriors.

One man in the brothers' ranks was named Lodin.[17] He carried their banner. He was from Poland. He was as tall as a giant, and unlike other men on account of his strength and hideous appearance. His spear was six ells in length and three handspans in thickness.[18] He rode an elephant and thrashed both men and horses with his banner-staff, so that everyone was terrified of this foe. He charged out a long way ahead of the host, and dealt death to fifteen men before the battle-lines came together. When Sorli saw that, he rode at Lodin and stabbed at him with his own staff. Then he lifted Lodin up and flung him out of the saddle more than fifteen feet, so that every bone in his body was broken.

When the brothers saw that Lodin had fallen, they began raging fiercely, with such madness that men could think of nothing else but how savage they had become. Tofi rode at Prince Sigvald, and he thought that he should lay down his life. But in the nick of time, Sorli the Strong came at Tofi and struck at him—but the blow had no effect, for it did not bite into his accursed body any more than stone. Now they both dismounted from their horses and attacked each other briskly, and neither one spared the other. Tofi used all sorts of tricks, wading through the earth up to his knees like soft snow, but Sorli boldly defended againt all his ploys.

Sorli said, "I thought it was said that no men in the world were greater than those from Africa. Now I find that to be lies and idlest chatter, if you have no more valor than you have shown, as great a fighter as you seem to be." And at that, Tofi raged as ferociously as he could.

Then Sorli said, "You craven fool and cursed filth, now you shall find out how we Norsemen receive guests such as you. You'll hardly be longing to meet us then."

Sorli grabbed Tofi's ear and tore off the entire side of his face and all his beard down to the chest. Tofi became quite hideous in appearance. Then he turned into the likeness of a dragon, for he was a great shape-shifter, and he blew so much venom and black choking smoke at Sorli that it was a wonder. But Sorli hewed the dragon asunder, and Tofi lost his life. Then Sorli fell in a swoon from his exertions and the blast of venom.

When Gardar saw his brother fall on the field, he was filled with trollish ferocity beyond all measure, and he rode at King Erling. He stabbed at the king with his spear and flung him more than twenty feet out of the saddle, so that three ribs were broken on one side of the king. At that moment, Sorli came to his senses, and when he saw his father fall, he rode at Gardar and struck at him with his sword so that he split his head and trunk all the way down to the saddle. Gardar fell dead from his horse.

Now the brothers Sorli and Sigvald pursued the fleeing army and killed everyone that they caught, so that few escaped with their lives.

CHAPTER IX

Then they turned back to the fallen, and had the field searched for the slain. They were brought home to the towns of King Harald and King Erling, along with those wounded men who could be healed, and care was given to them all. The wounds of King Harald and King Erling were soon healed, and at once a splendid feast was prepared for all the mighty men. King Harald thanked Erling and his sons for their noble assistance, but most of all he thanked Sorli the Strong. No one in the Northlands was thought to be a more renowned man than Sorli.

King Harald said to Sorli, "Now choose any reward that you wish from us, in return for the aid which you have provided us. For if we had not had the benefit of your bravery, all Norway would be out of our hands. I now make it known to you that no part of my possessions shall be too good for you, whatever you wish."

All the people said that the king would be willing to marry his daughter to Sorli, if he should wish to choose her. But Sorli answered the king's speech in this way: "Lord king," he said, "I am not so stingy, like a needy slave, that I would accept a fee for my might. Rather than accept gifts from you, it seems far more honorable to us that our fame might be borne as far as possible, so that it might be carried to the far-lying rivers."

After that the feast was concluded, and all the chieftains set out, each to his own household. Erling and his sons went to the kingdom of Oppland, after being sent away with fitting gifts by King Harald. And now Storli stayed quietly that winter.

CHAPTER X

When spring began, Sorli had his ship made ready, and made it known that he wanted to set out raiding over the summer. Then he sailed away from Norway. His foster-father Karmon was with him, as before.

Sorli now raided in the western quarter of the world and most of all around Africa, all the way to the Red Sea. He gained many good treasures on sea and on land. He captured twelve ships, all laden with gold and precious treasures, and chose the boldest warriors.

When most of the summer had passed, the prince wanted to turn back to Norway. It was very late one evening when they came to eastern Morland. There Sorli made a great raid on the coast: he plundered forts and markets and pillaged whatever he came across, but struck dead everyone who opposed him. There Prince Sorli captured twelve men, and two brothers named Bork and Bolverk[19]. They were the most wicked men, and great shape-shifters as well.[20]

From there, Prince Sorli sailed to Denmark, all the way to the Øresund. There they dropped anchor and laid up that night.

CHAPTER XI

In the morning, when the men on the prince's ships awoke, they saw seven ships anchored farther in the sound. Among them was a dragon-ship so splendidly ornamented that they thought they had never seen its like before, neither in size nor in fittings. It was all plated with steel and bathed in gold down to the waterline, with its prows carved with masterful skill, adorned with the brightest gold, and inlaid all over with enamelled silver. It was also beautifully stained and painted with all sorts of variegated hues: green and white, yellow and blue, pale and dark.

On this handsome ship there stood a man next to the sail, very tall and elderly in appearance. He was in a hooded cloak which was worked all over with lace. He held a sword in his hand, bright and keen. When Sorli approached the dragon-ship, he hailed this tall man and asked, "Who is this proud man who captains this great dragon-ship, which sails forward with such great magnificence and splendor that I have never seen the like before?"

The tall man who stood on the dragon-ship said, "This is a man who will not fear you, nor tremble before you or the slaves who follow you. I have little more to say to you."

Sorli said, "I believe that you think yourself too good to speak with us, but we will dare to find out who you are before you sail out to sea. But my greatest suspicion is that this must be King Halfdan Brana's Fosterling the son of Hring, from Scythia, which you won from Agnar the Rich, my father's brother, when you did slay him. I would not wish to refuse to give you a chance. I will now offer you the choice to surrender your fine dragon-ship into my power, and you may go wherever you wish."

King Halfdan said, "Long have we sailed this dragon-ship, and it has ever been lucky. Often, more has been offered to me for it than to give it away for nothing. And though I might have won land from your father's kin, you will have to let that stand as it is."

Then the king became very angry, and he paced back and forth on the ship. He ordered his men to prepare swiftly for battle against these knaves and kill them at once. There was a great uproar on the ships. First, large beams and rocks were thrown, corded-spears[21] and arrows, javelins and axes, pikes and polearms and all sorts of weapons. There was a great slaughter of men, and it wasn't long before all of Sorli's ships were cleared of men and broken apart, except for the one that he himself captained. But King Halfdan had lost three ships.

There was one man with King Halfdan, named Thorir the Strong. He was the son of Jarl Thorvid[22] and was fifteen years old, yet he was the best and most fearless of men, so that no one was his equal in valor and prowess throughout all Sweden.

Now there is this to be told about Sorli. As soon as he saw that things could not go on in this way, he leaped up onto the dragon-ship when it was least expected, and Bork and Bolverk came up with him onto another location. Now they all fought as bravely as each one had the courage and manliness for. Sorli slashed and stabbed every man who stood before him, and spared no one, but Bork and Bolverk went along the other side of the ship, where Thorir was.

King Halfdan Brana's-Fosterling now saw that they had come up onto the dragon-ship. He attacked Sorli furiously, and they struck at each other fiercely. There one might see blows both numerous and mighty. It went on for a long time, and neither one retreated before the other in the least. But it happened at last that King Halfdan began to grow weary, because he was a very aged man, while Sorli became more eager to strike blows the longer he fought. King Halfdan began to stagger, so he fell back to the afterdeck, and he was nearly worn out from exhaustion.

Then Sorli said, "Accept a truce, King Halfdan, and let the two of us settle this. I will leave whatever honors you will grant me up to your warrior's heart."

The king said, "I find that you obviously have a weakling soul. Now I will make you fearful, like most of your Norwegian kin. You may be sure of this: I have never humbled my spirits for any man, and I will certainly not do so for you."

Sorli said, "You must decide, king, though I tell you that a truce is wise."

Then they began to fight a second time, so furiously that neither one spared the other. The fight lasted a long time, and it happened, as before, that the king retreated and had almost reached the stern of the dragonship. Such great weariness overcame him that he could hardly hold his sword.

Then Sorli said, "Still I offer you a truce, king. Let us settle this. I will leave whatever honors you bestow upon me up to your warrior's heart."

King Halfdan said, "May he be damned who accepts any of your offers. I will lay down my life with boldness and manliness before I accept this offer of yours."

Then Sorli spoke up, and told him that no honor would come to him from this. He then struck so hard and fast that the king couldn't defend against him because of his exhaustion, and the sword dropped from his hand. Sorli caught it in the air and ran the king through.

King Halfdan had never been wounded or forced to his knees by any man. The king laid down his life with great honor.

CHAPTER XII

Now the story turns to Thorir the Strong. He cut down Sorli's men as if they were brushwood, so that death was certain for all of those who would not retreat from him. When Bork saw that, he cleared a path forward and struck at Thorir as hard as he could. But when Thorir saw his certain death, he leaped up and backwards over the sail-boom, and the sword cut down into it and stuck fast there. It took a long time for Bork to pull his sword out. When Thorir saw that, he grabbed up a great beam that was next to him and swung it at Bork's head, shattering his skull. Thorir was staggered from the blow, and at that moment Bolverk struck him across the shoulders so that Thorir was almost killed, but it didn't cut into his mailcoat. Now Thorir turned to face Bolverk, gripped each of his legs with one hand, and slung him down, so that Bolverk's skull shattered into fragments.

By then, so many of Sorli's men had boarded the ship that Thorir saw that his situation was hopeless and that he would shortly be overwhelmed. At the same time he saw that King Halfdan had fallen. He made the decision to leap over the side of the warship, and he swam as directly as possible to the land ruled by Sigurd, who had been allied with King Halfdan Brana's-Fosterling for a long time. Sigurd gave him a warm welcome.

After the battle, Sorli took the dragon-ship under his command, along with all the treasures that King Halfdan had owned. Now he sailed home to Norway, and soon met his father, kinfolk and friends, safe and sound. There was a joyful reunion. Prince Sorli told them everything about his travels, and many thought that he had greatly increased his fame from this journey. They wanted most of all to see the dragon-ship Skrauti.[23] Everyone said that a better or more splendid ship could not be found, neither for its great size nor for its fittings.

CHAPTER XIII

On one occasion the father and son, King Erling and Sorli, had a talk. King Erling said that Sorli should be prepared, since he could soon expect enmity towards him from the brothers, Halfdan's sons, who had heard about the loss of their father's life. The father and son quickly set to work and mustered forces from all of Norway. They also sent word to King Harald for him to send them some men. When all these plans were made, they kept a close watch, day and night, and they expected violence at any moment.

CHAPTER XIV

Next it should be told that Thorir the Strong reached land, as was said before. He met King Sigurd and told him the whole truth about the death of King Halfdan. Everyone felt this to be harsh news, and King Sigurd most of all.

Thorir did not stay there for long before the king gave him a ship and men to go to Sweden. Thorir sailed as straight as he could to Sweden, and made harbor near the town of Litidorum[24], which was then the capital of the kingdom. King Halfdan had two sons there. One was named Hogni, and the other was named Sigmund. He had a daughter who was named Marsibil, like her mother.

When Thorir spoke with people, they informed him that Hogni had sailed away to visit Astro, Duke of England. Thorir now went into the hall before Prince Sigmund, where he sat with all the chieftains and finest men. Thorir greeted the prince, who immediately asked for news, and whether King Halfdan had returned safe and sound. Thorir answered him in this way: "Many and evil tidings are now to be told of our journey: the death of King Halfdan your father, and the theft and loss of the dragon-ship Skrauti and all the king's treasures."

Now Thorir told the whole truth of how King Halfdan was slain by Sorli the Strong and all his men put to death. Everyone was greatly moved by these tidings, and the queen most of all, for she suffered one swoon after another until her heart burst from grief. Now there was even more sorrow than before. She was splendidly buried in a mound according to the old customs, and an inheritance-feast[25] was held for both the king and the queen. Many chieftains in that land were summoned.

When the worst sorrow and grieving for the king and queen had abated, Prince Sigmund held a council to decide what would be most proper in such a circumstance as they had on their hands. It seemed most advisable to all that a letter with a summons should be sent as soon as possible to Hogni and Duke Astro in England. So it was done. Messengers set out and sailed for England. Their journey went well, and they brought the letter to Hogni and the duke. When Hogni received the news, he had his ship made ready as quickly as possible, and asked the duke to come after him with as great a host as he could muster. The duke quickly agreed that it would be done.

CHAPTER XV

Before Hogni had to go to his ship, he went to meet Queen Marsibil, who was married to Duke Astro, and he told her everything about the death of King Halfdan, their father. When she heard that, she became so upset and distressed that she fell in one swoon after another. But when she recovered her senses and came to, she asked that the duke be called to her, and he came to meet her at once.

She then began to speak, and said, "I believe that I understand clearly that the death of my father seems important neither to you nor to Hogni, and it is obvious that all your zeal to wreak vengeance for him will leave you. That shame will last as long as the Northlands are settled, and it will be remembered by all, for ages, that King Halfdan left after him such faithless scoundrels and worthless nanny-goats[26] as you, who know that you are as completely terrified as the most cowardly rabbits. I have a mind for you to give me weapons and armor, and it would never go worse with me than it went for you and all of his liegemen. May it be an endless shame and disgrace to all of you as long as you live, and yet so much the worse after death. It would be better to be fallen with honor before the weapons of one's enemies."[27]

And as the greatest anger was flowing through her, she stood up, took the duke in her embrace and laid her arms around his neck, weeping, and said: "Think of my love and your own manhood, that you may avenge my father on those hideous and loathsome sons of slaves who have put him to death."

Hogni said, "Be at ease, sister, for we shall bring about vengeance for our father that will please you well."

She said, "I trust most of all, brother, that it will go best with you out of all our family."

After that, Hogni said farewell to the duke and to his sister, and sailed home to the Swedish realm. He summoned together a mob and a multitude. Then Hogni said, "I will go away from here and find out what I can about Sorli the Strong, because he is no more likely to be in Norway than anywhere else. Sigmund my brother shall have the rulership here and wage war against him should he come here, with the support of Thorir the Strong and other chieftains, and be prepared for him day and night, if he should attack this place. I will come back as soon as possible, when the opportunity presents itself."

What Hogni said seemed to all to be most fitting. Now he sailed away to Sweden, and then straight for Norway.

CHAPTER XVI

Now we must tell how Prince Sorli stayed at home by his father's side in the kingdom of Oppland. Father and son had assembled a countless host.

One day, Prince Sorli spoke with his father: "Now I want to sail away from here to Sweden," he said, "and try to reconcile with the brothers, if there is any chance. You should stay behind with half of the forces, together with King Harald and my brother Sigvald. The dragon-ship Skrauti shall stay here, equipped for the defense of this place."

This seemed advisable to everyone. Once this was decided, Prince Sorli the Strong sailed away from Norway, eastwards around the land, all the way to the island of Most,[28] which is surrounded by great crags and overgrown with forest. He sailed between the mainland and the island. At that same moment, Prince Hogni sailed around the seaward side of the island, and they passed each other, but neither one encountered the other. Sorli sailed directly to Sweden and reached harbor near the town, and had his tents pitched there.

Now we must tell how Prince Hogni sailed directly around Norway. His forces had a favorable wind and landed at the harbors which lie near the kingdom of Oppland. As they approached, they saw forty ships lying before them, and there they saw and recognized the dragon-ship Skrauti. Fierceness and wrath filled Hogni's heart, and he said, "It's clear now that Sorli the Strong must be home, because I recognize the dragon-ship Skrauti here." Hogni then gave the order to attack the ships at once, and it was done.

The man in command of the dragon-ship was named Ivar. He was from Finnmark in the east, a good knight.

Hogni said, "You vile slaves should know that I am giving you two choices. One is that you give me control of this good ship. If you don't want that, the other is for you to defend your wealth and your life against us, while your courage holds out."

Ivar answered his speech, and said that there was no way that he would give up the dragon-ship. Hogni became extremely angry at that. Immediately the fiercest battle broke out between them, and there was no need to ask what happened.

Hogni urged his men to the attack, and said to one of his men, who was named Sval,[29] "I think that you will be a good knight, but I don't want to put that to the test now."

Sval said, "If none of your men advances more briskly than I, Prince, then I may properly avoid disgrace."

And at that, Hogni leaped up into the dragon-ship first, and Sval with him. Hogni slashed and stabbed every man who stood before him, and spared no one, and Sval advanced along the other side. Then Ivar came against Sval and struck at him, so that Sval fell flat and blood gushed from his mouth and nostrils.

Ivar said, "When you get back to Sweden, tell them that you have met us Norwegians before. Now I am ready to let you have some more, if you don't think that was enough."

Then Sval said, "Little do you know, weakling, whether we two have parted as yet, or not."

Sval now sprang nimbly to his feet, gripped each of Ivar's legs with his hands, and slung him down so that his skull shattered into pieces. Then Sval said, "That's what we Swedes are accustomed to do to foxes when they get caught in the trap. It makes me cheerful that you won't be telling the news to King Erling at home."

At exactly the same moment that Ivar fell, Hogni had completely cleared the dragon-ship. All of those who survived went into Hogni's power. Hogni took command of the dragon-ship and sailed into the harbor straight away, and had his tents pitched a short distance from King Erling's town.

CHAPTER XVII

At dawn, when there was still little light, Hogni sent twelve men to the hall, with Sval leading them. Hogni ordered them to tell Sorli the Strong and his father King Erling that he would offer them battle at that very moment. The messengers set out and didn't stop until they came to the hall where King Erling was sitting with all his chieftains and landholders.

Sval greeted the king and spoke in this way: "Hogni, the son of King Halfdan, has sent us hither and lets it be known to you, king, that he offers battle to Sorli the Strong, if he is here in the land, or else to you yourself if he is not at home. Hogni now wishes to avenge his disgrace in a suitable fashion on you, father and son. I am afraid that you will fare no better than the loathsome slaves who had to defend your land and the dragon-ship Skrauti, who swiftly fell before us like cowardly goats. It appears to me that your men are quite faint-hearted, king, and best fitted to serve here in your hall, rather than to join battle with valiant warriors from Courland[30] and Scythia. So this is the best advice I can give: for you to let yourself be captured, and give all your kingdom into Hogni's power, under such mercy as he shall see fit to allow you."

Then King Erling said, "Luck hasn't left Hogni if he has one such as you, because many would be less minded than you to deliver the message of their own lord. You don't trouble the minds of us Norwegians, with your grandiloquence and your overweening arrogance. It would be most fitting for me to have you hanged on a gallows for your impudence, and so teach you not to play games like this any more."

Sval said, "I am not afraid of that, or for anything that may happen. Your reputation would be more widely villified than all other chieftains', if you were to give any less of a truce to messengers."

King Erling said, "Go away and tell Hogni that we will come out to fight him."

Then Sval went out of the town and met Hogni to speak with him. He repeated his conversation with King Erling exactly. Once Sval had left the hall, those who remained wished all evil upon him.

CHAPTER XVIII

When Hogni had heard Sval's message, as was told before, he put on a shirt which no iron could bite, and girded himself with the sword named Sigrljomi,[31] which King Hrolf Kraki had once owned. Then Hogni summoned all his forces to battle, and he stood at the forefront of his men. King Erling came out of the town with all his forces, together with King Harald and his son Sigvald. The man who bore the standard before King Erling was named Sverri. He was from Finnmark in the east, a good knight.

Hogni now rode forward into the ranks of the men of Norway. He slashed and stabbed every man before him, and he spared no one. At that moment he met Sverri, King Erling's standard-bearer, and struck at him with his sword, and Sverri crashed down to earth. Hogni now rode through the battle-lines and felled one man after another. But as he was most eager to strike down the men, such a huge lion came up out of the earth that everyone was struck with terror.[32] The lion quickly turned on Hogni and struck his horse so hard with its tail that Hogni was flung far away and landed in a patch of woods. Hogni sprang quickly and nimbly to his feet and struck at the animal, but that had no effect, because it didn't cut the lion in the least, and that happened with every one of his thrusts. Now Hogni flung his sword away and charged the beast, and they wrestled so fiercely that everything was knocked out of place. Even oak trees were broken from their stumps. This wrestling match lasted for three whole hours.

Then the prince made use of his strength and evil powers. He heaved the beast up to his chest and slung it down against a tree-stump, so that its back was broken. At that, the beast spewed poison, with dreadful snortings and black smoke, but the shirt's power protected the prince so that nothing harmed him, although he collapsed onto the lion in a swoon. King Erling saw that and rode to where Hogni was lying and struck three blows between his shoulders, but the sword didn't bite him at all.

When the king realized that a weapon would not bite him, he called to one of his men, named Gellir[33], and ordered him to beat Hogni to death with his club. But when Sval saw King Erling standing over Hogni with a naked sword, he set his horse to galloping as fast as he could. He rode at King Erling, stabbed his spear at him when he least expected it, and flung the king out of the saddle more than forty feet, so that every bone in his body was broken.

Now Gellir turned on Sval. He picked up the club and wanted to beat him to death. Sval saw that it would certainly be his death if the club should hit him. He leaped backwards out of the saddle, and the club landed on the horse, breaking its back. Sval attacked Gellir, and they wrestled fiercely until Gellir fell to the ground.

Then Gellir said, "I wish my foster-mother would come now."[34]

Next Sval found that he was being pulled backwards by his shoulders, most unmercifully, so that Sval ended up underneath with Gellir on top of him, and Gellir thought that Sval should lose his life. At that moment, Hogni regained his senses, gripped his sword, and cut Gellir in two at the middle. With that, Sval got to his feet, although he was stiff from wrestling. But as Hogni bent down to strike the blow, King Harald struck him across the shoulders, so that Hogni was almost killed. Now Hogni turned on Harald, brandished his sword and struck at King Harald so that he cleaved him all the way down to the saddle. Then Hogni rode at Sigvald and aimed his sword at his neck, so that he cut off his head.

Now there were few of the Norwegians left. All who were left standing fled to the town and told the queen all about the fall of the kings and Sigvald. There was such great sorrow in the town that no one heeded the need for either sleep or food.

CHAPTER XIX

On the morning after the battle, when it was still dim, Hogni entered the town with all his men. First he went into the king's hall and found no one inside, except for slaves of no importance. Hogni asked them where the queen might be, and they said that she had gone into her daughter's hall. But when Hogni and his men thought they would pay a visit, and they had come to the plank fence that surrounded the bower, such a great mist burst out that they couldn't see each other, and they found neither the fence nor the bower; they never found the way. And suddenly there was a river in front of Hogni's men, so huge that many plunged down into the water and splashed in it all through the night, laboring mightily. It was difficult for them to climb up the cliffs which made up the two banks of the river. This went on all the way till morning.

But when day broke, the men saw no river. They had been clawing at each other all along the base of the ring fence, which they had imagined to be a cliff, and so they'd been falling off the fence and accomplishing nothing. When they realized what a perplexing thing had happened, Hogni ordered them to break down the gate and take the door off its hinges.

When that was done, Hogni and his men went into the bower, and when they came there, they saw no one. Most of the men held back. Hogni had all the treasure chests broken up, and had the gold and silver and costly clothing taken away. Then he went away with all his men.

When they had gone a very short distance, Hogni happened to look back. He saw an unattractive woman who appeared quite elderly standing on the walls. Next to her stood a maiden so fair and refined in appearance that her loveliness appealed to Hogni's mind.

Hogni said to Sval, "Who do you suppose that that fair one might be, who stands there on the ramparts next to the ugly old crone?"

Sval said, "That must be King Erling's daughter Ingibjorg, and her foster-mother. They must be scheming against you and wishing death on us."

Hogni said, "We should return later and take the fair maid."

Sval said, "We had better not, lord, because in the night we got wretched treatment and hard labor, and we'll get certain death if we turn back now."

Hogni said that Sval should decide.

Now they rode to their tents and packed up all their camp. Then they boarded their ships, embarked from land and sailed their fleet away from Norway. There were fifty ships in all, including the dragon-ship Skrauti. They now sailed directly, with a fair wind all the way, until they came to Sweden.

CHAPTER XX

Now it is time to pick up where we left off with Prince Sorli's arrival in Sweden. He reached harbor near the town and had his tents pitched there. He had many bold men in his forces. Two Finnish brothers were with him. One of them was named Fal, and the other was Frodel.[35] Both of them were very learned in all magical crafts and ancient sorcery, so that when they chose, they could sink into the earth in an instant. It appeared to men as if an arrow flew from each of their fingers, and a man was marked for death from each arrow.[36] With Sorli were three other brothers, who never had been wearied nor defeated in any battle. They were named Amund, Austmund, and Arnljot of Gautland.

When the prince and his men had set up their camp, they sent twelve men to the hall, and Sverri led the expedition. And when the messengers came into the hall where Sigmund sat with his chieftains, Sverri said, "Sorli the Strong, son of the king of Norway, has sent us here. He makes it known to you that he offers you a settlement with honor for your father King Halfdan, and all the riches which the king had, along with his own friendship and sworn brotherhood and all the honors which he is best able to offer you brothers."

When Sigmund heard this speech and message, he flew into a furious rage, with terrible fierceness and wrath in his heart, and he spoke thus: "Pack up and leave quickly, and tell that worthless wretch who sent you that he will be torn by dogs and ravens and then burned up in flames, he and all his forces."

Sverrir said, "Sorli will not be afraid of these threats."

Sigmund said, "Get out of my sight quickly, you loathsome slaves, and tell Sorli that he has no hope of mercy from us. That damned one shall receive fitting rewards for his shameful foul deeds, such as few would wish for."

Sverri now went away and told Sorli all about how their conversation with Sigmund had gone. He said that there was no more hope of a settlement between them.

After that was said, Sorli the Strong prepared all of his forces for battle. Sigmund and Thorir the Strong drove all their forces out of the town. Now both sides raised their loudest battle-cry, with loud blasts on trumpets and blaring of horns. And when the battle-lines came together, Sorli slashed and stabbed every man who stood before him, and he broke Sigmund's ranks many times, charging both through them and along them.

When Prince Sigmund saw that, he thought that he should firm up his battle-lines. He rode forth boldly and encountered the brothers Fal and Frodel in the ranks, and he saw them striking down so many of his men that it was a wonder. Sigmund wanted to avenge his men. He brought up his sword and struck at Frodel, but Frodel slipped down into the earth at the blow. Sigmund snatched at him and wanted to drag him up. At that moment, Fal came up out of the ground behind Sigmund's back, and struck him in the belly from below, under his armor, and that was the death of him. Sigmund fell down dead, and all his tyranny was at an end. When Thorir the Strong saw that, and saw that it would be no use to fight against Sorli any longer, he fled back into the town with those few men who were left.

CHAPTER XXI

When Sorli saw that, he brought his camp near the town. Carrying spears and blades, they went to break down the walls, but Thorir and his men poured boiling pitch and brimstone onto them from the ramparts, so that Sorli suffered many casualties from that. He had his tents taken back up and brought farther away from the town, to where they had first pitched them.

CHAPTER XXII

Now as this was happening, Duke Astro arrived from England with an overwhelming host on many ships, and the fiercest battle broke out anew between him and Prince Sorli. The men of both armies fell dead like sapling brushwood cut down in a forest. Sorli the Strong rode forward fiercely and killed men with both hands, and Duke Astro did just the same in return. So the battle stood for the next two days. It seemed uncertain who would win.

CHAPTER XXIII

When the third day came, men saw many ships sailing in and making for a landing there. They were all well-equipped, yet one was far superior to all the others. Men recognized the dragon-ship Skrauti, and they guessed that this must be the expedition of Hogni, the son of Halfdan Brana's-Fosterling.

When Sorli realized this, he was somewhat grieved, and said, "Some turn of events which is still not clear to us must have befallen the people in Norway, because I recognize the dragon-ship Skrauti, and the contest between us is still not ended. We shall fall with honor, rather than prove to be unmanly." Everyone firmly swore to the king's son that they would follow him and not separate from him until death should part them.

This ship soon came to land. Hogni steered the dragon-ship into a good harbor close to the town, and so did all the ships' steersmen. Hogni now had the anchor dropped to the bottom of the sea. After that he had his silken, gold-woven tent pitched, and then went inside with all his best men. They drank there and were glad.

When Duke Astro and Thorir the Strong saw clearly that Hogni had landed and that the dragon-ship Skrauti had made harbor, they became very cheerful at his arrival. They rode to Hogni's camp, and there were joyous greetings among them all. Thorir told Hogni everything about their dealings with Sorli and Sigmund, Hogni's brother, and also about the offer that Sorli had made to Sigmund. Hogni listened to that, but had little to say. Afterwards they all went to the town with their forces and drank freely in the hall for the next three days, merry and cheerful.

CHAPTER XXIV

When the fourth day came, Hogni sent twelve men to Sorli's camp and told him to be prepared to meet him and begin the battle anew. He said that that day should be the end of their contest. When Sorli heard that, he said at once that he was ready, and that they must not delay. Both of them deployed their forces, and there was a fierce and terrible battle. Because the slaughter was greatest in Sorli's ranks, the tide soon turned against him, and few of his men were left standing. Thorir the Strong rode at Karmon, Sorli's foster-father, and dealt death to him. When Sorli saw that, he became fiercely angry, and he charged after Thorir on his horse, intending to deal death to him or else lose his own life.

When Hogni saw that, he said, "It will be best, Sorli, for the two of us to contend with each other, for it won't be any better to put it off."

Sorli said that he was ready for it.

CHAPTER XXV

Now each of them rode so hard against the other that both horses nearly collapsed, and each one hewed the other's horse in two at the withers, but neither one wounded the other because their armor protected them so excellently well. For a long time they kept on striking at each other, and neither could be accused of failing both to defend and attack.

Sorli saw that it was no use to trade blows with Hogni any longer. He flung his sword far away and charged straight at Hogni and grappled him with all his strength, and they wrestled fiercely. There was no need to ask about their fighting. Neither one cared to beg for peace or truce from the other, and their combat was so very ferocious that no one thought he had seen such wrestling before between two human beings.

Now Sorli noticed a very deep brook close by him, and he thought that Hogni should fall in. He pulled Hogni towards him as strongly as he could, so that they came close to the brook. But when Hogni saw what Sorli had devised, he charged into his grip as hard as he could. More weight was thrown onto Sorli than he had expected, and he fell backwards. Hogni now leaped onto him and pressed his knee into Sorli's belly.[37]

Then Hogni said, "Far from me is the sword Sigrljomi, which I need most, and it will seem ill-done if I bite your windpipe as a troll does. If it is true, as it is said, that you are called the most bold and dauntless of men, then lie here quietly and wait for me while I take up the sword."[38]

Hogni stood up and went over to where the sword lay, and Sorli lay as quietly as before. Hogni saw that Sorli never lost heart, and he said, "Sorli, I have no great dishonors to avenge on you, and I say that the game between us is nearly a draw. You shall now accept your life from me, if you will. This decides it the most: you offered to spare my father's life three times, although he did not want to accept your offer. That was excusable for you, although it ended up for you as fate would have it. And your offer to my brother Sigmund was very well done, although he didn't want to consent. For that, I offer you my friendship and sworn brotherhood, here and now. Give me an answer to my offer as you like."

Sorli said, "No one has ever made such an offer to me. It will be an honor for me to accept this offer from such a man as I believe that you must be."

After that, Hogni let him stand up. They made a firm pact between themselves. Now they went to where Duke Astro and Thorir the Strong were, and Hogni made a settlement for Sorli the Strong with both of them, so that now he liked both of them better than before. Afterwards they all went home to the hall together and drank now, glad and cheerful for many days afterwards, so that all their warlike nature was put aside.

CHAPTER XXVI

Then they sailed away from Sweden and came to England. They had a favorable wind and soon arrived safe and sound. And when Hogni went to speak with his sister, Queen Marsibil, he told her everything about his dealings with Sorli the Strong, and also told her that now they were reconciled and had become sworn brothers. When she heard that, she became so full of grief and rage that no one could calm her. She let it be known that she would never have peace from that day forward until Sorli were put to death, or else that he should rot like rubbish and never have peace.

Sorli heard that where he was sitting, and said quietly to himself, so that no one heard, "Now I wish that the old crone Mana, my lady friend, were here to still your arrogance."

After that, Sorli went to where the queen sat and laid his head on her knee. He said, "So has it come to pass, queen, that here you may get to look upon Sorli the Strong, as men call him. Now do as you like with him."

When the queen saw him, all her anger dwindled and she was completely dumbstruck. Then Hogni reconciled Sorli with his sister the queen. Now wine was eagerly drunk, and games were held with courtesy and politeness for the next three days.

At the conclusion of the feast, they sailed away to Norway. From there, they brought Ingibjorg and Steinvor, the daughters of King Erling and King Harald Valdimarson. Then they sailed back from Norway and home to Sweden with all their company. A lavish feast was held, and the celebrations continued. Hogni married Ingibjorg, Sorli's sister. In return, Sorli married Hogni's sister, who is not named. But Thorir the Strong married Steinvor, the daughter of King Harald Valdimarsson. These weddings were all celebrated together, with good cheer and fine celebrations and all manner of delightful entertainments that were customary for the people of that land.

At the end of the feasting, Sorli sailed back home to Norway and became king over it, but Hogni became king over Sweden and ruled it all until his dying day. He made Thorir the Strong a jarl in his kingdom. Hogni and Sorli never broke their friendship as long as they both lived, and it is not recorded whether or not any children were granted to them.

Here ends the saga of Sorli the Strong and his great deeds of valor, coming to an end in the way that has been told.

THE SAGA OF ILLUGI, GRID'S FOSTERLING

Illuga saga Gríðarfóstra

CHAPTER I

A king named Hring once ruled Denmark. He was the son of Skjold, the son of Dag. That Skjold fought with Hermann, as is told in their saga.[1]

King Hring was a wise man, well-beloved and generous with his wealth, and the greatest of warriors. He was married to a queen named Sigrid, the daughter of King William of Normandy.[2] With her he had a son named Sigurd, the handsomest of all men, and the most accomplished at sports and skills. He was kind to his friends and open-handed with wealth, but fierce to his enemies.

There was an old man named Svidi. He lived in a tenant's cottage, a very short way from the king's hall. He was married to an old woman named Hild. With her he had one son named Illugi, who was tall and strong, and adept at all games. His father was called Svidi the Bold-Attacker.[3]

Sigurd the king's son and Illugi used to play with each other. Sigurd had many playmates, and he was far above them, no matter what they competed in—but Illugi beat him in everything. And so it happened that they swore brotherhood; each one had to avenge the other, in case they were attacked with weapons. There was great affection between them.

CHAPTER II

There was a man named Bjorn. He was the king's counsellor. He did all the evil in his power. He was a liar and a schemer in every respect. Nonetheless, he was the greatest champion and defended the king's land against raiders. The king valued him highly for that. Bjorn was envious that Illugi was so dear to Sigurd the king's son, and as it happened, he slandered Illugi to both father and son, and said that Illugi was untrue to the king's son. The king listened to him, but Sigurd didn't believe it.

For some time, Sigurd the king's son stayed at home with his father, held in great honor and esteem. One day, Sigurd asked his father to give him ships and men, and said that he wanted to leave his homeland to win wealth and fame for himself. The king said that would be arranged in a month's time. "Bjorn shall go with you," said the king, "but I want Illugi to stay home."

Sigurd answered, "I very much want Illugi to go."

But the king said that Bjorn had to go with him—"because he is the greatest of all champions and never fails in combat. He will be gracious and true to you, as he has been to me." And so they ended their conversation.

After that, the king's son went to Svidi's home and told Hild what he and his father had discussed. She said that her son was young and could not go on the raid. "He is untested," she said, "and I don't want Bjorn to blame him because he doesn't dare to fight alongside you in battle." So Hild ended her speech, and the king's son returned to the hall, very unhappy.

A bondsmaid named Sunnlod was close beside Hild. She was a sorceress, and the worst of night-riding witches. She had done many men a bad turn.

Hild came to speak with Illugi, and asked him to fetch the spade which Svidi had left behind in the cowshed. He agreed. It was late in the day when Illugi set out. He went quickly and came to the shed, and found the spade there. By then night had fallen, yet he left the shed anyway. When he had gone a short distance, he was struck on the back so hard that his feet flew out from under him. The creature had a switch in hand and beat Illugi with it. It was Sunnlod who had come. Nevertheless, Illugi carried this ogress a long way, until he came to a certain large stone. He slammed the ogress down so hard against the stone that her back broke, and she lost her life. He didn't stop until he came home.

Hild, his mother, was outside when he came home. Illugi was frowning. Hild was happy. "Has anything noteworthy happened on your journey, my son?" she said. "Did you find the spade where I showed you?"

"Yes," said Illugi.

She said, "Did you find that serving-girl of mine, whom I sent to gather firewood for me?"

Illugi said, "I can hardly believe that I found a worse girl, because she rode me.[4] But I killed her like this: I broke her back against a stone."

Hild said that he could go on the journey. "And I want you to serve Sigurd the king's son, and go raiding with him," she said.

Illugi eagerly agreed and was glad to hear it. He went inside with his mother and slept that night.

In the morning, Illugi got ready to go to the king's hall. First he said farewell to his father and mother. Then he went to the hall and arrived when the king was at his morning drinking. He went before the king and greeted him warmly. The king welcomed him. But when Sigurd the king's son saw Illugi, he gave him a grand welcome and offered him a seat next to himself, and Illugi accepted. Several days passed while Sigurd stayed at home with his father and Illugi.

CHAPTER III

When Sigurd's ships were ready, the time came to sail away from land. It was decided that Bjorn and Illugi should both go. The king's son now took leave of his father. He sailed first to Orkney and Scotland, and he made many raids in both places and won many victories against the Scots, and he gained much wealth. They never headed to a place where they couldn't win a victory. All the folk were afraid of them.

In the autumn, Sigurd wanted to head for home, but they were struck by a great storm. The ship began yawing off course and was driven northwards over the sea. The sail was so strained that the seams[5] were on the verge of ripping, and all the ropes began to snap. They saw no land anywhere. The sea began to get rough, and such a great storm blew up that water poured into the ship on both sides, but so valiant were those men on the ship that they never spoke a word of fear. Now the ship began leaking badly, and they were all blown eastwards for eight days.

The ship was driven far north into the bay known as the White Sea.[6] They tied the sail down with strong ropes, but were hit by a huge wave that broke over the ship, so that it was on the verge of splintering apart. Most of the men were exhausted by then. Just then they saw land, surrounded by crags, and then the ship was driven into a bay. The sailors saved the ship and the men.

The king's son said that they should wait there for a favorable wind. Most of his men were completely worn out from their labor, and they felt so cold that death seemed likely and close at hand, for they had no fire. Sigurd the king's son bore up wonderfully well, but everyone eagerly wanted to light a fire, yet they couldn't manage it.

Then Bjorn began to get severely chilled, and he spoke in this way: "You, Illugi, must row over this fjord and search for fire. If you don't find it, then I shall claim your head. But if you do get it, then you shall have this ring which I have always had."

Illugi answered, "I certainly don't want to wager my head against you, Bjorn, but I will gladly search for fire, if it may be of help to our men." Now he rowed, alone, away from his men.

CHAPTER IV

A certain cave stood on the other side of that fjord, which Grid[7] the troll-woman ruled. She was the worst of troll-women. Illugi reached the shore and tied up his boat, and went up onto land and entered the cave. By that time, evening had come. He heard hard footfalls on the earth, and Grid came home. She asked him his name. He said that he was called Illugi.

So much snot was hanging down in front of her mouth that it looked to him as if a snowstorm or a rainstorm was pouring out of her nose. She had a beard, but was bald-headed. Her hands were like eagle's talons. Both of her sleeves were burned, and the blouse which she was wearing hung down only to her buttocks in the back, but all the way to her toes in the front. Her eyes were green, her forehead was broad, and her ears were wide and drooping down. No one could call her beautiful.

Illugi said that he wanted to fetch fire from her. Grid answered, "You'll get no fire from me unless you speak three truths[8]. If you can do that quickly, then you shall lie next to my daughter. And if you don't want to run the risk, then I don't care what happens, even if Bjorn freezes to death."

Illugi said that he was willing. And then a woman came forth. She was so beautiful that Illugi thought that he had never seen a lovelier woman. As soon as he saw her, he fell deeply in love with her. She was melancholy and spoke little.

Then Illugi spoke up: "It's time for me to offer these truths," he said. "Your cave is so high and wide that I've never seen a larger or stronger dwelling. Also, the nose on your face is so huge that I have never seen a greater monstrosity than you, and you're so dark that the floor looks bright next to you, and I have never seen anything more hideous than you. But your daughter is certainly lovely, and I see the greatest difference between the two of you, and anyone who saw you both would say the same."

Then Grid spoke. "It's certain that you want neither to praise me nor flatter me," she said, "but you don't dislike me as much as you claim. But I believe it's best for you to go to bed with my daughter and play all the games that you feel like playing, since you prefer my daughter to me. You must do it all quickly; there's not much time before daybreak."[9]

Illugi said that he would. He went to bed and took off his clothes. The old crone made her daughter ready, and she and Illugi both came together in the same bed. Illugi turned towards her[10] and enjoyed himself, but she didn't cheer up.

Then Grid grabbed Illugi by the hair and pulled him over to a tree-trunk. With her other hand, she drew a sharp and glittering knife and pointed it at his head. But Illugi lay quietly and didn't stir at all.

Grid then said very angrily, "Listen, you wicked son of a fiend,[11] why did you think I would put up with you shaming my daughter? No, you shall die on the spot."

Illugi said, "My heart has never been fearful. I came into your cave because fate intended it. Yet I can't die more than once, so I'm not afraid of your threats."

Hearing these words, Grid threw him back. He turned to his bride and was quite cheerful. And when he was at his happiest with her, Grid wrapped his hair around her hand and pulled him to the tree trunk and aimed the knife right at his head. "You're a foolhardy one, and now you'll die on the spot."

But Illugi said that he wasn't afraid of his own death.

She said, laughing, "I have never met anyone who hasn't feared death, except for you. Now go to sleep and sleep well!"

Illugi went and turned to his woman, and now she was quite happy.

Then Grid rushed at the bed once again and dragged him to the tree trunk. She waved the knife, and she scowled most horribly to see, but it all went as before. Illugi said that he wasn't afraid.

Then Grid said, "You are not like other men. Your pulse never wavered, and you aren't afraid. Now you shall accept your life from me, and with it I give you my daughter, who is named Hild. Yet I can never repay your good deed, because you have broken a great spell that was on me, because in similar encounters I have murdered and killed many, and all have been afraid of my terrible knife. I have killed sixteen brave men with this knife, though such things may not be women's work. Now I must tell you my life story. You listen."

CHAPTER V

"A king named Ali ruled over Alfheim.[12] He was married to a queen named Alfrun. They had one daughter, named Signy. She was accomplished in every way. As soon as Signy came of age, she was betrothed to a king called Eirik. He died on a Viking expedition in the west. They had a daughter together named Hild, and she was the loveliest maiden. Then Signy went to her father's home and stayed with him. The queen caught a sickness which brought about her death. The king wasn't much concerned, but Signy stayed in her bower and deeply mourned her husband and her mother.

"Then the king took a queen named Grimhild. She was fair to see, but on the inside she was the worst ogre. The king loved her very much. They were able to have seven daughters, and they all took after their mother and became the most dreadful ogre-women. With Grimhild's coming, it happened that a man in the kingdom would disappear every night, and everyone supposed that Grimhild must be the cause.

"Now the king grew old, and the queen felt that their relationship was less satisfactory than she wanted. She planned to betray the king and get another young man for herself. She poisoned him, and he died at once and was laid in a mound next to his queen. Grimhild became so evil that she despoiled the entire kingdom of both riches and men.

"After this deed of Grimhild's, she went to the bower where Signy and her daughter were sitting, and when she came there, she said this: 'You, Signy, 'have long stayed here in great honor and happiness, but I shall take all that away from you. I lay this upon you: you shall depart from here and dwell in a cave and become the worst of troll-women. You shall be named Grid. Your daughter shall go with you, and every man who sees her shall fall deeply in love with her. You shall murder every one whom you see in her bed. You have seven sisters. They shall battle with you every night. They shall tear you all to pieces, slash you and maim you, but you shall never die. Never shall you escape from this spell, until you meet the man who is not afraid of your terrible knife when you brandish it. And because men will find it horrifying, he will never be found.'

"Signy could not speak for her grief and weeping. Hild said, 'Grimhild, I want to pay you back for your spell. I hereby declare that you shall stand with one foot on this bower, and the other foot on the king's hall. Slaves shall kindle a bonfire between your feet. That fire shall burn both night and day, and all your lower parts shall burn from the fire, but your upper parts shall freeze, so that you will never get your rest. But if we two, mother and daughter, get out of this spell, then you shall die and tumble down into the fire.'[13]

"Then Grimhild spoke up. 'Our talk is very foolish, and I wish neither of these curses to be valid.'

"Hild said that these words would stand.

"The mother and her daughter departed into the cave, and I am that same Signy, and here is Hild, my daughter. Now I want to betroth you to her and so reward you, for you have brought me out of the spell."

As this story was ending, seven ogres with sharp blades entered the cave, and they rushed at Grid and struck at her, hard and often. Hild was terribly afraid. Illugi lent his aid to Grid and struck at them both furiously and often, and he didn't stop until they had killed them all. They burned them all in a bonfire.

Then Grid said, "Now, Illugi, you have freed us both from these ogres. I have dealt with them for eleven winters."

Illugi said that had been long enough.

CHAPTER VI

After that, Grid went with Illugi and his bride to his boat, and she gave them gold and many costly treasures, and she brought fire with her.

She parted with them there. Illugi rowed back to his men. They were glad of that and got themselves warm.

For a month the king's son was anchored there, never getting a favorable wind. Bjorn recognized Hild, and said that Illugi had frequently visited her in the cave, and he said that she was the greatest troll-woman. Sigurd ordered Bjorn to be silent; he didn't want to believe what Bjorn said.

It happened one night that the king's son's men were sleeping on the ship, and when they woke up, they saw that Bjorn had disappeared. They looked for him and saw that he was hanging from the sail-yard. They didn't know what Bjorn's death meant, but Grid had hanged Bjorn that night because he had called Hild a troll-woman.[14]

After that, Sigurd sailed away from Finnmark, and there he got a favorable wind and came home to Denmark. He had gotten much wealth, and he gave away gold with both hands. Now he stayed home with his father. Illugi lived with Sigurd for a long time, even though he had a large farm next to the king's hall.

A little later, King Hring caught the illness that brought about his death. Right away, Sigurd held an inheritance-feast for his father and had all the best men in the land summoned, and then Sigurd was raised to the kingship over the realm that his father had owned. King Hring had been a petty king in Denmark, and he had ruled Skåne.[15]

Now Signy came to Denmark, and Illugi and Hild welcomed her. Illugi said that he would share everything with her. King Sigurd asked for her hand in marriage. Signy said that Illugi should be the man to give her in marriage. Sigurd then talked the matter over with him, and with her consent, Illugi betrothed Signy to him. Their married life was good, and they had many children who all became men of distinction. King Sigurd and Queen Signy lived very long, and Illugi lived longer, but nothing is known about any children that he and Hild may have had. This Illugi later became the sworn-brother of Gnod-Asmund.[16]

And so we end this saga.

THE TALE OF ASMUND OGRE-LUCKY

Inntak úr söguþætti af Ásmundi flagðagæfu

In a valley far from the populated areas of Norway, there lived an old man and an old woman. They had three sons. The oldest was called Grim, the second was Thorir, and the third was Asmund. Grim and Thorir were handsome and well-mannered. They had the task of tending the old couple's sheep, and bringing useful things to their farm. This verse tells about it:

An old man lived in a far-off land,
his sons they numbered three,
in many ways a kindly man,
as you can plainly see.
Grim and Thorir tended sheep,
and served him as sons should,
and so a careful watch they'd keep
o'er their parents' worldly goods.[1]

Asmund wasn't like his brothers. He lay in the hearth-house[2] and didn't concern himself with anything that had to be done. His father loved him little, but his mother loved him much.[3]

At the time, Olaf Haraldsson was king over Norway. Many bold young men who wanted to seek their fortunes felt that it was the greatest honor to go to meet him and offer to serve him. The same idea occurred to Grim and Thorir; they wanted to take this course of action, and they informed their father. He welcomed this, and said that their manliness would increase, and that this journey would certainly bring them honor and fame. He prepared them to leave home as best he could, and he gave them everything they needed, except for a horse to ride.

They left their home on foot, and traveled continuously for three days, until they came to a certain lake. They saw a man there, tall and stout, walking along the lake. He was herding his cattle together, and walking with a dog. The man looked hideous to them, and fear gripped their chests at once. They said that they would much rather be poor and close to their father than have their lives in the hands of a troll. They turned back and went home to their father. The old man was astonished that they had come back so quickly. He became quite vexed and spoke to them sharply, and said it was bad to have sons who accomplished nothing. He talked so much and so loudly that Asmund heard it in the hearth-house. He burst out laughing, but didn't say a word. The old man became even more annoyed, and said that the idiot didn't need to chuckle at this, since it all would have gone worse for him.

"I don't know until I've tried," said Asmund.

So ended their conversation.

Some time later, Grim and Thorir wanted to leave their home again. The old man's urgings, more than their own desire, drove them to do what had to be done. They said that now their trip must not go as it had before, and they must not give up before they had met King Olaf and become his men. Then the old man got them ready for their journey as best he could. But meanwhile, the old woman went to Asmund in the hearth-house and told him what his brothers intended to do. Out of affection, she begged him to go with them. "I think no less of you than them," she said, "and it seems wrong to me that they should become men of renown, and not you."

Asmund said that he was very reluctant, and he didn't accept what she said at all. But as they conversed, she told him to stand up, go to his father and ask for supplies for the journey. He said that he wouldn't do it. She took off all the rags and tatters that he had on. She washed and combed his hair, and then it was as golden as silk and fell down to his shoulders. Then she put good clothes on him. Outfitted in this way, he stood up, and he was more handsome and magnificent than any man.

Then the old woman went to her husband and told him what had happened between her and Asmund, and she asked him to give him something for the journey, like his brothers. The old man was dumbfounded and said that she was too stupid for words, if she imagined that such a filthy man could accomplish anything. "Still, I'm willing to let him have something" he said, "but don't let that dunce come into my sight."

With that, the old man went to his smithy, which was set apart from the hearth-house. A fire had been newly made on the ground in front of it. The old man stepped up into the smithy and reached up to the roof, and he took down a mailcoat, a helmet, and a shield, all of them rusted through. But when he tried to step down, he and the smithy tumbled down into the fire; the armor fell out of his hands and went every which way. Asmund let the old man lie there, but picked up the armor and scraped off the rust.

Then the old woman came up and said to Asmund, "Now, my son, you must be able to hold onto what you have in your hands, because your father won't outfit you with any more weaponry than he already has, both because he's in a bad mood and because he's been hurt in the fire. I will now contribute something that may turn out to be somewhat helpful, and give you my poker."

She put a knife in his hand, large and black and well worth having. She said, "I received this knife as an inheritance from my father, but I haven't done with it as I should, and I've used it to poke the fire in a pinch. Keep it, my son, and carry it always.[4] I now pronounce that from now on, all your dealings shall yield good fortune and prosperity for you."

Asmund accepted the knife and went out behind the hut to a great stone that was standing there. He struck the stone with the knife, and it didn't stop, but split the stone completely through. Asmund looked around and saw that the old woman lay dead on the floor with a gaping wound on her. She had died at the instant that he struck the stone, because it was her life-stone.[5] Asmund found this to be a terrible and evil deed.

Now the three brothers went from the place together, and left their cold household. Thorir and Grim begged Asmund not to go the way that they went before, and they said that certain death was there. Asmund paid no attention to that, and they went that same way. They didn't stop their journey until they came into a great forest, and then to a certain moor. There they saw a large hut, and a very tall man walking. He was carrying a bear on his back, and was heading for the hut, though he still had quite a way to go. The moment that Grim and Thorir saw the man, fear flew into their breasts, and they earnestly begged Asmund not to go to the hut—"or else we'll all be killed."

Asmund had to gather moss to cover them up. They stayed behind, but Asmund went to the hut. He walked in through the open door, and let the door swing halfway shut, then dashed behind the door and stood there. A hound ran in front of the giant, huge and ferocious, but the giant came more slowly, because he had a heavy load to carry. The hound charged fiercely into the hut, but Asmund hurriedly got out and slammed the door behind him, and now the dog was inside. Then the giant arrived and threw down his burden: the bear and a large bundle of birds.[6] Asmund greeted him and said, "Welcome, good sir."

"You'll never be welcome," said the giant. "But where are your brothers, those miserable cowards? They won't have any bolder hearts the next time we meet. But from you I can expect evil. Still, you may skin the animal with me, if you want."

"We may well brag, sir," said Asmund, "but what is your name?"

"That's not lacking," said the giant, "I'm called Nadd."[7]

Then they skinned the bear, and Asmund finished first. He wrapped the skin around his hand and struck Nadd in the ear with it. Nadd got angry at that and asked why this knave had beaten him. Asmund laughed and said that it was customary when two people were skinning together that the one who finished first had to box the slower one's ear with the skin. The poet tells of this:

"If you slap me with that skin,
soon you'll have regrets."
Asmund jumped up with a grin:
"You really shouldn't fret.
Those who win a skinning bout
must show their skill and pride,
and give the loser's ear a clout
with the bloody hide."

Then Asmund and Nadd leaped to their feet and began to fight in earnest. Their fight was the fiercest, and neither spared the other. The dog in the hut heard what was happening outside. He was in a bad situation, separated from his master, and he began to howl ferociously and tear at the door, but he didn't get out. And the encounter between Asmund and Nadd ended thus: Asmund felled Nadd and killed him.

Asmund's brothers lay in the moss while Asmund and Nadd were fighting, and now and then they peeked out from underneath. But when Nadd had fallen, Asmund began running towards where they lay, and he cried out in a loud voice and said that the giant was chasing him, and begged them to help him. He did this to test them. They were all the more terrified and crouched down for as long as they could. Then Asmund tore the moss from them and said that Nadd was dead. They were overjoyed. They jumped up and went with Asmund to the hut. Now they showed their manful courage and gave Nadd many great blows where he was lying there dead. Then they took his corpse and burned it to ashes.

Asmund cut a stick for himself and took it to the doors, and opened them up. The dog rushed at him with gaping jaws and wanted to tear him up. At once Asmund stuck the stick crosswise into his maw.[8] At that, the dog lay down and crept to Asmund's feet, and tears ran down his muzzle. Asmund petted the dog and said these words to him: "Now I will become your master, in place of Nadd. You must render me all the same services that you rendered him."

Then the dog stood up and fawned on Asmund and followed him ever after, and he became the greatest help to Asmund when he had to deal with evil beings. This is remembered in the poem:

Asmund petted his hound's fur,
his words made it glad:
"All your life you'll serve me, cur,
just as you served Nadd."

They went away from there soon, and Asmund didn't stop until he met King Olaf and became his retainer. He proved himself to be the boldest man in all dangerous situations, and he always accompanied the king. The king held him very dear. Asmund was the foremost retainer, wherever hardships were shared.

It's said that at one time, King Olaf was resting quietly, after he had traveled throughout Norway and made all the folk of the land Christian. A decree came from him that there would be no man in Norway who had not accepted Christianity, neither along the mountains nor along the seacoast. As the poet said:

We've made Norway Christian now,
from mountains to the sea.

His retainers answered the king's summons and said, "We don't think that all the folk in Norway are Christian, because on an island in the north, along the coast, lives that woman named Thorgerd, called Holdatroll.[9] She has not accepted the faith, and she has settled on that island for a long time but paid no tribute. Some of your men have been sent there to fetch the tribute, but none has come back. Thorgerd is full of sorcery and is the worst to deal with."

This seemed a serious matter to the king, and he discussed with his men whether someone would go to the island and get the tribute. All said that they were unwilling. They said that anyone who went into Thorgerd's clutches would certainly perish, and they listed all the dangers. In the end, no one volunteered for the journey.

Then the king talked with Asmund and asked him to go. Asmund said, "I'm not very capable for this journey which everyone refuses. But for the sake of what you command, lord, I offer myself, as the man most obliged to do what you want. I shall venture on the journey, whatever may happen."

The king was happy with Asmund's words, and he asked him to promise to avenge his men. Then he had a ship made ready, and brought to it the men that Asmund wanted to have. And when they were prepared, Asmund talked to the king and asked him to lend him his own luck; he said that there was great need of it, considering what he had to face. The king agreed to this.[10]

Asmund and his men sailed away, and they didn't swerve from their course until they came to the island and landed at a certain place. They saw a large and stately house on the island, and they were certain that Thorgerd must have her abode there.

Then Asmund said to his men, "Now you must wait for me here at the ship, and I will go to the house and find out what's going on."

They begged him to be careful. So he went to the house, and when he arrived, he saw no one outside. He went around the farm, and made tracks in a ring all around the farm. The doors weren't locked. Asmund went in, and he called out in every building, but he never found anyone.

Finally, he came to a certain building, a long way inside the farm. He entered and saw a young and outstandingly beautiful woman, sitting at her sewing. Asmund addressed her courteously. She received his greeting well. She asked who he might be and what his name was. He said that his name was Asmund and that he was a retainer of King Olaf, and then he asked her name and family.

She answered, "I am called Hladvor. My mother is called Thorgerd, and she rules over this island and lives at this farm. My father is dead."

"Where is your mother now?" said Asmund.

"She is out fishing," said Hladvor.

"When is she coming home?" said Asmund.

"In a little while," said Hladvor. "Do you have business with her?"

"I certainly do," said Asmund. "I've been sent from King Olaf to fetch tribute from you, which she has long withheld from the chieftains in Norway. He has called for the tribute to be sent to where he is king over the land."

Hladvor said, "Many have come here for this reason. I feel certain that you won't be here any longer than any of them. But it will be said that you've had good luck if you succeed in getting the tribute."

Asmund said, "Will you come with me to meet King Olaf? That's much better for you than to stay here in heathenry and idolatry."

"I won't be unwilling, if you beat my mother and get the tribute," said Hladvor. "But I will ask this of you: if your fortune proves greater, do not abandon my mother dead. And you must not stay here for long, since my mother is so little disposed to let men talk with me."

Then Asmund went outside and concealed himself somewhere by the farm. Now Thorgerd came home and didn't see Asmund. She went inside to her daughter and said that a guest had come.

"How do you know that?" said Hladvor.

Thorgerd answered, "When I came to the farm, I saw his tracks on all sides. And when I walked over the tracks, my feet burned. The one who has done this must certainly have greater power than the others who have sought our home."

Then Thorgerd went back outside and saw Asmund, and she said, "Here you have come, Asmund. I recognize you clearly. You killed Nadd, and his hound goes with you. I know why you have come here: you have to fetch tribute from this island for King Olaf."

"It's as you say," said Asmund. "Now you must do one of two things: pay tribute, or get off the island."

Thorgerd replied, "This choice must be put off until I have put you through the same tests as the others who have come on this mission. Yet I don't know whether I'll stand the heat better than you."

"That may be," said Asmund, "but I will certainly risk whatever test you want to try."

This was Thorgerd's first trick: she could wade through fire so that she wasn't hurt. Now she had a fire built, and she walked up to it and waded as she had done before. Then she asked Asmund to come up and do the same. Asmund went up to the fire and made the sign of the cross over it. He waded through the fire and took no harm at all.

Her second trick was this: he had to take a sword and strike at Thorgerd's bare foot, which she would place on a stump. They went to the stump, and he struck with all his might, but the sword bit no more than if it were cutting stone. Now Thorgerd had to strike. Asmund laid his foot on the stump and made the sign of the cross over it. Thorgerd struck with both hands and thought the sword would pass clean through, but the sword turned in her hands and injured them.[11]

Thorgerd said, "You're not alone in these games, Asmund. Yet the tests aren't complete unless you've been tested three times. There's one test left that we have to try. I promise that if you beat me, I shall abandon the island and take nothing from it for myself, from now on. Now you must come with me to my smithy, and we shall try the heat-game." Asmund wasn't familiar with that game.

They went to the smithy, and Asmund sat down in the cinder-pit. Thorgerd brought him an iron rod and asked him to forge six nails and heat each one glowing hot. "You shall swallow three," she said, "and I the other three."

Asmund did as she said. He forged two nails, one after the other, and brought them to Thorgerd. She took them and swallowed them both.[12] Then Asmund forged the third, and he blessed it with the sign of the cross. He gave it to Thorgerd, and she did the same as with the others. As soon as that nail came into her mouth, it burned her so terribly that it took away her speech and all her strength. She lay there, but Asmund left and went off to his men, and ordered them to go to the farm and carry off all the valuables from there. They did so.

Asmund went to Hladvor and told her what had happened with him and Thorgerd, and where her possessions were being taken. He asked whether she should be brought away or left there in peace. Hladvor said, "My mother's nature is little suited for other people, and she will turn to her own kin. For that reason, it's best for her to be left here."

Asmund had all the money and treasures that had been found taken and brought to the ship. He took Hladvor and brought her away with him, but Thorgerd was left behind and is out of the saga. Leaving matters as they stood, Asmund and his crew sailed away. Their journey went well, and they met with King Olaf. He welcomed Asmund and asked him to accept his thanks for the journey. Asmund gave the king all the wealth that he took on the island, and that was a great deal. Hladvor was brought before the king, and was thought to be the loveliest and most well-mannered of women. She was baptized and made a Christian.

With this accomplished, Asmund brought forth his suit and asked the king to marry Hladvor to him. He said the king should arrange for her betrothal. The king gave a favorable answer and said that there was no more fitting match, and so it was that Asmund betrothed himself to Hladvor, and the king held their wedding feast. Later, the king let people settle on the island, but Asmund and Hladvor stayed with him, highly honored.

Somewhat later, a report came to King Olaf that there were still men, up against a mountain range away from human habitation, who didn't hold to the Christian faith. It was said that there were apparently some folk who lived in some hidden valley north of Namdalen, just a few on a farm, who practiced the old ways and worshipped some monstrous beast. The king was astonished at this and wanted to know the truth with certainty. He swiftly had an expedition prepared and rode north to the valley. Asmund was with him, and as always, the dog Nadd's Gift went with him. There are two other men named here, Grim and Sigurd; they were bold and excellent men.

They now rode following the path out of the inhabited regions, until they came into a certain valley. There they saw a large farm and headed for it. But when they came close to the farm, the king rode off and circled the entire farm. There was no one outside.

A little later, an old man came out. He greeted the king and said that he and his men were welcome, and invited him to come into the house.

The king accepted and went in with all his men. There were good living quarters, and a common room laid out with everything. A fine feast soon began, and there was no lack of good ale or anything else to drink. The housewife came into the room, with the couple's son. Their daughter sat on a dais in the room with her sewing, and she was both young and beautiful. The feast went on splendidly, but the king was always looking around to see whether or not he might see some other strange new thing. The old man was most hospitable, and begged the king to condescend to eat something. The king said that he would accept some food.

At once there came into the room a strange and monstrous beast. It carried a most magnificent linen cloth decorated with gold, the greatest treasure. The beast came up to the table and spread the cloth on it. This was the trusted deity of the old man and woman and their son, but their daughter didn't worship it and was always annoyed by it. Mother and daughter often quarreled over it. It was nothing but a horse's cock, which the old man and wife had worshipped with sacrifices and made powerful with such great devilish craft that it walked around with them like a man, and worked at everything that they needed done. It also went to various dwellings, stole money and treasures, and brought them home.

Now two different things at once seemed ominous to the king: first, how wretched that thing was that spread the tablecloth, but on the other hand, how handsome the cloth was; it seemed to the king to be a fitting possession for worthy folk.

Asmund sat at the head of the table. He spoke up and asked what sort of devil that was who spread the tablecloth. The old woman heard that and said, "I don't let any man blaspheme my god."

"Is that your god?" said the king.

"It certainly is," said the old woman. "All three of us believe in him, my husband and I and our son, but my daughter is so ill-disposed that she won't offer him any service, however I ask."

"Does your god have any name?" said the king.

"He certainly has," said the old woman. "He's called Volski."

At that moment, it brought food to the table: it was bear meat and enormously fat sausages. So said the poet:

On the table there was bear meat and a jug of beer,
sausages of monstrous size,
the king's men stared with open eyes.[13]

Then the king said, "I have come here on a mission to preach Christianity. You must no longer believe in this devil, but rather in Almighty God, who shaped heaven and earth and all things."

The old woman answered, "It seems to me, king, that the god whom you preach couldn't bring me more treasures and other goods than this one, whom I have long served."

The king said, "That thing which you have served is nothing but an evil spirit which you all have summoned from Hell with wicked words. It has only brought you what it stole from others, and what it intends for you in the end is the eternal loss of your life and soul."

The king spoke long and bravely of his mission and preached the true faith to them. The old woman spoke harshly against him, and asked the king not to go on with this stupid notion that she should believe in a different god than Volski, come what may.

Now Volski came to serve them at the table. It happened that he reached out over the table to where Asmund was sitting. Asmund quickly stood up and grabbed Volski, shoved him face down, and ordered the demon to come out. At once, Volski turned into a troll and grabbed Asmund, but Asmund shoved the table forward with everything on it. A fierce fight broke out between him and Volski. The old woman rose up and attacked the king. The old man attacked Sigurd, and the man's son attacked Grim, but the maiden sat quietly and didn't take part.

Now all of them were grappling so ferociously that no one held back his strength. Most of the things in the common room was knocked out of place, and many were broken. The first thing that happened was that the old woman got the king onto one knee. Then he wrapped his arms around her, flung her down onto her back, and broke her spine, and so she lost her life. She was the first to perish of those that the king had to deal with. The king said that he had never wrestled with a worse ogre than that old woman.

Now the king rushed to where Asmund and Volski were fighting. He felt that Asmund was in great need of help, but the others needed it less. Asmund and Volski were fighting savagely. The dog growled with all the fierceness that he had, and he tore at Volski mercilessly. Now there were three surrounding him all together: the king, Asmund, and the dog, and all of them had all they could handle.

Next it happened that Sigurd slew the old man, for he was weary on account of old age. Not long after, Grim killed the old man's son; their fighting had been the fiercest, for both were young and very strong. They hurried to help the king and Asmund, and so they had four in all against Volski. In the end, after a long struggle, by the grace of God and by King Olaf's luck, they were able to overcome the fiend, although they were all exhausted. Asmund said later that he never had to deal with such overwhelming strength, nor come into such a trial, as when he fought Volski. Some people said that Asmund came away from this more irritable in mood than before.[14] So ended the fight.

Now the old man's daughter began to weep, not because her family was diminished, but she thought that the king would take her as punishment for the evil deeds of her elders and kill her at their feet. The king quickly noticed that, and told her to cheer up, and said that he intended nothing else for her but what would suit her well. "You shall go with me," he said, "and accept Christianity. Then I will make your lot in life so good that you may enjoy it well."

The king now took everything of value on the farm. Much wealth was brought together, and many good treasures. Then he ordered his men to burn the farm and those who had been left inside. He said that he didn't want evil-doers to be drawn there, and so it was all burned to ashes.

Then the king said to Asmund, "Now I will augment your name and call you Asmund Ogre-Lucky. I think that very few men now living have had such good luck in triumphing over ogres and monsters as you."

"Your words are good," said Asmund, "but what should go with the name?"

The king gave him a gold ring and said that he should keep that as a name-fastening.[15] Ever since then, he was called Asmund Ogre-Lucky, and he bore that nickname as long as he lived. After that, the king went home and brought the farmer's daughter with him. So said the poet:

The king brought the farmer's daughter from a northern dale,
never did she cast a spell,
the wise rings'-prop° did quite well.[16] *rings' prop*: woman

It's said that some time afterwards, Asmund went to visit his father, and found him still living. When they met, the old man didn't recognize his own son, and asked who he was.

Asmund said, "I remember the day when you blamed me that you fell from your smithy into the fire and nearly died."

The poem tells about this:

"You knew me once, you silly soul,
when you suffered disgrace;
you fell headfirst into the coals
and landed on your face."

And so ends this summary of the saga-tale of Asmund Ogre-Lucky.

NOTES

Introduction

1 *History of the Danes* I.19-23, ed. Ellis-Davidson and Fisher, pp. 21-24.

2 *Fornaldarsögur* dealing with giant fosterage include *Örvar-Odds saga*, *Hjálmþers saga ok Ölvis*, *Ketils saga hængs*, *Gríms saga loðinkinna*, and *Egils saga einhenda*, besides those in this book. For *riddarasögur*, see Matyushina, "Magic Mirrors, Monsters, Maiden-Kings," p. 3.

3 Gallo, "Giantess as Foster-Mother," p. 12-17. *Bárðar saga Snæfellsáss*, *Orms þáttr Stórolfssonar*, *Grettis saga*, and *Gunnars saga Keldugnúpsfífls* depict versions of fosterage by giants, as do "post-classical" sagas such as *Þorsteins saga Geirnefjufóstra* and *Ármanns saga in fyrri*. Human *fóstrur* who resemble giantesses include Þorgerðr Brák in *Egils saga Skallagrímssonar*, Þuríðr in *Grettis saga*, and Syrpa in *Finnboga saga ramma*.

4 For an older but still useful review, see Ellis, "Fostering by Giants."

5 Kalinké, "Norse Romance," pp. 316-317.

6 Hume, "From Saga to Romance," p. 3.

7 Straubhaar, "Nasty, Brutish, and Large", p. 106.

8 For a recent overview of opinions, see Quinn, "Interrogating Genre". Scholars who have argued against the existence of definable saga genres include Ross, *Prolonged Echoes*, vol. 2, pp. 50-51; O'Connor, *Icelandic Histories and Romances*, pp. 41-46; Waggoner, *Sagas of Ragnar Lodbrok*, pp. xi-xiv.

9 Haraldsdóttir, "Flateyjarbók", pp. 197-198.

10 Transl. Hollander, *Heimskringla*, pp. 51-58.

11 *Haralds saga Hárfagra* ch. 25; transl. Hollander, *Heimskringla*, pp. 80-81.

12 *Bárðar saga Snæfellsáss* ch. 1-2, transl. O'Connor, *Iceland Histories & Romances*, pp. 185-188.

13 e.g. *Flóamanna saga* ch. 1; *Orms þáttr Stórolfssonar* ch. 1.

14 It may not be wholly without interest that Kjalarnes is just north of the modern city of Reykjavík. Many of the saga locations can now be reached by the Reykjavík city bus system.

15 Danielson, "*Kjalnesinga saga*," p. 356.

16 This motif also appears in "sagas of poets" such as *Gunnlaugs saga örmstungu* and *Bjarnar saga Hítdælakappa*.

17 Norwegian folktales about giants and trolls in the Dovrefjell were a source for Henrik Ibsen's play *Peer Gynt*. Peer fathers a child on the daughter of Dovregubben (the Dovre-Master or Old Man of Dovre), the king of the trolls of the Dovrefjell, and he is almost adopted by the Dovre-Master as a troll himself (Act II). He later encounters the king's daughter and their son but refuses to admit paternity (Act III). This is in fact a fairly close parallel to *Kjalnesinga saga*, although the saga was probably not his source.

18 Danielson, "*Kjalnesinga saga*," p. 356; Gísli Sigurðsson, *Gaelic Influence in Iceland*, pp. 90-93.

19 Danielson, "*Jökuls þáttr Búasonar*," p. 348.

20 Finlay, "*Brandkrossa þáttr*," p. 56.

21 *FN* vol. 2, pp. 95-110; translated in Bachman and Erlingsson, *Six Old Icelandic Sagas*, pp. 72-84.

22 Jorgensen, "*Hálfdanar saga Brönufóstra*," p. 261.

23 Jesch, "*Illuga saga Gríðarfóstra*", pp. 322-333.

24 D732 in Thompson, *Motif-Index*, vol. 2, p. 84. See Folks and Lindahl, "Loathly Lady", pp. 600-602. Three other *fornaldarsögur* make use of the Loathly Lady: *Hrólfs saga kraka*, *Þorsteins saga Víkingssonar*, and *Gríms saga loðinkinna*.

25 Z116 in Thompson, vol. 5, p. 560. See MacKillop, "Sovereignty, Lady", pp. 390-391.

26 Jesch, "*Ásmundar saga Flagðagæfu*", pp. 103-107.

27 Driscoll, "Editing the *Fornaldarsögur Norðurlanda*", p. 208.

28 Vígfusson and Unger, *Flateyjarbók*, vol. 2, pp. 331-336.

29 Vígfusson and Unger, *Flateyjarbók*, vol. 1, pp. 337-338.

30 Vígfusson and Unger, *Flateyjarbók*, vol. 1, pp. 292, 296-298.

31 Kvideland and Sehmsdorf, *Scandinavian Folk Belief and Legend*, ch. 39,

pp. 175-179.

32 *Skáldskaparmál* ch. 54, st. 300a; ed. Faulkes, p. 83.

33 *Bárðar saga snæfellsáss* ch. 1; transl. O'Connor, *Icelandic Histories & Romances*, pp. 185-186.

34 *Þorsteins þáttr bæjarmagns* chs. 5, 6; transl. Pálsson and Edwards, *Seven Viking Romances*, pp. 263-265.

35 *Þorsteins saga Víkingssonar* ch. 1; transl. Waggoner, *Sagas of Fridthjof the Bold*, p. 2.

36 *Örvar-Odds saga* ch. 18; transl. Pálsson and Edwards, *Seven Viking Romances*, p. 76.

37 *Þrymskviða* 22; transl. Hollander, *Poetic Edda*, p. 108.

38 *Helgakviða Hjörvarðssonar* 25; transl. Hollander, *Poetic Edda*, p. 175.

39 Motz, "Old Icelandic Giants and their Names," p. 314.

40 *Gylfaginning* 15, ed. Faulkes, p. 17.

41 *Hávamál* 140, transl. Hollander, *Poetic Edda*, p. 36.

42 *Skáldskaparmál* G58, ed. Faulkes, p. 4. Odin is often interpreted as cheating Gunnlod and stealing the mead, but the text clearly says that *lofaði hon honum*, "she permitted him," to take three drinks of the mead.

43 *Skírnismál*, transl. Hollander, *Poetic Edda*, pp. 65-73.

44 *Gylfaginning* 23, ed. Faulkes, pp. 23-24.

45 Motz, "Giants in Mythology and Folklore," pp. 75-76.

46 *Landnámabók* (*Sturlubók*) 208; transl. Pálsson and Edwards, p. 94

47 Einar Svensson, *Folk-Stories of Iceland*, pp. 163-170.

48 Kvideland and Sehmsdorf, *Scandinavian Folk Belief and Legend*, ch. 55, pp. 299-313.

49 Motz, "The Families of Giants," p. 232.

50 Motz, "The Families of Giants," p. 222.

51 Motz, "The Families of Giants," p. 235.

52 Cleasby and Vigfusson, *Dictionary*, p. 498.

53 Motz, "The Families of Giants," pp. 229-230.

54 Einar Svensson, *Folk-Stories of Iceland*, p. 163.

55 *Hrólfs saga kraka* ch. 23, transl. Byock, p. 50.

56 *Eyrbyggja saga* ch. 63; Thorolf Lame-Foot's body had to be cremated to stop him from walking after death and causing harm. A cow who licked up the ashes from his pyre gave birth to the trollish bull.

57 *Örvar-Odds saga* ch. 19, transl. Pálsson and Edwards, *Seven Viking*

Romances, pp. 81-82.

58 *Flateyjarbók*, vol. II, p. 7.

59 *Orkneyinga saga* ch. 88, transl. Pálsson and Edwards, pp. 175-177; *Magnússona saga* ch. 6, transl. Hollander, *Heimskringla*, p. 692.

60 *Óláfs saga Tryggvasonar* ch. 33; transl. Hollander, *Heimskringla*, pp. 173-174. These four guardians are depicted on Iceland's modern coat of arms.

61 *Landnámabók*, *Sturlubók* ch. 329; transl. Pálsson and Edwards, p. 126.

62 Hastrup, *Culture and History*, pp. 60-64.

63 Hastrup, *Culture and History*, pp. 147-154. Ross (*Prolonged Echoes*, vol. 1, pp. 50-56) argues for a more complex conceptual model with multiple concentric circles (such as an outermost one for beings like Útgarða-Loki and the Midgard Serpent, which are literally anti-social beings that the gods cannot control) and with both vertical and horizontal dimensions. I believe that Hastrup's model is adequate, as long as it is remembered that it is fractal: the *Innangarðr/Útgarðr* division repeats itself on multiple spatial scales.

64 Hastrup, *Culture and History*, pp. 136-137.

65 Hastrup, *Culture and History*, p. 121.

66 *Njáls saga* ch. 70.

67 *Sörla saga sterka* ch. 8; *FN* vol. 3, p. 204.

68 Hastrup, *Culture and History*, p. 151.

69 e.g. *Óláfs saga helga* ch. 133; transl. Hollander, *Heimskringla*, pp. 403-408.

70 *Orkneyinga saga* chs. 87-88, transl. Pálsson and Edwards, pp. 169-177.

71 For example, in the myths of the building of the walls of Asgard, told in *Gylfaginning* 42, ed. Faulkes, p. 34, and alluded to in *Völuspá* 25-26, transl. Hollander, *Poetic Edda*, p. 5. Ross's *Prolonged Echoes*, vol. 1, expands on this theme of "the gods' designs upon the giants" in far more detail than I can go into here.

72 e.g. Thorolf's alliance with King Faravið of Kvenland in *Egils saga*, chs. 14, 17, or the crusaders' trading in *Orkneyinga saga* ch. 88, transl. Pálsson and Edwards, p. 177.

73 e.g. Skaði's acceptance among the gods in *Skáldskaparmál* G56, ed. Faulkes, p. 2; Thor carrying Aurvandil and being healed by Gróa

in *Skáldskaparmál* 17, ed. Faulkes, p. 22; Thor's friendly liaison with the giantess Arinnefja in *Egils saga einhenda* ch. 12 (*FN* vol. 3, p. 172).

74 e.g. Odin giving up his eye as a pledge when he drinks from Mimir's Well, in *Gylfaginning* 15, ed. Faulkes, p. 17.)

75 e.g. Hrungnir's story in *Skáldskaparmál* 17, ed. Faulkes, pp. 20-22.

76 *Hálfdanar saga Brönufóstra* ch. 6.

77 Hastrup, *Culture and History*, pp. 148-149.

78 *Grettis saga* chs. 64-67, 72; *Völsunga saga* ch. 8, *FN*, vol. 1, pp. 15-16.

79 *Skáldskaparmál* 18, ed. Faulkes, pp. 24-25.

80 *Skáldskaparmál* 1, ed. Faulkes, p. 1; *ibid.* 33, pp. 40-41; *Hymiskviða* 39, transl. Hollander, *Poetic Edda*, p. 89; *Lokasenna*, Introduction, *ibid.*, pp. 90-91.

81 *Völsunga saga* ch. 22; *FN*, vol. 1, p. 46.

82 *Norna-Gests þáttr* ch. 7; *FN*, vol. 1, p. 181.

83 Motz, "Giants in Folklore and Mythology," pp. 73-74.

84 *History of the Danes* I.21-22; transl. Davidson and Fisher, pp. 22-23. Note that Ellis-Davidson suggests that the giantess's variable shape has been borrowed from Boethius's *Consolation of Philosophy* (*ibid.*, n27).

85 In a poem by Bragi Boddason, quoted as stanza 52 in *Skáldskaparmál* 4, ed. Faulkes, p. 16.

86 *Gautreks saga* ch. 7; Saxo Grammaticus, *History of the Danes* VI.182-183; transl. Davidson and Fisher, p. 170.

87 *Skirnismál* 31, transl. Hollander, *Poetic Edda*, p. 71.

88 *Hymiskviða* 8, transl. Hollander, *Poetic Edda*, p. 84. See stanza 36 of the same poem for a reference to giants as *folkdrótt fjölhöfðaðr*, "a many-headed host."

89 Hume, "From Saga to Romance", p. 5.

90 Eremenko, "Dual World", pp. 2, 6.

91 Motz, "Giants in Folklore and Mythology", p. 71.

92 *Grettis saga* ch. 66.

93 *Þorsteins saga Víkingssonar* ch. 2; transl. Waggoner, *Sagas of Fridthjof the Bold*, p. 3.

94 *Hjálmþés saga ok Ölvis* ch. 13; transl. O'Connor, *Icelandic Histories & Romances*, pp. 146-147.

95 *Hrólfs saga Gautrekssonar* ch. 19; *FN*, vol. 3, p. 99.

96 *Hálfdanar saga Brönufóstra* ch. 4.

97 e.g. *Þorsteins þáttr bæjarmagns* chs. 6-7, *FN* vol. 3, pp. 406-407; *Bárðar saga Snæfellsáss* chs. 10, 12; Saxo Grammaticus, *History of the Danes* VII.290, transl. Davidson and Fisher, p. 265; *Hymiskviða* 28-32, transl. Hollander, *Poetic Edda*, p. 88.

98 *Kjalnesinga saga* ch. 14.

99 *Sörla saga sterka* ch. 25.

100 Saxo, *History of the Danes* I.23, ed. Ellis-Davidson and Fisher, p. 24.

101 *Sörla saga sterka* ch. 5.

102 Osborn and Overing, "Bone-Crones Have No Hearth," pp. 345-350.

103 Osborn and Overing, "Bone-Crones Have No Hearth," pp. 340-345.

104 Ross, *Prolonged Echoes*, vol. 1, pp. 69-70.

105 *Hjálmþés saga ok Ölvis* ch. 8; transl. O'Connor, *Icelandic Histories & Romances*, p. 141.

106 *Sturlaugs saga starfsama* ch. 16; *FN*, vol. 2, pp. 332-335.

107 *Egils saga einhenda ok Ásmundar berserkjabana* ch. 12, transl. Pálsson and Edwards, *Seven Viking Romances*, p. 246.

108 *Örvar-Odds saga* ch. 18; transl. Pálsson and Edwards, *Seven Viking Romances*, p. 76.

109 Ström, *Níð, Ergi, and Old Norse Moral Attitudes*, p. 4.

110 *Gríms saga loðinkinna* ch. 1; *FN*, vol. 1, p. 272.

111 *Egils saga einhenda ok Ásmundar berserkjabana* ch. 11; *FN*, vol. 3, p. 244.

112 The Hunnestad stone probably depicts the giantess Hyrrokin, who pushed the funeral ship out at the funeral of the god Balder; see Ewing, *Viking Clothing*, pp. 43-44, fig. 20.

113 Ewing, *Viking Clothing*, e.g. figs. 25-31. See also Saxo Grammaticus, *History of the Danes* I.13, ed. Ellis-Davidson and Fisher, p. 16.

114 Jochens, *Women in Old Norse Society*, pp. 134-140.

115 These include the undead Thorgunna in *Eyrbyggja saga* ch. 51, and an unnamed dead woman in a dream in *Hemings þáttr* ch. 18, ed. Vigfússon, *Icelandic Sagas*, vol. 1, p. 373.

116 Kunin, *A History of Norway*, p. 15.

117 See translation and commentary in Bately and Englert, *Ohthere's*

Voyages.

118 *Óláfs saga Tryggvassonar* chs. 78-80; transl. Hollander, *Heimskringla*, p. 232.

119 e.g. *Egils saga Skallagrímssonar* chs. 10, 14; *Óláfs saga helga* ch. 133, transl. Hollander, *Heimskringla*, pp. 403-408.

120 Tambets, "The Western and Eastern Roots of the Saami", pp. 671, 677.

121 Hofstra and Samplonius, "Viking Expansion Northwards," p. 242.

122 *Ynglinga saga* chs. 13, 19, transl. Hollander, *Heimskringla*, pp. 16-17, 22-23.

123 *Haralds saga hárfagra* ch. 25, transl. Hollander, *Heimskringla*, pp. 80-81.

124 *Haralds saga hárfagra* ch. 32, transl. Hollander, *Heimskringla*, pp. 86-87; see also *Egils saga* ch. 37.

125 Straubhaar, "Nasty, Brutish, and Large", p. 110; Mundal, "Coexistence of Saami and Norse Culture," p. 352-353.

126 Mundal, "Coexistence of Saami and Norse Culture," pp. 353-355.

127 e.g. Beach, *A Year in Lapland*, p. 5.

128 Motz. . . .

129 Jochens, "Race and Ethnicity," pp. 80-81.

130 *Ynglinga saga* ch. 1, in *Heimskringla*, transl. Hollander, p. 6.

131 Lindow, "Supernatural and Ethnic Others," pp. 8-31.

132 Jochens, "Race and Ethnicity," pp. 85-92.

133 Jochens, "Race and Ethnicity," p. 102.

134 Quoted in Steinsland, "Giants as Recipients of Cult", pp. 212-213.

135 *Lokasenna* 51, transl. Hollander, *Poetic Edda*, p. 100.

136 Steinsland, "Giants as Recipients of Cult", pp. 213-214.

137 *Grímnismál* 11, transl. Hollander, *Poetic Edda*, p. 56.

138 Snorri Sturluson, *Gylfaginning* 23, ed. Faulkes, p. 24. Snorri refers to Skaði as *öndurgoð eða öndurdís*, "snowshoe-god or snowshoe-goddess."

139 For examples of *blótnaut* as a receiver of sacrifices, see *Hjálmþés saga ok Ölvis* ch. 10 (*FN* vol. 3, pp. 267-268; transl. O'Connor, *Icelandic Histories & Romances*, pp. 157-160); *Þorsteins þáttr wafts* ch. 14. Also compare the cow Sibilja in *Ragnars saga loðbrókar* chs. 9-12 (*FN* vol.

1, pp. 113-127); the bull in *Bósa saga* ch. 8 (*FN* vol. 2, pp. 478-479); and the aurochs in *Sturlaugs saga starfsama* ch. 22 (*FN* vol. 2, p. 347).

140 Vígfusson and Unger, *Flateyjarbók*, vol. 2, p. 7.

141 Motz, "The Great Goddess of the North," p. 475.

142 Røthe, "Þorgerðr Hölgabrúðr," pp. 46-47.

143 *Ketils saga hængs* ch. 5; *FN*, vol. 1, p. 261.

144 Motz, "The Storm of Troll-Women", pp. 32-33.

145 Motz, "The Storm of Troll-Women", pp. 34-35; a well-known example is Hræsvelg in *Vafþrúðnismál* in the *Poetic Edda.* In several sagas in this book, the hero is blown to the giants' lands by a storm, and it is stated or implied that the giants have sent the storm.

146 Motz, "The Storm of Troll-Women", pp. 35-37; examples include *Hyndluljóð* and *Vafþrúðnismál* in the *Poetic Edda.* In this book, see *Hálfdans þáttr* ch. 6, in which Dofri teaches Harald. Elsewhere, see *Bárðar saga Snæfellsáss*, in which Bárð learns lore from Dofri and later teaches it to Odd Onundson.

147 Motz, "The Storm of Troll-Women", pp. 37-38.

148 Motz, "Families of Giants," pp. 217-222.

149 Motz, "Families of Giants," pp. 222-229.

150 Motz, "Rulers of the Mountain," pp. 412-414.

151 Motz, "The Storm of Troll-Women," p. 38.

152 Straubhaar, "Nasty, Brutish, and Large," p. 119.

153 Hume, "From Saga to Romance", pp. 3-4.

154 McKinnell, *Meeting the Other*, pp. 32-36.

155 Stitt, *Beowulf and the Bear's Son*, pp. 43-94. Stitt classifies major episodes in *Ketils saga hængs*, *Gríms saga loðinkinna*, *Örvar-Odds saga*, *Þorsteins þáttr uxafóts*, and *Hjálmþés saga ok Ölvis* as examples of the Two-Troll tradition.

156 McKinnell, pp. 126-139.

157 McKinnell, p. 195. An Icelandic folktale also depicts a female troll defeated by red-hot iron; see "How Kraka Lost Her Lover", transl. Simpson, *Icelandic Folktales and Legends*, pp. 76-78.

158 McKinnell, pp. 172-176.

159 McKinnell, pp. 181-186.

160 *Þorsteins saga Víkingssonar* chs. 17, 19, transl. Waggoner, *Sagas of Fridthjof the Bold*, pp. 33-34, 38.

161 *Gríms saga loðinkinna* chs. 1-2; *FN*, vol. 1, pp. 270-273.
162 McKinnell, pp. 186-195.
163 "Vígð Drangey", in Árnason, *Íslenzkar Þjóðsögur og Æfintýri*, vol. 1, pp. 144-146; transl. Hallmundsson and Hallmundsson, *Icelandic Folk and Fairy Tales*, pp. 31-34.
164 Tulinius, *Matter of the North*, pp. 40-43, 184-186.
165 Ross, *Prolonged Echoes*, vol. 1, pp. 88-102.
166 Osborn and Overing, "Bone-Crones Have No Hearth," p. 350.
167 Óláfur Halldórsson, "*Óláfs saga Tryggvasonar*", p. 449.
168 Kolbrún Haraldsdóttir, "*Flateyjarbók*," pp. 197-198.
169 Nordal, *Flateyjarbók*, vol. II, pp. 47-52 (*Hálfdanar þáttr svarta*), pp. 63-70 (*Hauks þáttr hábrokar*).
170 Vígfusson and Unger, *Flateyjarbók*, vol. I, pp. 561-567 (*Hálfdanar þáttr svarta*), pp. 577-583 (*Hauks þáttr hábrokar*).
171 Jóhannes Halldórsson, *Íslenzk Fornrit XIV: Kjalnesinga Saga*, pp. xvii-xx.
172 Jóhannes Halldórsson, *Íslenzk Fornrit XIV: Kjalnesinga Saga*, pp. xxx-xxiii.
173 Finlay, "*Fljótsdæla saga*," pp. 198-199.
174 Jón Jóhannesson, *Íslenzk Fornrit XI: Austfirðinga Sögur*, pp. lxxxii-lxxxvi.
175 Jón Jóhannesson, *Austfirðinga Sögur*, pp. xcii-c.
176 Hufnagel, "*Sörla saga sterka* and Rafn's edition." pp. 398-404.
177 Kennedy, "English Translations", pp. 285-303.
178 For example, see Desmond Slay's criticism of Jesse Byock's translation of *Hrólfs saga kraka*.

Tale of Halfdan the Black

1 Agder is at the southern tip of present-day Norway. Gudrod was killed when his son Halfdan was one year old; Halfdan succeeded to the kingship at the age of nineteen. (*Ynglinga saga* ch. 48; transl. Hollander, *Heimskringla*, pp. 48-49)
2 A hersir was a local leader, ranking below a jarl.
3 Up to this point the text has been a condensed summary of *Hálfdanar saga svarta* in *Heimskringla*. From here on it begins to follow the saga text much more closely. Olaf Geirstad-Alf's story follows Halfdan

the Black's story in *Flateyjarbók* (Nordal, ed., vol. 2, pp. 74-78).

4 These are the sons of Hálfdan's rival Gandálf.

5 In the saga in *Heimskringla*, Olvir is killed in the first battle.

6 At this point, *Heimskringla*, inserts the life-story of Sigurd Hart, which is repeated nearly identically in *Þáttr af Ragnars sonum* ch. 5 (transl. Waggoner, *Sagas of Ragnar Lodbrok*, pp. 72-73).

7 Here the tale resumes following the *Heimskringla* saga.

8 In the sagas, a more usual way of gaining insight through dreams is to sleep on a burial mound. It's been suggested that "pigsty" might have once been a kenning for "burial mound", given that the god Freyr is associated with both burial mounds and boars (Davidson, *Lost Beliefs of Northern Europe*, pp. 123-124).

9 Here the tale and the *Heimskringla* saga diverge. At this point in *Hálfdanar saga svarta* in *Heimskringla*, the chieftain tells Harald that his father is dead, and that he must now take the kingship. The two texts do not reconverge until their respective final chapters, recounting the death of King Halfdan.

10 All of these names are recorded in poetry as names of Odin (e.g. *Grimnismál* 47, transl. Hollander, *Poetic Edda*, p. 63). *Viðrir* means "master of winds"; *Hár* means "high"; *Þriði* means "third", and *Jólnir* means "Yule-being" (from *Jól*, "Yule").

11 This paragraph is paralleled by one in the twelfth-century *Ágrip af Nóregskonungasögum* ch. 1 (transl. Driscoll, pp. 1-2), which lists the same four names of Odin and contrasts his Yule feast with the Christian Nativity, albeit somewhat less polemically.

12 The Dovrefjell range in central Norway (Old Norse *Dofrafjall*).

13 The Old Norse is *hvárki sá af honum veðr ne reyk*—"he saw neither wind nor smoke of him."

14 Harald was said to have vowed not to cut or comb his hair until he had won all of Norway; he was called Haraldr *lúfa* ("matted-hair") before his final victory, and Haraldr *hárfagri* ("fair-hair") afterwards. *Heimskringla* (*Haralds saga hárfagra* chs. 3-4, transl. Hollander, pp. 61-62) and a later chapter in *Flateyjarbók* (Nordal, vol. 1, p. 55) tell a different story; Haraldr makes his vow after Gyða refuses to marry him unless he can conquer all Norway.

15 Halfdan's brother Olaf Geirstad-Alf was also said to be buried in a mound and worshipped to bring good harvests (Nordal, *Flateyjarbók*,

vol. 2, 76). A euhemerized account in *Ynglinga saga* (ch. 10; transl. Hollander, *Heimskringla*, pp. 13-14) tells how the god Freyr was also buried in a mound and worshipped for good harvests and peace.

Tale of Hauk Habrok

1 Bjorn on the Mound (*Björn at Haugi*) was said to be the grandson of Bjorn Ironside who was the son of the legendary Ragnar Lodbrok, and Onund was his brother, according to *Hervarar saga*. *Hervarar saga* gives a slightly different chronology from the one given here, in which Harald Fairhair wins the throne of Norway while Eirek is king of Sweden (ed. transl. Tolkien, *Saga of King Heidrek*, pp. 60-61). Rimbert's *Vita Anskarii* mentions early 9th-century Swedish kings named Bernus and Anoundus, who may be Bjorn and Onund. (Robinson, *Anskar*, ch. 11, p. 48; ch. 19, p. 65)

2 Old Norse *Hólmgarðr*, "enclosure on an island", the usual name for the city now called Novgorod.

3 Salgard's nickname *Serkr* is translated as "Saracen" by some (e.g. Bachman, *Forty Old Icelandic Tales*, p. 10). In the sagas, *Serkland*, "Saracen-Land", means the Middle East, more or less. However, there is no other indication that Salgard is an Arab or a Muslim (although, given the existence of trade routes between Scandinavia and the Middle East, this would not be implausible). The more usual meaning of *serkr* is "shirt, tunic." Since there are many other cases in the sagas of people whose nicknames derive from their customary clothing (including the protagonist of this tale), I've chosen to translate *serkr* as "tunic".

4 The Old Norse word translated "cloak" is *skikkja*. Ewing (*Viking Clothing*, pp. 104-105) points out that *skikkja* almost always refers to a costly and elaborately crafted garment of delicate fabric.

5 The verb is *hábrókast*, literally "to wear high breeches." Ewing (*Viking Clothing*, pp. 96-98) suggests that *hábrók*, "high breeches," refers to extremely baggy knee-length trousers, either open or gathered at the knee, as depicted on several Viking-era carvings (*Viking Clothing*, figs. 60, 66-67). Since such trousers required a great deal of cloth, they implied high status and proud, aristocratic bearing.

6 Hauk had tricked Athelstan into agreeing to foster Harald's son

Hakon. In this way Athelstan inadvertently admitted to Harald's superiority, since a man who fostered another man's child was considered to have lesser standing. The story is told in full in *Haralds saga hárfagra* ch. 39 (transl. Hollander, *Heimskringla*, pp. 92-93).

7 The name *Haukr* means "Hawk". "High-Breeches" (*Hábrók*) is a poetic name for a hawk, and also the name of the legendary King Hrólf Kraki's hawk. Wide, baggy breeches may have been known as *hábrók* from their resemblance to a hawk's leg feathers. See Note 5 above. (Ewing, *Viking Clothing*, p. 97)

8 The motif of a man coming to a royal court by traversing an uncrossable mountain, hidden in a cloud of snow or dust, appears in the *riddarasaga Þjalar-Jóns saga* ch. 2 (ed. Gunnlaug Þórðarson, p. 7). In *Ketils saga hængs* ch. 3 (FN vol. 1, p. 253), Gusir the king of the Finns travels in a whirlwind of snow, and it's not quite clear whether this is supernatural or not. The author may be hinting that there is something a bit uncanny about Vighard.

9 The coast of the White Sea, home of the *Bjarmar*, a Finnic-speaking people. Norse trading voyages to Bjarmaland are historically attested (reviewed in Hofstra and Samplonius, "Viking Expansion Northwards"), but the area had a reputation in the legendary sagas as a place of monsters, sorcerors, and trolls.

10 Old Norse *Gandvík*. The name may have been derived from the Finnish *kanta-*, "base", but most hearers would have understood the first element as *gandr*, "magic wand or creature", and interpreted *Gandvík* as "Magic Bay." (Hofstra and Samplonius, "Viking Expansion Northwards, p. 238) The shores of Gandvík were the haunt of monsters, giants, and dangerous magic in Norse legend; see note 6 to *Illuga saga Gríðarfóstra.*

11 The giantess Arinnefja in *Egins saga einhenda* esteems a gift of bacon and butter more than gold (*FN* vol. 3, p. 187). Butter is also mentioned in *Ketils saga hængs* (ch. 3; *FN* vol. 1, p. 252) as a trade item prized by the Saami.

12 Location unknown, but the name means "Surtr's Valley". In the myths, Surtr is the leader of the giants who is destined to destroy the world in flames. A few more mundane giants in the legendary sagas also bear the name (e.g. *Jökuls þáttr Búasonar* chs. 1-2). Certainly the name reinforces the "trollish" nature of the far north.

13 The name *Lýtir* may be related to Old Norse *lýta*, "to deform, to blemish" and *lýti*, "a flaw; a deformity"; the word is used in poetry to mean "damager; destroyer." (Jónsson, *Lexicon Poeticum*, p. 387) Alternatively, *Lýtir* could be related to *lúta*, "to bow down; to worship". Lytir is not known from any other saga, but the details of his worship link him with the gods known as the Vanir, and it's possible that he is equivalent to the god Frey; see the next footnote.

14 Lytir's worship is remarkably similar to Nerthus, a Roman-era goddess worshipped in present-day Jutland and documented by the historian Tacitus (*Germania* XL.2-5, transl. Hutton, pp. 196-197). Like Lytir, Nerthus was only present at certain times, travelled in a wagon, and was veiled from the eyes of ordinary humans. Nerthus's name is closely related to the name of the Norse god Njörðr, whose son Freyr was especially worshipped at Uppsala, and who also travelled in a wagon (see *Ögmundar þáttr dytts*). The geography here is a little confused, since Hauk apparently sails up the Atlantic coast of Norway, while Bjorn and Salgard sail into the Gulf of Bothnia.

15 Persons in the sagas who speak prophecy or work magic often yawn or gape (*geispa*) as they do. A seeress named Heid yawns as she prophesies in *Hrólfs saga kraka* (ch. 3, transl. Byock, pp. 6-7). Other examples include Thorhall in *Eiríks saga rauða* (ch. 8), Svan in *Njáls saga* (ch. 12), and Skjaldvor in *Þorsteins þáttr uxafóts* (ch. 10).

16 In both legendary sagas (*Sturlaugs saga starfsama* ch. 9, *FN* vol. 2 p. 320) and sagas of Icelanders (e.g. *Heiðarvíga saga* ch. 23; *Kjalnesinga saga* ch. 9; *Kormaks saga* ch. 1; *Reykdæla saga* ch. 5), wise women stroke a man's body as a way to foretell whether he will be wounded in battle, and/or to give him strength and protection in battle.

17 The passages about Harald's death, his burial mound, and his excellent qualities are paralleled in *Haralds saga hárfagri* ch. 42 (transl. Hollander, *Heimskringla*, p. 94). The account that follows of Harald's infatuation with Snjofrid is paralleled in *Haralds saga hárfagri* ch. 25 (transl. Hollander, p. 80), but with many differences in detail.

18 In *Haralds saga hárfagri* in *Heimskringla*, Svasi is a "Finn".

19 According to *Heimskringla*, they had four sons: Sigurd *Hrísi* ("Bastard"), Halfdan *Hálegg* ("Long-Leg"), Gudrod *Ljómi* ("Gleam"),

and Rognvald *Rettilbeini* ("Straight-Limbs").

20 *Flateyjarbók* has *at endódum þeirra órlógum* here. Sigurður Nordal's edition (p. 70) has *at enduðum þeirra örlögum*, "at the end of their fates". An earlier edition (*Fornmanna sögur*, vol. 10, p. 207) emends this to *at endöðum þeirra álógum*, "at the end of that magic spell".

21 The Norse skaldic form has not been duplicated exactly, but the end-rhymes are present in the original. The kennings "waves of the lord of graves" (literally *kerlaug drauga dróttins*, "bath of the lord of the undead"), "Regin's brew", and "Dvalin's grip" all refer to the myth of dwarves brewing the mead which conferred poetic inspiration. Odin stole that mead from a giant and was said to dispense it to favored poets. (*Skáldskaparmál*, ed. Faulkes, pp. 3-5)

22 The Norse verse uses end-rhyme, which I've replicated.

Kjalnesinga Saga

1 Helgi's name *Bjóla* (*Bjólan* in other sources) is Gaelic, apparently derived from the name Béollán (Craigie, "Gaelic Words and Names", p. 444)

2 Helgi Bjola's settlement is also mentioned in *Landnámabók* ch. 14 (transl. Pálsson and Edwards, p. 23. He and his descendants also appear in *Laxdæla saga* chs. 1-5, and briefly in *Eyrbyggja saga* ch. 1.

3 A plenarium was a book that contained all the texts on a given topic. In the medieval Church, the word could mean a book containing all four Gospels, or else a book containing all of the prayers and psalms needed to celebrate the daily offices.

4 *Landnámabók* (*Sturlubók* 15; transl. Pálsson and Edwards, pp. 23-24) gives a different version of this story: Orlyg is the son of Hrapp, and grandson of the powerful Norwegian chieftain Bjorn Buna, but is fostered by Bishop Patrick in the Hebrides, not Iceland. The details of his voyage are also a little different, and Helgi Bjola is said to be Orlyg's uncle.

5 The people on this ship are not documented in *Landnámabók* or any other historical sources.

6 *Brautarholt* means "path in a forest."

7 Probably the same as Thord Skeggi, mentioned in *Landnámabók* (*Sturlubók* 11; transl. Pálsson and Edwards, p. 22), which makes him

Orlyg's brother and thus Helgi Bjola's nephew.

8 Old Norse *goði* originally meant "priest", and the *goðar* originally maintained temples and kept up sacrifices. In Iceland, the *goðar* held considerable secular power, and the office of *goði* was retained as a secular rank even after Christianity was adopted. Each *goði* held the allegiance of a certain number of free farmers, but but originally did not rule defined territories; the fact that Thorgrim is depicted as having a definite territory has been claimed as evidence for a relatively late date of composition, after Iceland lost its independence in 1268, when sherrifs (*sýslumenn*) governed defined territories (Einar Sveinsson, *Dating the Icelandic Sagas*, pp. 69-71). However, some powerful *goðar* were claiming territories (*héraðsríki*) as early as the late 12th century and possibly before (Helgi Torláksson, "Historical Background," p. 149). See note 2 to *Fljótsdæla saga*.

9 The word *kennslamál*, literally "evidence case", is a legal term for a case in which there are no eyewitnesses. This rare word first appeared in Iceland in the law code *Járnsíða*, written in 1271 after Iceland's union with Norway; this sets a limit on the date of composition. (Jóhannes Halldórsson, *Kjalnesinga saga*, p. 7 n6)

10 Old Norse *hlaut* means the blood of a sacrificed animal, but the word is also related to words for "share; allotment" (*hlutr*, *hleyti*).

11 *Blótkelda* means "sacrifice well". It is hard to know how much of this temple description might be historical and how much is literary convention. Jóhannes Halldórsson notes that the sacred fire may have been borrowed from accounts of Greek or Roman temples, and a sacrificial well outside the temple also appears in Adam of Bremen's account of the great temple at Uppsala. On the other hand, he claims that two carved boards from Hof have survived in a museum in Copenhagen, and that oral tradition has it that they formed part of the temple. (*Kjálnesinga saga* pp. 7-8, n8, n1)

12 Olaf Jonsson is briefly mentioned in *Árna saga biskups* as living at Hof in the mid-13th century. (Jóhannes Halldórsson, *Kjálnesinga saga* p. 8, n1.)

13 The Althing (*alþing*, "General Assembly") was the annual summer assembly of men from all Iceland, where the law was recited, new law was made, and legal cases could be tried. A Spring Assembly (*varþing*) dealt with cases within one district; larger cases could be

heard at the Quarter Assembly (*fjórðungsþing*); and still larger ones at the Althing. Shelters (*búðir*) were built to provide temporary housing during an assembly.

14 A newborn was sprinkled with water (*ausa vatni*) as part of the ritual of naming. Despite outward similarities with the Christian rite of infant baptism, this rite has pagan origins.

15 Kolfid is a *kolbítr* or "coal-biter", an unpromising lad who does nothing but sit by the fire. It's a common trope in the sagas that a *kolbítr* rises to the occasion and becomes a mighty man when urged on. Compare Asmund in *The Tale of Asmund Ogre-Lucky*.

16 Since Bui has been compared with the Irish hero Cú Chulainn, it's noteworthy that Cú Chulainn's name also means "dog", specifically "Culann's Hound". (Gísli Sigurðsson, *Gaelic Influence*, pp. 91-93)

17 This detail seems strange; several settlers of Iceland were allegedly *goðlauss*, "godless," without being outlawed (*Landnámabók* (*Sturlubók*) 12, 57; transl. Pálsson and Edwards, pp. 22, 35-36). However, before Christianity, those who did not pay the tax for temple upkeep could be prosecuted (e.g. *Vápnfirðinga saga* ch. 5), and it's possible that the saga author has confused this with later Christian prohibitions against heresy.

18 Iceland had laws and courts, but no police or any other way to enforce its judgments. Outlawry (*skóggangr*, literally "going into the forest") meant that a man was outside the protection of the laws. He could not keep his property, could not be helped by anyone, and could be killed with impunity. *Skóggangr* was permanent; lesser outlawry (*fjörbaugsgarðr*, literally "sanctuary") lasted three years. (Hastrup, *Culture and History*, pp. 137-142)

19 Literally, *nú er við ramman reip at draga*, "now we have to pull a rope with a strong man", referring to a metaphorical tug-of-war.

20 A proverbial expression.

21 Icelandic law required that a man who killed another had to announce that he had done the deed.

22 This phrase is my attempt to render the Norse word *einstigi*, "a path only wide enough for one person". Jorgensen points out that *einstigi* is a rare word in Old Norse, but it is used specifically for a trail leading to a monsters' or outlaws' cave in several sagas (including ch. 4 of *Hálfdanar saga Brönufóstra* and ch. 3 of *Jökuls þáttr Búasonar*

in this book). *Beowulf* also contains a narrow path to a monster's dwelling, described in very similar language: *steap stanhliðo, stige nearwe, / enge anpaðas*, "steep stone slopes, narrow ways, / tight paths for one person" (lines 1409-1410; ed. Dobbie, p. 44). This is one of many motifs shared between *Beowulf* and various Icelandic sagas. ("Icelandic Analogues", pp. 202-203)

23 *Laugargnipa* means "bath peak" or "hot spring peak." Jóhannes Halldórsson notes that there is a hill called Búi overlooking the site of Esjuberg, with a cave known as Búahellir (Bui's Cave), although there is no path leading to it now. (*Kjalnesinga saga* p. 14 n1)

24 Esja's use of smoke could be entirely non-magical, but the author probably intended this to be understood as an example of magic. In several sagas, a woman hides a man from searchers using illusionary magic; the closest parallel is *Fostbræðra saga* (ch. 23), in which the woman also uses floor-sweepings to generate concealing smoke.

25 Literally, *austmaðr*, "easterner, man from the east," used in the sagas to mean a man from continental Scandinavia, often (though not always) a Norwegian, typically a merchant. In the sagas of Icelanders, visiting *austmenn* have something of a reputation for trying to seduce their hosts' daughters; e.g. *Þórsteins saga uxafóts* ch. 3; *Hrómundar þáttr halta* chs. 1-2.

26 A proverb; see also *Sturlaugs saga starfsama* ch. 7, in Jónsson and Vilhjálmsson, *Fornaldarsögur Norðurlanda* vol. 2, p. 316.

27 The *eldhús*, "fire-house" or "hearth-house", was an outbuilding with a fire, where cooking was done. Since cooking was women's work on a farmstead, Kolfid's lying around the *eldhús* implies that he is not only lazy, but unmasculine. (Jochens, *Women in Old Norse Society*, pp. 129-130)

28 Old Norse *kollhetta*, literally "hood for the crown of the head". Exactly what this garment was has been debated. Ewing suggests that it was a tight-fitting cap (*Viking Clothing*, pp. 118-119), but elsewhere suggests that it is a hooded garment open at the sides, something like a poncho, but with skirts that could be fastened between the legs when necessary (p. 91-92). *Eiríks saga rauða* (ch. 8) mentions a similar garment worn by Scottish slaves, the *kjafall* (probably from Irish *cabhail*, "trunk of a shirt").

29 Ewing points out that hairy calfskin or rawhide shoes were worn

by slaves and laborers (*Viking Clothing*, pp. 123-124), and that long breeches (*ökulbrækr*) are also low-status clothing in the sagas (pp. 98-99). Again, the saga author is emphasizing Kolfid's poor dress.

30 There may be a link between Kolfid and the Irish hero Cú Chulainn; in a story in the *Táin Bó Cúailnge*, Cú Chulainn goes to some games, amusing himself by throwing his spear and running after it. Like Kolfid, Cú Chulainn ends up killing someone and receiving protection from his mother's brother. (Gísli Sigurðsson, *Gaelic Influence*, pp. 90-91) There are also parallels between Búi and Cú Chulainnn (see notes 16, 45, and Introduction p. xi).

31 Most manuscripts read *hæðiligr*, "ludicrous"; some have *hræðiligr*, "frightening". (Jóhannes Halldórsson, *Kjalnesinga saga*, p. 18 n3)

32 Women give magically protective shirts or cloaks to favored men in both sagas of Icelanders (e.g. *Eyrbyggja saga* ch. 18, *Vatnsdæla saga* ch. 19) and legendary sagas (e.g. *Ragnars saga loðbrókar* ch. 15; transl. Waggoner, *Sagas of Ragnar Lodbrok*, p. 29; *Örvar-Odds saga* ch. 12; transl. Pálsson and Edwards, *Seven Viking Romances*, pp. 52-55)

33 In both legendary and historical sagas, wise women stroke a man's body to foretell whether he will be wounded and/or to give him strength and protection in battle; see note 16 to the *Hauks þáttr Hábrokar*.

34 Very similar dueling customs are described in *Kormaks saga* ch. 10; there may be a direct connection between *Kormaks saga* and this one (Gísli Sigurðsson, *Gaelic Influence*, p. 97 n43).

35 The Old Norse *berkykvendi* can mean any female animal. Comparing a man to a female animal was one of the worst possible insults; for example, in the Gulaþing Law of Norway, someone who called a man a female animal (*berendi*, literally "bearing offspring") had to pay the highest level of compensation. (Ström, *Níð, Ergi, and Old Norse Moral Attitudes*, p. 6)

36 *Orrustuhóll* means "Battle Hill"; Jóhannes Halldórsson notes that a sandhill by that name is located south of Eilifsdal, just east of *Skeiðhlíð*, "Warship Slope". (*Kjalnesinga saga*, p. 26 n1)

37 Under Icelandic law, a full outlaw could not take passage from Iceland. If he did leave, he could not return, and Icelanders abroad could kill him with impunity. (Hastrup, *Culture and Society*, p. 139)

38 Old Norse *tafl* means any boardgame; several different boardgames

were known to the Norse. Game boards and pieces, including some with elaborate workmanship, have been found in Viking-era burials (Bayless, "Tabletop Tactics"), and boards made of costly materials such as ivory or precious metals are mentioned in some sagas (*Gull-Þóris saga* ch. 20; *Króka-Refs saga* chs. 11-12).

39 Red dyes had to be imported into Scandinavia in the Viking era; thus red clothing is especially associated in the sagas with luxury and nobility. (Ewing, *Viking Clothing*, p. 156; see also *Hálfdanar saga Brönufóstra* ch. 6)

40 *Hávamál* 4 (transl. Hollander, *Poetic Edda*, p. 15) mentions that a guest at a feast should be given water and a towel to wash, and then an invitation to partake of the feast.

41 The expression *skemmta sér*, "to amuse oneself", often has sexual connotations. (Jochens, *Women in Old Norse Society*, pp. 68-69)

42 In a hall, the chieftain sat in the high seat (*öndvegi*) in the middle of one bench. The opposite high seat (*öndvegi it óæðra*), in the center of the other bench, was reserved for important guests or others whom the chieftain wanted to honor.

43 *Blámaðr*, "black man", is used for Africans in a few sagas, but most of the *blámenn* in the sagas have nothing to do with actual Africans; they are primarily savage troll-like villains. See Introduction p. xi; *Sörla saga* note 4.

44 A thong-spear (*snarspjót*, *snærispjót*) is a spear thrown by means of a cord. It's possible that they were like the Roman *hasta amentata*, in which a cord wrapped around the handle was used to make the spear spin in flight and fly straighter. (Short, *Viking Weapons*, p. 92; Speidel, *Ancient Germanic Warriors*, pp. 145, 260 n26-27)

45 This episode resembles stories of both Hildebrand and Cú Chulainn, as has been noted (see Introduction, p. xi). A similar story also appears in *Landnámabók*, in which Ævar wrestles and almost kills his son Vefrod, not knowing who he is; however, the two are reconciled in the end (*Sturlubók* 184; transl. Pálsson and Edwards, p. 87).

46 The oldest manuscript of this saga ends Jokul's story here. A second group of manuscripts adds: "Most men suppose that he must have gone back to his mother and stayed there with his mother's kin." (Jóhannes Halldórsson, *Kjalnesinga saga*, p. 43 n1) Still other

manuscripts add *Jökuls þáttr Búasonar* to the end of this saga.

47 It was the usual heathen custom to bury men of distinction with treasures and favorite possessions; Bui's burial without such grave-goods underscores his estrangement from traditional Norse religion.

48 Arni Thorlaksson was the bishop at Skalholt between 1269 and 1298; this sets another limit on the maximum age of the saga. (Jóhannes Halldórsson, *Kjalnesinga saga*, pp. 43-44 n3)

49 Halldór Laxness's novel *Iceland's Bell*, set in the late 17th century, opens by describing an ancient iron bell hanging at Þingvellir. Laxness may have had this saga in mind.

The Tale of Jokul Buason

1 A sexual invitation.

2 *Öllumlengri* means "longest of all." It's true that the longest fjord in the world, Scoresby Sund / Kangertittivaq, is located on the eastern side of Greenland, although it's not likely that the tale's author knew this. However, a 14th-century description of Greenland, written by one Ivar Bardarson, identifies Öllumlengri with Prince Christian Sund / Ikerasassuaq, near the southernmost tip of Greenland (Jóhannes Halldórsson, *Kjalnesinga saga*, p. 50 n4).

3 Once again, the Norse word *einstigi*, "a path only wide enough for one person", is used for a trail leading to a monster's lair, a motif shared with *Beowulf*. (Jorgensen, "Icelandic Analogues", pp. 202-203; see note 22 to *Kjalnesinga saga* and 11 to *Hálfdanar saga*)

4 As in *Sörla saga*, the giantess is called *vínkona*, "female friend" rather than *fóstra*, and no sexual relationship is explicitly depicted between the giantess and the hero. See note 13 to *Sörla saga*.

5 Old Norse *Serkland*, "Saracen-Land", refers to the Muslim realms of North Africa and the Middle East. *Soldan*, the usual name of the ruler of Serkland in legendary sagas, is derived from "sultan"; however, his son has a Norse name (*Hvítserkr*, "white shirt").

6 Norns are embodiments of fate; there are three great Norns that embody the fate of the universe, but also "personal Norns" that shape an individual's destiny (*Gylfaginning* 15, ed. Faulkes, p. 18). In some later legendary sagas (e.g. *Hrólfs saga kraka* ch. 48, *FN* vol. 2

p. 83) Norns are grouped with wicked beings such as trolls.

7 Norse *pímet ok klaret*, "pyment and claret". *Pyment* is used today for mead brewed with grapes or grape juice (Schramm, *The Compleat Meadmaker*, pp. 121-128) but in the Middle Ages, *pyment* usually meant a sweetened spiced wine. *Claret* or *clary* was not necessarily a red wine, as the word means today; it referred to wine poured through a bag of spices. (*Middle English Dictionary*; Adamson, *Food in Medieval Times*, pp. 50-51) The influence from the "chivalric sagas" is obvious.

8 A fairly standard way of justifying a bloody Viking career in the legendary sagas. See, for example, *Friðþjófs saga inn frækni* ch. 11; *Þorsteins saga Víkingssonar* ch. 22; *Sturlaugs saga starfsama* ch. 4.

9 Old Norse *Bláland*, "black [men's] land". See note 8 to *Sörla saga.*

The Tale of Brindle-Cross

1 The "story of the two Helgis" is *Droplaugarsona saga*, which tells of a conflict between Helgi Droplaugarson and Helgi Asbjarnarson. This tale was written as a "prequel" to the saga.

2 This is the same Hrafnkel whose story is told in *Hrafnkels saga Freysgoða*, but the details differ: In *Hrafnkels saga* (ch. 1), it is Hrafnkel's father (named Hallfred in that saga) who is warned in a dream to move away, just in time to avoid a landslide that claims two of his animals (a pair of goats). *Landnámabók*, however, tells the same story as *Brandkrossa þáttr* and was presumably its source (*Sturlubók* 283, transl. Pálsson and Edwards, pp. 113-114).

3 At the end of *Hrafnkels saga Freysgoða* (ch. 20), Thorir gets Hrafnkelsstadir and Asbjorn gets his father's old farm, which is called Aðalból.

4 *Ósvifr* means "coarse."

5 *Ótryggr* means "untrustworthy."

6 The Moving Days (*fardagar*) were four consecutive days towards the end of May. Under Icelandic law, this was the only time when Icelanders could change their residences.

7 A foreboding of events in *Droplaugarsona saga* ch. 3 and *Fljótsdæla saga* ch. 10: Helgi's wife Droplaug is killed in an accident, after which a grieving Helgi sells the farm at Oddstad and moves elsewhere.

This curse may have been borrowed from a similar event in *Víga-Glúms saga* ch. 9, in which a man who has lost his land through legal machinations offers an ox to Frey and asks that the new owner of his land may be driven away, just as he is.

8 Vapnafjord (modern *Vopnafjörður*) is a broad bay in the northeast of Iceland. Inner and Outer Krossavik are two settlements located on the southwest side of Vapnafjord.

9 This episode may be borrowed from *Eyrbyggja saga* ch. 63, in which an uncanny bull goes wild, destroys haystacks, kills a man, and finally rushes into a bog and drowns.

10 Oxarfjord (modern *Öxarfjörður*) is another bay in the northeast of Iceland, north and west of Vapnafjord, surrounding the modern settlement of Kopasker.

11 Unaós ("Uni's Estuary", named for an early settler) is on the southeastern edge of the delta of the Lagar River (Lagarfljót), along the coast, southeast of Vapnafjord.

12 "Shaggy cloaks" (*vararfeldar*) were cloaks of homespun wool with tufts of wool worked into the weave, creating a shaggy or furry effect. They were typical of Iceland, but were widely traded abroad. See Jochens, *Women in Old Norse Society*, pp. 144-146.

13 *Kárhöfði* means "curly-haired."

14 *Geitishamrar* means "Geitir's Cliffs."

15 *Mardöll* is also a name of the goddess Freyja (*Gylfaginning* 35, ed. Faulkes, p. 29), meaning something like "brightness of the sea."

Fljotsdæla Saga (extract)

1 The Selfljót does not flow into the Lagarfljot today, but physical evidence and oral tradition suggest that it once did. This is a flat, deltaic region of Iceland where river channels have often shifted, making it uncertain exactly how large Thidrandi's district would have been. (Jón Jóhanneson, *Austfirðinga Saga*, pp. 218-219 n7)

2 *Útmannasveit* means "outsider's district." The fact that Thidrandi holds a geographically bounded chieftainship shows that the saga was written late; Icelandic chieftains or *goðar* did not originally govern defined territories (see note 8 to *Kjalnesinga saga*).

3 *Þrum-Ketill* means "Ketil the Taciturn." In other texts, including

Brandkrossa þáttr ch. 1, he is called *Þrym-Ketill* or *Ketill Þrymr*, which literally mean "Ketil Noise." This may be a rather sardonic pun.

4 Kjartan Olafsson is a leading character in *Laxdæla saga.*

5 Hoskuld Thorgeirsson appears in *Ljósvetninga saga.* A godi (Old Norse *goði*) was a chieftain with a group of free followers who pledged support; see note 8 to *Kjálnesinga saga.*

6 Ingolf Thorsteinsson the Handsome appears in *Vatnsdæla saga* and *Hallfreðar saga vandræðaskálds.*

7 The sagas sometimes contrast humble Icelandic clothing, usually undyed wool, with the fine *lítklæði* or "colored clothing" worn by high-ranking men who had acquired it abroad. (Ewing, *Viking Clothing*, pp. 166-168) With only undyed wool to wear, Thorvald cannot hope to be received as a man of importance.

8 Bjorgolf is not known from any other source, and this detail is probably fictitious: Viking-era Shetland was not an independent earldom, but was ruled by the jarls of Orkney. (Jón Johanneson, *Austfirðinga Sögur*, p. 223 n1)

9 The landscape resembles a tidal sandbar (tombolo). There are several in Shetland; the best known is St. Ninian's Isle.

10 Schlauch (*Romance in Iceland*, p. 104) points out that maidens abducted by giants are usually bound by their own hair, an image which may go back to Greek romances. See *Hálfdans saga Brönufóstra* ch. 5 in this book. An iron pillar is also found in the cave of Geirröðr, a giant killed by Thor (*Skáldskaparmál* 18, ed. Faulkes, p. 24).

11 *Geitishamar* means "Geitir's crag"; *Geitissulur* means "Geitir's pillar." *Geitishellir*, mentioned later, is "Geitir's caves."

12 Jóhannesson (*Austfirðinga Sögur*, p. 226 n2) notes that the jarl is hinting that he is willing to bestow a rich dowry on his daughter, and thus on her rescuer.

13 Giants' beds are sometimes quite luxurious as well as huge; e.g. *Vatnsdæla saga* ch. 3.

14 It's tempting to speculate that the green sword may have been based on a real find of a Bronze Age sword in Shetland (Short, *Viking Weapons*, p. 119). Bronze swords were made at Jarlshof in Shetland around 700 BCE; only casting molds have been found there in modern times, but it's not impossible that a Norseman might have found an actual sword at this or a similar site (Turner,

Ancient Shetland, pp. 58-60). A bronze knife found in Shetland was long kept as a "trow's [troll's] sword" until the 19th century (Black, *Printed Folk-Lore*, pp. 153-154). However, Jón Jóhannesson points out that tempered steel may take on a greenish color; green may simply indicate high-quality steel (*Austfirðinga Sögur*, p. 227 n1).

15 Stitt (*Beowulf and the Bear's Son*, p. 112) points out that giantesses often wear red tunics (see *Hálfdanar saga* and *Kjalnesinga saga* in this book). Even though Droplaug is fully human in this saga, there may be influence from a tradition in which she was not entirely of human descent, as in *Brandkrossa þáttr.*

16 The word *óheil* literally means "unwell", but it is also a euphemism for "pregnant." Droplaug is never said to give birth, and no child of hers is mentioned, but given the sexual nature of giants and Thorvald's wait to marry her, the meaning "pregnant" is reasonable in context.

17 This is an *álög*, a prophecy or curse similar to the Irish *géasa*, commonly spoken by dying enemies in the legendary sagas. (Schauch, *Romance in Iceland*, pp. 129-130; see also *Illuga saga Gríðarfóstra* ch. 5, note 13; *Hálfdanar saga Brönufóstra* ch. 16, note 2). The curse may be fulfilled in *Droplaugarsona saga* chs. 9-10, when Thorvald's descendant Helgi Droplaugarson gives up his sword before going on the journey on which he is killed. (Jón Jóhannesson, *Austfirðinga Sögur*, p. 229 n1)

18 Though a giant, Geitir seems to share some traits in common with *draugar*, the walking dead. Cutting off a dead man's head and placing it between his legs ensured that the corpse would not walk after death; see, e.g. *Grettis saga* ch. 18, 35.

19 Burning a body and scattering the ashes in the sea was another common way of defending a community against a dead man who might walk after death and cause harm; e.g. *Eyrbyggja saga* ch. 63; *Laxdæla saga* ch. 24; *Svarfdæla saga* ch. 30.

20 Possibly Thurso in Caithness at the northernmost tip of Britain, just across the Pentland Firth from Orkney. Old Norse *Þórsá*, literally "Thor's River", but probably derived from earlier *Þjórsá*, "Bull River."

Saga of Halfdan Brana's Fosterling

1 An older name for Jutland in present-day Denmark.

2 Although the word is not used, this curse belongs to a type known as *álög* (see footnote 13 to *Illuga saga*). Schlauch (*Romance in Iceland*, p. 128) points out the close resemblance between this curse and the *geis* of Irish legends.

3 In saga dreams, the dreamer often sees the *fylgjur* or "fetches" of people, spirits that take the shapes of animals whose nature is like that of their people. Warriors often appear as bears, kings appear as "noble beasts" such as stags or lions, and so on. (Turville-Petre, "Dreams", pp. 36-39) Foxes are usually the *fylgjur* of enemies who work evil magic; see *Hávarðar saga Ísfirðings* ch. 20, and the legendary *Þorsteins saga Víkingssonar* ch. 12 (*FN* vol. 2, p. 209; transl. Waggoner, *Sagas of Fridthjof the Bold*, p. 21).

4 The Norse word here is *ragr*, a hard word to translate simply; it can mean "passively homosexual", but in the absence of sexual connotations it typically means "cowardly; unmanly."

5 One mark (*mörk*) was equal to about 200 grams, although actual weights from the Viking era ranged from 180 to 216 grams. (Christensen, *Norsemen in the Viking Age*, p. 333.)

6 Biting one's shield was a sign of going into *berserksgang*, a heightened state of fury.

7 Like Esja in *Kjalnesinga saga*, Gríma is a human foster-mother who uses magic to defend her charges, foreshadowing the giantess *fóstra* to come.

8 Bjarmaland is the coast of the White Sea in what is now north Russia. Several historical Norse expeditions did go there; perhaps the best known is Ohthere's voyage, described in an Old English text (see Bately and Englert, *Ohthere's Voyages*). However, in the legendary sagas, Bjarmaland, like the rest of the far Arctic, is a semi-mythical land populated by wizards and giants (summarized in Hofstra and Samplonius, "Viking Expansion Northwards," pp. 244-245).

9 To help hold a ship together, a rope known as a *þvergyrðingr* ("cross-binding") could be passed beneath the keel and tightened by twisting pegs (*snarvelir*). (Kruse, *Die Geschichte von Halfdan*, pp. 83-84, n22)

10 *Helluland* ("rock slab land") is mentioned in *Grænlendinga saga* (ch. 3), and has been identified with Baffin Island. In this legendary saga,

geographic accuracy is beside the point; what matters is that it's big, rocky, and remote. The word *jökull* here could mean either "glacier" or "ice", but because Halfdan is said to get provisions by walking across it, I have assumed that he is walking across sea ice to fish.

11 The Norse word is *einstigi*, "a path only wide enough for one person". *Einstigi* is used specifically for a trail leading to a monster's or outlaw's lair in several sagas (including ch. 4 of *Kjalnesinga saga* and ch. 3 of *Jökuls þáttr Búasonar* in this book), which seems to be a motif shared with *Beowulf* (Jorgensen, "Icelandic Analogues", pp. 202-203; see note 22 to *Kjalnesinga saga*).

12 The Viking-era ell varied with place and time, but ranged from 47 cm to 63 cm, or between 18 and 25 inches. (Christensen, *Norsemen in the Viking Age*, p. 333)

13 Eating horseflesh was a pagan practice (*Njáls saga* ch. 101; see also *Hákonar saga góða* chs. 17-18, transl. Hollander, *Heimskringla* pp. 110-111.) Although the story takes place in nebulous pre-Christian times, the combination of human flesh and horsemeat would have doubly emphasized the otherness of giants to medieval Christian Icelandic audiences. See also *Sörla saga* ch. 3, note 6.

14 *Járnnef* means "iron nose"; *Sleggja* means "sledgehammer". Many giants have names related to iron; besides *Járnnef* and *Járnhauss* ("Iron Skull") in this saga, *Járnskjöldr* ("Iron Shield") appears in *Þorsteins þáttr uxafóts*, *Járngrímr* ("Iron Mask") appears in *Njáls saga*, while the giantess *Járnsaxa* ("Iron Knife") is a concubine of the god Thor, and the *Járnviðjur* ("Iron-Wood Dwellers") are hostile giantesses in *Völuspá*.

15 The verb translated "bewitch" is *seiða*, literally meaning "to work *seiðr*." *Seiðr* is a magical practice that can be used for protection or divining the future, but is more often used to create illusions and alter perceptions. *Ynglinga saga* ch. 7 (transl. Hollander, *Heimskringla*, p. 11) claims that *seiðr* carries such unmanliness (*ergi*) that it is not fitting for men to use it (see also Ström, *Níð, Ergi, and Old Norse Moral Attitudes*, pp. 8-10). The fact that a male giant says that he has used *seiðr* may point to the cultural and sexual otherness of *jötnar*.

16 Schlauch (*Romance in Iceland*, p. 104) points out that maidens abducted by giants are usually bound by their own hair, an image which may go back to Greek romances. See *Fljótsdæla saga* ch. 5 in this book.

17 The text reads *fóstbræðr*, which could mean "foster-brothers", i.e. children raised together by the same foster-parents. However, it could also mean "sworn brothers" or "blood brothers", i.e. men who have sworn an oath which essentially makes them siblings. This reading is preferable, although the text doesn't mention any oath between Halfdan, Sigurd and Sigmund.

18 Since red dyes had to be imported into Scandinavia in the Viking era, red clothing is especially associated in the sagas with luxury and nobility. This is a sign that Brana is no ordinary troll. Note, however, that several other giants in these sagas wear red; it may have been associated with trollishness. (Ewing, *Viking Clothing*, p. 156; see also *Kjalnesinga saga* ch. 13)

19 Molda probably comes from *mold*, "earth," while Mana may be derived from *máni*, "moon." Lukman ("An Irish Source," p. 56) suggested that both this saga and *Sörla saga* are based on an Irish chronicle; he derives Mana from Irish *mná*, "woman", Molda and Sleggja from the Irish name Maelsechlainn, and Brana from the Irish saint Brenann (Brandan). His argument is imaginative but unconvincing; it requires the Irish text to have been considerably rearranged.

20 The Old Norse text has *Valland*, which means northern France, more or less equal to Normandy and Brittany. The word means "land of foreigners", derived from the same root as Old English *Wælisc* and Modern English *Wales*. "William" (*Vilhjálmr*) cannot be identified with any historical ruler of Normandy; it's the standard name for any ruler of northern France in the legendary and chivalric sagas. See *Illuga saga Gríðarfóstra* ch. 1, note 2.

21 *Járnhauss* means "iron skull". *Járnhauss* is also the nickname of a berserk in *Víga-Glúms saga* ch. 6, of another berserk in *Flóamanna saga* ch. 15, and of a trollish being in *Þorsteins saga Víkingssonar* ch. 2; as noted in note 14, giant names having to do with iron are fairly common.

22 The Norse reads *sá í gaflhlaðit á henni*, "looked into her [house's] gable-end", which Stitt interprets as a sexual euphemism. The sisters' dress is not described (except that it is not like Brana's red tunic), but they are presumably wearing scanty tunics that reveal the buttocks and genitals, like many female giants in these sagas.

(*Beowulf and the Bear's Son*, p. 55 n5)

23 In some texts, and in folklore, giants and trolls are turned to stone by the light of the sun.

24 The idea of a cave with a trapdoor over the sea may be borrowed from the history *Morkinskinna* (ch. 13; transl. Anderson and Gade, p. 145). Haraldr Harðráði consorts with the Byzantine empress's niece in her *sjávarlopt*, a house built out over the sea; when the emperor arrives, he drops down into the ocean and escapes.

25 *ek fer eigi kona ein saman*, literally "I am not going as a lone woman"; a cute Norse idiom for "I'm pregnant."

26 This is a common stipulation in sagas about giants and humans, e.g. *Kjalnesinga saga* ch. 14; see also *Örvar-Odds saga* ch. 18 (transl. Pálsson and Edwards, *Seven Viking Romances*, p. 77). *Hálfdanar saga Brönufóstra* is unique in that the child is a girl and never enters the saga; in the others, the child is a boy who later meets his father.

27 *Brönugras* (Brana's herb) is the Icelandic name for a plant that is said to makes people who sleep on it fall in love. Jón Arnason recorded other names: *hjónagras* (couple's herb), *elskugras* (love herb), *Friggjargras* (Frigg's herb), and *vinagras* (friend-herb). (*Íslenzkar Þjóðsögur og Æfintýri*, p. 646) Cleasby and Vígfusson's *Dictionary* (p. 76) identifies *Brönugras* as *Satyrium albidum* (now *Pseudorchis albida*), the small-white orchid. However, more recent sources (e.g. Hörður Kristinsson, *Flora Íslands*) identify *Brönugras* with the heath-spotted orchid, *Dactylorhiza maculata*.

28 The original here just has *klæði*, "clothes", but it is made clear in ch. 11 that the clothes are in fact armor.

29 *Hnituðr* means "welded together." A ring with the same name, "welded together in seven places", appears in *Norna-Gests þáttr* (ch. 2; *FN* vol. 1, p. 170). *Þorsteins þáttr bæjarmagns* (ch. 2; *FN* vol. 3, p. 399) mentions a precious ring that can be taken apart into four parts. In *Sörla saga sterka* ch. 4 there is a magic ring made of nine parts screwed together.

30 *Skrauti* means "showy; decorated." This ship will appear again in *Sörla saga sterka*.

31 Hladgerd is the same name as the Norwegian warrior-woman Lathgertha, whom Saxo Grammaticus claims was the first wife of the hero Ragnar Lodbrok (*History of the Danes* IX.301; ed. Ellis-

Davidson and Fisher, pp. 280-281). Although Lathgertha is not said to be a giant, Saxo's story has similarities with the theme of the hero fostered by a giant woman, including the tale of how the giantess aids the hero even after he has left her for a human woman (IX.303-304, pp. 282-283). *Ála flekks saga* also mentions a giantess named Hladgerd; like Brana, she is half-giant, and she aids the hero to escape from her own family (ch. 5; transl. Bachman and Erlingsson, *Six Old Icelandic Sagas*, pp. 46-47). Ellis-Davidson and Fisher also suggest that Lathgertha may be the same as Thorgerd Holgabrud (pp. 151-152, n9).

32 *Alfífa* is the Norse form of Old English *Ælfgifu*, a well-attested woman's name meaning "elf-gift" (Kruse, *Die Geschichte von Halfdan*, p. 91 n53). Icelandic audiences may have understood the name differently, however: *fífa* means "cotton grass" (*Eriophorum* sp.), a common bog plant with seeds enclosed in cottony down. Since *fífa* down is proverbially light, *Alfífa* could be interpreted to mean something like "completely light."

33 The Norse reads *meir en eykt dags*, "more than *eykt* of a day." *Eykt* originally meant the time of day two-thirds of the way between noon and sunset, and so it could be translated as "until midafternoon." However, it later came to mean any period of three hours, and I have assumed that Halfdan held Aki under "for more than three hours of the day". (Cleasby and Vigfusson, *Dictionary*, p. 135)

34 Some scholars have compared this swimming contest to the contest between Beowulf and Breca in *Beowulf* (lines 506-581). Puhvel ("The Aquatic Contest"), however, is sceptical, pointing out that the *Beowulf* contest is an endurance race, whereas the contest here is an aquatic wrestling match, a popular entertainment mentioned in a number of sagas.

35 *Lóngant* and *Spóliant* are Old French names, meaning "hurrying" and "despoiling" respectively. The source is unknown, but the influence from continental chivalric romances is clear. (Kruse, *Die Geschichte von Halfdan*, p. 92 n56)

36 This incident might be borrowed from Icelandic and English saints' lives in which an offender is frozen in place or paralyzed (Fjalldal, *Anglo-Saxon England*, pp. 14-15; Crossley-Holland, transl., "The Passion of St. Edmund", *The Anglo-Saxon World*, p. 232).

37 It's a fairly common convention in Norse romances for dying men to place an *álög* or curse on their opponents, even if they are otherwise not skilled in magic. See note 2 above; cf. *Fljótsdæla saga* ch. 5 note 17; also Schlauch, *Romance in Iceland*, pp. 129-130.

38 There is a legendary saga about Ali Spot or *Áli Flekkr* (transl. Bachman and Erlingsson, *Six Old Icelandic Sagas*, pp. 41-61). King Richard (*Ríkardr*) does not correspond to any historical king.

Saga of Sorli the Strong

1 Literally, "Sweden the Cold" (*Svíþjóð inni kalda*), used by Snorri Sturluson (*Ynglinga saga* ch. 1) and others for the vast unknown lands north of the Black Sea, east of Russia.

2 *Sörla þáttr* (ch. 3; transl. Bachman and Erlingsson, *Six Old Icelandic Sagas*, p. 77) states that Erling ruled when twenty-four years had passed after the death of Peace-Frodi (*Frið-Fróði*). Peace-Frodi's legendary reign was noted for a long period of peace, and was thought of as taking place at the same time as the birth of Christ; see Saxo, *History of the Danes* V.170, ed. Ellis-Davidson and Fisher, p. 157; Miller, transl., "Fragments of Danish History," ch. 3, p. 10.

3 The same is said of Göngu-Hrólfr, the hero of the *fornaldarsaga Göngu-Hrólfs saga* (ch. 4; *FN*, vol. 2, pp. 368-369).

4 *Blámenn* are stock figures in legendary sagas; see discussion in the Introduction p. xi, *Kjalnesinga saga* note 43..

5 In the fictional *Íslendingasaga Víglundar saga* (ch. 16), the hero Víglund beat his enemy Jökull with the same maneuver of switching his weapon and shield.

6 Eating horseflesh was a pagan practice; human flesh is of course taboo as well. The audience would have understood the giants to be doubly Other. See note 13 to *Hálfdanar saga Brönufóstra.*

7 A common feat of magic in the legendary sagas is the ability to sink partially or completely into the earth, and to rise up out of it; e.g. this saga, chs. 8, 18, 20.

8 Literally *Bláland*, "black [men's] land". Chapter 10 of this saga uses the alternative name *Affríka.*

9 I have not been able to trace the origin of the name *Estróval*, but it seems to be Old French or at least inspired by Old French.

10 The verb translated as "bewitch" is *seiða*, "to work *seiðr*-magic". *Seiðr* is a magical practice put to several uses but frequently used to mislead or deceive others; see note 13 to *Hálfdanar saga Brönufóstra.*

11 In the sagas, *skikkja*, translated here as "cloak", always refers to a very fine garment of delicate fabric, fit for a king to give or receive. See Ewing, *Viking Clothing*, pp. 104-105; and note 4 to *Hauks þáttr hábrokar.*

12 Several rings in the legendary sagas are described as being made of several pieces screwed or welded together; see note 29 to *Hálfdanar saga Brönufóstra.*

13 Gallo ("Giantess as Foster-Mother," p. 10) points out that Mana is never called Sorli's *fóstra* in this saga, but is twice referred to as his *vinkona*, "female friend". This may be because relationship is based on mutual assistance, with no stated sexual encounter.

14 *Maskabert* is the Saracen ruler in *Elis saga ok Rosamundu*, a Norse translation of the Old French romance *Elie de Saint Gille*; in which the name appears as *Macabré*. (See Kölbing, *Elis saga*, p. 19 et seq.). *Pantíparus* may be a version of *Pandarus*; in the canonical Matter of Troy, Pandarus does not rule Greece after Agamemnon, but many variants of the Matter of Troy were in circulation in the Middle Ages. In any case, the influence from medieval romances on *Sörla saga* is clear.

15 It's not clear what land *Morland* refers to. Chapter 10 implies that Morland is part of Africa or at least along the sailing route to Africa; the name might derive from the "Moors," or from the Roman province of Mauretania. It could also be a variant of *Mornaland*, which appears in *Oddrúnarkviða* 1 (transl. Hollander, *Poetic Edda*, p. 279) and seems to be equivalent to the land of the Huns.

16 A war-token (*herboð*) was a wooden object passed from home to home, as a summons to an assembly or mustering for war. The most usual token was an arrow (*herör*, "war-arrow").

17 *Loðinn* means "shaggy; hairy." This Loðinn is not said to be a giant, but he has many trollish traits. A *jötunn* with the same name is mentioned in *Helgakviða Hjörvarðssonar* 25 (transl. Hollander, *Poetic Edda*, p. 175).

18 The Viking-era ell ranged from 47 cm to 63 cm, or between 18 and 25 inches. (Christensen, *Norsemen in the Viking Age*, p. 333). A

handspan (*spönn*) was the distance from the thumb to the middle finger when the fingers of the hand are outstretched, roughly 18 cm or seven inches (Cleasby and Vigfusson, *Dictionary*, p. 585).

19 *Börkr*, "bark", is a fairly common man's name in historical sagas. *Bölverkr* means "Bale-Worker" or "Evil-Doer"; in poetry and myths it is one of the many names of the god Odin (e.g. *Grímnismál* 48, transl. Hollander, *Poetic Edda*, p. 63).

20 Niels Lukman suggests, not always convincingly, that many elements in both *Sörla saga sterka* and *Hálfdanar saga Brönufóstra* are derived from Irish chronicles (see note 19 to *Hálfdanar saga*). He notes that an Irish text mentions an expedition to North Africa in 866 that brought captured "black men" back to Ireland, where they were "long to be seen", and suggests that this incident is the basis for Sorli's expedition to Africa and his capture of Bork and Bolverk. ("An Irish Source", p. 53)

21 The *flettiskepta*, "string-shaft", is probably the same as the "cord-spear" mentioned in several sagas. See note 44 to *Kjalnesinga saga*.

22 Possibly the same as Jarl Thorfid in *Hálfdanar saga Brönufóstra*, although this is not certain.

23 This is the first time the ship has been named; it is apparently the same ship that the giantess Brana made for Halfdan (*Hálfdans saga Brönufóstra* ch. 8).

24 Not identified with certainty, although the Latinate ending suggests influence from continental romances. Lukmann ("An Irish Source," p. 51) in keeping with his idea that *Sörla saga* is derived from Irish chronicles, links the name Litidorum with the Irish *leit-rí*, "half-king", on the basis of parallel events involving a pair of royal brothers or co-rulers.

25 An inheritance-feast (here, literally, *drykkja erfi*—"to drink the inheritance") was not only a commemmoration of a dead man, but a ceremony by which the man's heir formally claimed his inheritance.

26 She-goats were a byword for cowardice in Old Norse (compare English "sheep").

27 In sagas of all genres, women routinely urge their menfolk to fight with threats and accusations of cowardice.

28 An island off the coast of South Hordaland, Norway.

29 *Svalr* means "cool; fresh".

30 Courland (*Kúrland*) is in present-day western Latvia, between the Baltic Sea and the Gulf of Riga.

31 *Sigr-ljómi* means "victory-light". Compare Old English *hildeléoma*, "battle-light", a sword's name (or kenning for a sword) in *Beowulf* (1143). *Hrólfs saga kraka* (chs. 45-50, *FN* vol. 2 pp. 79, 87, 93) states that Hrólfr kraki's sword was named Sköfnungr; this sword was allegedly recovered from his grave and owned by several renowned Icelanders (e.g. *Kormaks saga* chs. 9-10; *Þórðar saga hreðu* ch. 2; *Laxdæla saga* ch. 57).

32 Since "Finns" are said to possess powerful magic in the sagas, and magic-workers are commonly said to be able to sink into the earth or rise up out of it, this lion is probably intended to be Sverri in shape-shifted form.

33 *Gellir* means "yeller; bellower".

34 Evidently Gellir has also been fostered by a giantess, and she intervenes invisibly in the battle, although this is not explicitly stated.

35 Once again, the *Finnar* have a reputation as masters of magic in Norse sagas and folklore.

36 Shooting arrows from each finger, literally or metaphorically, is recorded in several legendary sagas as a feat of hostile magic. See *Örvar-Odds saga* ch. 29 (transl. Pálsson and Edwards, *Seven Viking Romances*, pp. 112-113); *Jómsvíkinga saga* ch. 21 (transl. Hollander, p. 101); *Þorsteins saga Víkingssonar* ch. 23 (transl. Waggoner, *Sagas of Fridthjof the Bold*, p. 45).

37 Note the irony: Hogni defeats Sorli in the same way that Sorli defeated Mana.

38 The hero who waits calmly for his adversary to fetch his sword and finish him off also appears in *Egils saga einhenda* (ch. 4; transl. Pálsson and Edwards, *Seven Viking Romances*, p. 232). Again, the adversary is so touched by the display of courage that he spares the hero's life and does him honor.

The Saga of Illugi, Grid's Fosterling

1 The reference may be to an obscure, as yet unpublished romance,

Hrings saga ok Skjaldar, in which Skjold and Hermann fight a duel over the princess Dagmær. (Schauch, *Romance in Iceland*, p. 40)

2 The original text reads *Valland*, roughly equivalent to present-day Normandy and Brittany. See note 20 to *Hálfdanar saga Brönufóstra*.

3 *Sviði inn sókndjarfi* is said to be the illegitimate son of the hero Bósi in *Bósa saga ok Herrauðs* (ch. 16; FN vol. 2, p. 497), which claims that he is the father of Vilmundr *viðútan* ("the outsider"), the hero of his own chivalric saga. A character by the same name plays a role in the legendary *Hálfdanar saga Eysteinssonar* (*FN* vol. 3, pp. 283-319). It's not clear whether all these are meant to be the same person

4 The idea that witches can ride people at night, causing exhaustion or injury, appears in some sagas (e.g. *Eyrbyggja saga* ch. 16) and in later folklore (e.g. Kvideland and Sehmsdorf, *Scandinavian Folk Belief*, ch. 41, pp. 183-187). The implication in this scene seems to be that Sunnlod is riding Illugi through witchcraft, although she is not said to be doing anything supernatural.

5 Literally *rif*, "reefs in the sail", i.e. panel-like sections of the sail that could be taken in to decrease sail area and slow the ship down.

6 Old Norse *Gandvík*, "Magic Bay," had a reputation as the haunt of monsters and magic; see note 10 to *Hauks þáttr Hábrókar*.

7 The name *Gríðr* probably derives from *gríð*, "eagerness". In a myth told in the *Prose Edda*, the god Thor encounters a friendly giantess named *Gríðr*, the mother (by the god Odin) of the god Vidar the Silent. (*Skaldskáparmál* 18, ed. Faulkes, pp. 24-25)

8 In Saxo's *History of the Danes* (VIII.293-294, ed. Ellis-Davidson and Fisher, pp. 268-269), Thorkil, voyaging into the high Arctic and in desperate need of fire, encounters a giant who will only give him directions if he can speak three true statements. He must speak three more truths in order to obtain fire. Thorkil passes both tests; one of his truths is that the giant has the ugliest nose he's ever seen, identical with one of Illugi's truths. Another version of the "three truths" appears in the *Chronicon Lethrense*. The motif may come from the *Gesta Romanorum*, a popular medieval collection of anecdotes. (Ellis-Davidson and Fisher, pp. 146-147, n166)

9 A pun: *lýsingr* means both "daybreak" and "declaration of intent to marry."

10 A common saga euphemism for sexual relations; see Jochens, *Women*

in Old Norse Society, pp. 72-73.

11 Grid calls Illugi *herjansson. Herjan* is one of the names of the god Odin, meaning "leader of the host," but aChristianization, the name came to mean something like "devil".

12 *Álfheimr* is mentioned in some texts as mythological, the land of the spirits or deities known as *álfar* (alfs, elves). Other texts place it in the human world, between the present-day Glomma and Göta älv Rivers, roughly equivalent to the Swedish province of Bohuslän. A few texts blend the two traditions (e.g. *Þorsteins saga Víkingssonar* ch. 1, transl. Waggoner, *Sagas of Fridthjof the Bold*, p. 2). It's not clear which is referred to here.

13 Curses like these are known as *álög* ("laid on") in Norse. *Álög* closely resemble the *geasa* of Irish and Scots Gaelic tales, and were probably borrowed from such sources (Schauch, *Romance in Iceland*, pp. 125-134; Power, "Gaelic Love-Tales"). It's fairly common in the romantic sagas for the victim to have the chance to cast an elaborate counter-curse, even if he or she has no other magical powers; for examples, see *Hjálmþés saga ok Ölvis* ch. 8 (transl. O'Connor, *Icelandic Histories & Romances*, p. 138; *Ála flekks saga* chs. 4, 8 (transl. Bachman and Erlingsson, *Six Old Icelandic Sagas*, pp. 45, 50).

14 Evidently Signy/Grid retains her trollish form and powers at this point in the story; there may be some confusion as to exactly when she regains human form. Another woman-turned-giantess who is freed from the spell by a hero, and who then hangs the hero's enemy from his own ship's mast under cover of darkness, is Skellinefja in *Þorsteins saga Víkingssonar* (ch. 19; transl. Waggoner, *Sagas of Fridthjof*, pp. 36-37).

15 Skåne is at the southernmost tip of the Scandinavian peninsula. Now part of Sweden, it was traditionally Danish, from the Viking era until 1658.

16 *Egils saga einhenda ok Ásmundar berserkjabana* relates part of Asmund's life, and other legendary sagas mention him briefly (e.g. *Hrómundar saga Gripssonar* ch. 1, *FN* vol. 2, p. 275; *Gríms saga loðinkinna* ch. 3, *FN* vol. 1, pp. 277-278). His ship, the *Gnoð* or *Gnóð*, was said to have been one of the largest and most magnificent ships of all time.

The Tale of Asmund Ogre-Lucky

1 The verses in this tale are all in the traditional meters of *rímur*, the long, rhyming, alliterative ballad-like poems that began to be composed in Iceland in the 14th century. Many *rímur* are based on sagas, and some sagas were derived from *rímur*. This stanza, as well as the second and the last in this saga, are written in the meter known as *ferskeytt*. (Hughes, "Late Secular Poetry", pp. 206-208) The translator hasn't always followed the original meter perfectly, but has tried to capture something of the flavor.

2 The *eldhús*, "fire-house" or "hearth-house", was an outbuilding where food was prepared. See note to *Kjalnesinga saga*.

3 Asmund is another *kolbítr* or "coal-biter", a young man who lies idle by the fire until encouraged to rise to the occasion. See note 15 to *Kjalnesinga saga*.

4 There may be a parallel with *Grettis saga* ch. 17: Grettir's hostile father refuses to give him a sword, but his sympathetic mother gives him a sword that is an heirloom in her own family.

5 In several sagas, *lífsteinn*, "life-stone," refers to an amulet that can heal wounds (*Kormaks saga* ch. 9; *Laxdæla saga* ch. 57). Here, however, the *lífsteinn* is evidently a stone in which the woman's soul or life is kept. This is not a common theme in the sagas, but is a widespread folklore motif (e.g. Frazer, *Balder the Beautiful*, vol. 2, ch. 10, pp. 95-133; also motifs E710-711 in Thompson, *Motif-Index of Folk-Literature*, vol. 2, pp. 493-494). In a variant of the motif, the object that contains a person's soul can only be destroyed with that person's own sword (D1651.10, in Thompson, vol. 2, p. 296).

6 There are parallel scenes of a a hero arriving at a giant's hut, and then the giant returning from hunting, in the legendary sagas *Þorsteins saga Víkingssonar* (ch. 15) and *Ketils saga hængs* (ch. 2).

7 *Naddr* means "nail" or "stud."

8 It's just possible that this preserves a bit of myth: the gods fettered the wolf Fenrir and then gagged him with a sword propping open his jaws. (*Gylfaginning* 34; ed. Faulkes, p. 29)

9 Thorgerd Holgabrud or Holdatroll appears in several sagas as a deity worshipped by the Jarls of Hladir. See Introduction.

10 Several sagas mention that luck (called *gipta* here; also known as

gæfa or *hamingja*) can be lent from one person to another, especially from a king to those who carry out his will (e.g. *Óláfs saga helga* ch. 69, Hollander, transl., *Heimskringla*, pp. 300-301; *Hallfreðar saga vandræðaskálds* ch. 6).

11 The foot-chopping contest is somewhat reminiscent of the head-chopping contest in *Sir Gawain and the Green Knight.*

12 Human berserks, who overlap somewhat with trolls in the sagas, were also said to be able to walk through fire, swallow hot objects, and withstand sword blows when in their frenzy. See *Ynglinga saga* ch. 6, transl. Hollander, *Heimskringla*, p. 10; Saxo, *History of the Danes* VII.221, ed. Ellis-Davidson and Fisher, p. 205. In *Kristni saga* (ch. 2, ed. Kahle, p. 8; ch. 9, p. 29), berserks' ability to survive fire and sword blows are nullified when a bishop consecrates the fire.

13 This *ríma* verse is in *braghent* meter, in a version known as *frárímuð* in which the first line does not rhyme with the other two. (Hughes, "Late Secular Poetry", pp. 207-208)

14 In several Norwegian and Icelandic folk tales, a person who encounters elves or trolls is often mentally changed by the experience when he returns to human society. The change may be anything from moodiness to complete insanity. See for example Kvideland and Sehmsdorf, *Scandinavian Folk Belief and Legend*, ch. 45, pp. 212-213.

15 The one who gave a name to someone was obliged to give a gift along with the name, called a *nafnfestr* or "name-fastening". See, for example, *Hrólfs saga kraka* ch. 28; *Þorsteins saga uxafóts* ch. 14; *Þorsteins þáttr skelks.*

16 This *ríma* verse is in *braghent* meter, in a version known as *baksneidd* in which the first line rhymes imperfectly with the other two. (Hughes, "Late Secular Poetry", pp. 207-208)

BIBLIOGRAPHY

Note that Icelandic authors have been alphabetized by first name, as is common practice. All Icelandic sagas mentioned in the text whose publication information is not specifically cited may be found in translation in *Complete Sagas of Icelanders*, edited by Viðar Hreinsson. All sagas cited as *FN* are taken from Guðni Jónsson and Bjarni Vilhjálmson's 1943-44 edition of *Fornaldarsögur Norðurlanda.*

Adamson, Melitta Weiss. *Food in Medieval Times.* Westport, Conn.: Greenwood Press, 2004.

Andersson, Theodore M. and Kari Ellen Gade, transl. *Morkinskinna: The Earliest Icelandic Chronicle of the Norse Kings (1030-1157).* Ithaca, N.Y.: Cornell University Press, 2000.

Bachman, W. Bryant, transl. *Forty Old Icelandic Tales.* Lanham, Md.: University Press of America, 1992.

— and Guðmundur Erlingsson, transl. *Six Old Icelandic Sagas.* Lanham, Md.: University Press of America, 1993.

Bately, Janet and Anton Englert. *Ohthere's Voyages.* Roskilde: Viking Ship Museum, 2007.

Bayless, Martha. "Tabletop Tactics." *Archaeology*, vol. 58, no. 1 (Jan-Feb 2005), pp. 36-40.

Beach, Hugh. *A Year in Lapland: Guest of the Reindeer Herders.* Seattle: University of Washington Press, 2001.

Black, G. F., coll.; Northcote W. Thomas, ed. *County Folk-Lore Vol. III: Printed Extracts No. 5: Examples of Printed Folk-Lore Concerning the Orkney & Shetland Islands.* Publications of The Folk-Lore Society XLIX. London: David Nutt, 1903.

Byock, Jesse, transl. *The Saga of King Hrolf Kraki.* London: Penguin, 1998.

Christiansen, Eric. *The Norsemen in the Viking Age.* Oxford: Blackwell, 2002.

Cleasby, Richard, and Gudbrand Vigfusson. *An Icelandic-English Dictionary.* Oxford: Clarendon Press, 1874.

Craigie, William A. "Gaelic Words and Names in the Icelandic Sagas." *Zeitschrift für celtische Philologie*, vol. 1 (1897), pp. 439-454.

Crossley-Holland, Kevin. *The Anglo-Saxon World.* Oxford: Oxford University Press, 2009.

Danielsson, Tommy. "*Jökuls þáttr Búasonar.*" *Medieval Scandinavia.* Ed. Phillip Pulsiano and Kirsten Wolf. London: Routledge, 1993. p. 348.

—. "*Kjálnesinga saga.*" *Medieval Scandinavia.* Ed. Phillip Pulsiano and Kirsten Wolf. London: Routledge, 1993. pp. 355-356.

Davidson, Hilda Ellis. *The Lost Beliefs of Northern Europe.* London: Routledge, 1993.

Dobbie, Elliott van Kirk, ed. *Beowulf and Judith. The Anglo-Saxon Poetic Records*, vol. 4. New York: Columbia University Press, 1953.

Driscoll, Matthew J. (ed. transl.) *Ágrip af Nóregskonungasögum: A Twelfth-Century Synoptic History of the Kings of Norway.* London: Viking Society for Northern Research, 2008.

—. "Editing the *Fornaldarsögur Norðurlanda.*" Agneta Ney, Henrik Williams and Fredrik Charpentier Ljungqvist. *Á austrvega: Saga and East Scandinavia. Preprint Papers of the 14th International Saga Conference, Uppsala, 9th-15th August 2009.* Gävle: Gävle University Press, 2009. pp. 207-212.

— and Silvia Hufnagel. "*Fornaldarsögur Norðurlanda*: a Bibliography of Manuscripts, Editions, Translations and Secondary Literature." Arnamagnæan Institute, Copenhagen. http://www.staff.hum.ku.dk/mjd/fornaldarsagas/

Einar Ólafur Sveinsson. *Dating the Icelandic Sagas: An Essay in Method.* London: Viking Society for Northern Research, 1958.

—. *The Folk-Stories of Iceland.* Transl. Benedikt Benedikz; ed. Anthony Faulkes. London: Viking Society for Northern Research, 2003.

Ellis, Hilda R. "Fostering by Giants in Old Norse Literature.". *Medium Ævum* vol. 10 (1941): pp. 70-85.

Eremenko, Alexey. "The Dual World of the *Fornaldarsögur.*" *Proceedings of the 13th International Saga Conference, Durham and York, 6th-12th August, 2006.* http://www.dur.ac.uk/medieval.www/sagaconf/eremenko.htm

Ewing, Thor. *Viking Clothing.* Stroud: The History Press, 2009.

Finlay, Alison. "*Brandkrossa þáttr.*" *Medieval Scandinavia.* Ed. Phillip Pulsiano and Kirsten Wolf. London: Routledge, 1993. p. 56.

—. "*Fljótsdæla saga.*" *Medieval Scandinavia.* Ed. Phillip Pulsiano and Kirsten Wolf. London: Routledge, 1993. pp. 198-199.

Finnur Jónsson. *Lexicon Poeticum Antiquæ Linguæ Septentrionalis: Ordbog over det Norsk-Islandske Skjaldesprog.* 2nd ed. Copenhagen: S. L. Møller, 1931.

Fjalldal, Magnús. *Anglo-Saxon England in Icelandic Medieval Texts.* Toronto: University of Toronto Press, 2005.

Folks, Cathalin B. and Carl Lindahl. "Loathly Lady." *Medieval Folklore: An Encyclopedia of Myths, Legends, Tales, Beliefs, and Customs.* Ed. Carl Lindahl, John McNamara, and John Lindow. Santa Barbara, Calif.: ABC-CLIO, 2000.

Frazer, James George. *The Golden Bough. Third Edition. Part VII: Balder the Beautiful*, vol. 2. New York: MacMillan, 1935.

Gallo, Lorenzo Lozzi. "The Giantess as Foster-Mother in Old Norse Literature." *Scandinavian Studies* vol. 78 (2006), pp. 1-20.

Gísli Sigurðsson. *Gaelic Influence in Ireland: Historical and Literary Contacts, A Survey of Research.* 2nd ed. Reykjavík: University of Iceland, 2000.

Guðbrandur Vigfússon and C. R. Unger, eds. *Flateyjarbók.* 3 vols. Christiania: P. T. Malling, 1860-1868.

Gudbrand Vigfusson, ed. *Icelandic Sagas and Other Historical Documents Relating to the Settlements and Descents of the Northmen on the British Isles. Volume I: Orkneyinga saga, and Magnus saga, with Appendices.* London: Eyre and Spottiswode, 1887.

Guðni Jónsson and Bjarni Vilhjálmson, eds. *Fornaldarsögur Norðurlanda.* 3 vols. Reykjavík: Bókaútgáfan Forni, 1943.

Gunnlaug Þórðarson, ed. *Sagan af Þjalar-Jóni.* Reykjavík: E. Þórðarson, 1857.

Hallmundsson, May and Hallberg Hamundsson, ed. transl. *Icelandic Folk and Fairy Tales.*

Hastrup, Kirsten. *Culture and History in Medieval Iceland: An Anthropological Analysis of Structure and Change.* Oxford: Clarendon Press, 1985.

Helgi Þorláksson. "Historical Background: Iceland 870-1400. *A Companion to Old Norse–Icelandic Literature and Culture*. Rory McTurk, ed. Oxford: Blackwell, 2007. pp. 136-154.

Hofstra, Tette and Kees Samplonius. "Viking Expansion Northwards: Mediæval Sources." *Arctic*, vol. 48, no. 3 (1995), pp. 235-247.

Hollander, Lee M., ed. transl. *Jómsvíkinga saga*. Austin: University of Texas Press, 1955.

Hörður Kristinsson. *Flóra Íslands*. Akureyri: Náttúrufræðistofnun Íslands. http://www.floraislands.is/

Hufnagel, Silvia. "*Sörla saga sterka* and Rafn's edition." Agneta Ney, Henrik Williams and Fredrik Charpentier Ljungqvist. *Á austrvega: Saga and East Scandinavia. Preprint Papers of the 14th International Saga Conference, Uppsala, 9th-15th August 2009*. Gävle: Gävle University Press, 2009. pp. 398-404.

Hughes, Shaun. "Late Secular Poetry." *A Companion to Old Norse–Icelandic Literature and Culture*. Rory McTurk, ed. Oxford: Blackwell, 2007. pp. 205-222.

Hume, Kathryn. "From Saga to Romance: The Use of Monsters in Old Norse Literature." *Studies in Philology*, vol. 77 (1980), pp. 1-25.

Ibsen, Henrik. *Peer Gynt. The Oxford Ibsen, Volume III*. Ed. James Walter McFarlane. London: Oxford University Press, 1972.

Jesch, Judith. "*Ásmundar saga Flagðagaefu*". *Arv*, vol. 38 (1982), pp. 103-131.

—. "*Illuga saga Gríðarfóstra*". *Medieval Scandinavia*. Ed. Phillip Pulsiano and Kirsten Wolf. London: Routledge, 1993. pp. 322-333.

Jochens, Jenny. *Women in Old Norse Society*. Ithaca, N.Y.: Cornell University

Press, 1995.

—. "Race and Ethnicity in the Old Norse World." *Viator*, vol. 30 (1999), pp. 79-103.

Jóhannes Halldórsson, ed. *Kjalnesinga Saga. Íslenzk Fornrit XIV*. Reyjkavík: Hið Íslenzka Fornritafélag, 1959.

Jón Árnason. *Íslenzkar Þjóðsögur og Æfintýri. Fyrsta Bindi.* Leipzig: J. C. Hinrich, 1862.

Jón Jóhanneson, ed. *Austfirðinga Sögur. Íslenzk Fornrit XI*. Reyjkavík: Hið Íslenzka Fornritafélag, 1950.

Jorgensen, Peter A. "Additional Icelandic Analogues to *Beowulf*." *Sagnaskemmtun: Studies in Honour of Hermann Pálsson.* Ed. Rudolf Simek, Jónas Kristjánsson, and Hans Bekker-Nielsen. Vienna: Hermann Böhlaus, 1986. pp. 201-208.

—. "*Hálfdanar saga Brönufóstra*." *Medieval Scandinavia.* Ed. Phillip Pulsiano and Kirsten Wolf. London: Routledge, 1993. pp. 260-261.

Kahle, B., ed. *Kristnisaga. Þáttr Þorvalds ens Víðforla. Þáttr Ísleifs Biskups Gizurarsonar. Hungrvaka. Altnordische Saga-Bibliothek. Heft 11.* Gustaf Cederschiöld, Hugo Gering, and Eugen Mogk, eds. Halle: Max Niemeyer, 1905.

Kalinké, Marianne E. "Norse Romance (*riddarasögur*)." *Old Norse–Icelandic Literature: A Critical Guide.* Ed. Carol J. Clover and John Lindow. Toronto: University of Toronto Press / Medieval Academy of America, 2005. pp. 316-363.

Kennedy, John. "The English Translations of *Völsunga saga*". *Northern Antiquity: The Post-Medieval Reception of Edda and Saga.* Ed. Andrew Wawn. Enfield Lock: Hisarlik Press, 1994. 285-303.

Kölbing, Eugen. *Elis saga ok Rósamundu.* Heilbronn: Henninger, 1882.

Kolbrún Haraldsdóttir. "Flateyjarbók". *Medieval Scandinavia*. Ed. Phillip Pulsiano and Kirsten Wolf. London: Routledge, 1993. pp. 197-198.

Konúnglega Norræna Fornfræði Félag. *Fornmanna Sögur. Túnda Bindi.* Copenhagen: S. L. Möller, 1835.

Kruse, Mathias. *Die Geschichte von Halfdan, dem Schuutzling der Brana / Hálfdanar saga Brönufóstra: Übersetzung und Kommentar.* Munich: Herbert Utz, 2009.

Kunin, Devra, transl., Carl Phelpstead, ed. *A History of Norway and the Passion and Miracles of the Blessed Óláfr.* London: Viking Society for Northern Research, 2001.

Kvideland, Reimund and Henning K. Sehmsdorf. *Scandinavian Folk Belief and Legend.* Minneapolis: University of Minnesota Press, 1988.

Lindow, John. "Supernatural Others and Ethnic Others: A Millennium of Worldview." *Scandinavian Studies*, vol. 67 (1995), pp. 8-31.

Lukman, Niels. "An Irish Source and Some Icelandic *Fornaldarsögur.*" *Mediaeval Scandinavia*, vol. 10 (1977), pp. 41-57.

MacKillop, James. *A Dictionary of Celtic Mythology.* Oxford: Oxford University Press, 2004.

Matyushina, Inna. "Magic Mirrors, Monsters, Maiden-Kings (the Fantastic in *Riddarasögur*)". *Proceedings of the 13th International Saga Conference, Durham and York, 6th-12th August, 2006.* http://www.dur.ac.uk/medieval.www/sagaconf/matyushina.htm

McKinnell, John. *Meeting the Other in Norse Myth and Legend.* Cambridge: D. S. Brewer, 2005.

Middle English Dictionary. Ann Arbor: University of Michigan, 2001. http://quod.lib.umich.edu/m/med/

Miller, Clarence H., ed. transl. "Fragments of Danish History". *ANQ* vol. 20, no. 3 (2007), pp. 9-22.

Motz, Lotte. 1980. "The Rulers of the Mountain: A Study of the Giants of the Old Icelandic Texts." *Mankind Quarterly*, vol. 20 (1979-80), pp. 393-416.

—. "Giants in Folklore and Mythology: A New Approach." *Folklore*, vol. 93 (1982), pp. 70-84.

—. "The Families of Giants." *Arkiv för Nordisk Filologi*, vol. 102 (1987), pp. 216–236.

—. "The Storm of Troll-Women." *Maal og Minne*, vol. 1-2 (1988), pp. 31-41.

—. "The Great Goddess of the North." *Sagas and the Norwegian Experience. Preprints for the 10th International Saga Conference, Trondheim, 3-9 August 1997*. Trondheim: Senter for Middelalderstudier, pp. 471-477.

Mundal, Else. "Coexistence of Saami and Norse Cultures—Reflected In and Interpreted By Old Norse Myths." In: Geraldine Burnes & Margaret Clunies Ross (eds), *Old Norse Myths, Literature and Society. Proceedings from the 11th International Saga Conference 2-7 July 2000*. University of Sydney. Sydney: University of Sydney, pp. 346–355.

O'Connor, Ralph, ed. trans. *Icelandic Histories & Romances*. 2nd ed. Stroud, Gloucestershire: Tempus, 2006.

Óláfur Halldórsson. "*Óláfs saga Tryggvasonar*." *Medieval Scandinavia*. Ed. Phillip Pulsiano and Kirsten Wolf. London: Routledge, 1993. pp. 448-449.

Osborne, Marijane and Gillian R. Overing. "Bone-Crones Have No Hearth: Some Women in the Medieval Wilderness." *Textures of Place: Exploring Humanist Geographies*. Ed. Paul C. Adams, Steven D.

Hoelscher, and Karen E. Till. Minneapolis: University of Minnesota Press, 2001.

Pálsson, Hermann and Paul Edwards, transl. *Orkneyinga Saga: The History of the Earls of Orkney*. London: Penguin, 1981.

—. *Seven Viking Romances*. London: Penguin, 1985.

Power, Rosemary. "Gaelic Love-Tales in Iceland: a Case of Multiple Introduction?" *Proceedings of the 13th International Saga Conference, Durham and York, 6th-12th August, 2006*. http://www.dur.ac.uk/medieval.www/sagaconf/power.htm

Puhvel, Martin. "The Aquatic Contest in *Hálfdanar saga Brönufóstra* and Beowulf's Adventure with Breca: Any Connection?" *Neuphilologische Mitteilungen* vol. 99, no. 2 (1998), pp. 131-138.

Quinn, Judy, ed. "Interrogating Genre in the *Fornaldarsögur*: Round-Table Discussion." *Viking and Medieval Studies*, vol. 2 (2006), pp. 275-96.

Robinson, Charles H. *Anskar: The Apostle of the North, 801-865*. London: Society for the Propagation of the Gospel in Foreign Parts, 1921.

Ross, Margaret Clunies. *Prolonged Echoes: Old Norse Myths in Medieval Northern Society. Volume 2: The Reception of Norse Myths in Medieval Iceland.* Odense: Odense University Press, 1998.

Røthe, Gunnhild. "Þorgerðr Hölgabrúðr: The *Fylgja* of the Háleygjar Family." *Scripta Islandica* vol. 58 (2007), pp. 33-55.

Saxo Grammaticus. *The History of the Danes: Books I-IX*. Ed. Hilda R. Ellis-Davidson, trans. Peter Fisher. Rochester, N.Y.: D.S. Brewer, 1996.

Short, William R. *Viking Weapons and Combat Techniques.* Yardley, Pa.: Westholme, 2009.

Sigurður Nordal, ed. *Flateyjarbók*. 4 vols. Akureyri: Flateyjarútgáfan, Prentverk Akraness H.F., 1944-1945.

Simpson, Jacqueline. *Icelandic Folktales and Legends.* Berkeley and Los Angeles: University of California, 1972.

Slay, Desmond. "*The Saga of Hrolf Kraki.*" [Book review] *Saga-Book*, vol. 25 (1998-2001), pp. 329-332.

Snorri Sturluson. *Edda. Prologue and Gylfaginning.* 2nd ed. Ed. Anthony M. Faulkes. London: Viking Society for Northern Research, 2005.

—. *Edda. Skáldskaparmál. 1: Introduction, Text and Notes.* Ed. Anthony M. Faulkes. London: Viking Society for Northern Research, 1998.

—. *Heimskringla: History of the Kings of Norway.* Transl. Lee M. Hollander. Austin: University of Texas Press, 1992.

Speidel, Michael P. *Ancient Germanic Warriors: Warrior Styles from Trajan's Column to Icelandic Sagas.* Abingdon: Routledge, 2004.

Steinsland, Gro. "Giants as Recipients of Cult in the Viking Age?" *Words and Objects: Towards a Dialogue Between Archaeology and History of Religion.* Ed. Gro Steinsland. Oslo: Norwegian University Press, 1986. pp. 212-222.

Stitt, J. Michael. *Beowulf and the Bear's Son: Epic, Saga, and Fairytale in Northern Germanic Tradition.* New York and London: Garland, 1992.

Straubhaar, Sandra. "Nasty, Brutish, and Large: Cultural Difference and Otherness in the Figuration of the Trollwomen of the *Fornaldar sögur.*" *Scandinavian Studies*, vol. 73, no. 2 (2001), pp. 105-124.

Ström, Folke. *Níð, Ergi, and Old Norse Moral Attitudes.* London: Viking Society for Northern Research, 1974.

Tacitus, Cornelius. *Germania.* Transl. M. Hutton, rev. E. H. Warrington. *Tacitus I: Agricola, Germania, Dialogus.* Loeb Classical Library. Cambridge, Mass.: Harvard University Press, 1970.

Tambets, Kristiina, and 45 others. "The Western and Eastern Roots of the Saami—the Story of Genetic 'Outliers' Told by Mitochondrial DNA and Y Chromosomes." *American Journal of Human Genetics*, vol. 74 (2004), 661-682.

Thompson, Stith. *Motif-Index of Folk-Literature.* 5 vols. Bloomington: Indiana University Press, 1973.

Tolkien, Christopher, ed. transl. *The Saga of King Heidrek the Wise.* London: Thomas Nelson, 1960.

Tulinius, Torfi. *The Matter of the North: The Rise of Literary Fiction in Thirteenth-Century Iceland.* Odense: Odense University Press, 2002.

Turner, Val. *Ancient Shetland.* London: Batsford / Historic Scotland, 1998.

Viðar Hreinsson, ed. *Complete Sagas of the Icelanders.* 5 vols. Reykjavík: Leifur Eiriksson Publishing, 1997.

Waggoner, Ben. *The Sagas of Ragnar Lodbrok.* New Haven: Troth Publications, 2009.

—. *The Sagas of Fridthjof the Bold.* New Haven: Troth Publications, 2009.

CPSIA information can be obtained
at www.ICGtesting.com
Printed in the USA
LVOW11s2013141116
512905LV00001BA/363/P

9 780578 059334